Creative Colour
Photography

CLB 1570
© 1986 Text: Colour Library Books Ltd., Guildford, Surrey, England.
© 1986 Illustrations: Colour Library Books Ltd., Alan Bedding,
    Colin Glanfield and Roger Hicks.
Text filmsetting by Acesetters Ltd., Richmond, Surrey, England.
Printed and bound in Barcelona. Spain by Cronion, S.A.
All rights reserved.
ISBN 0 86283 417 1

Creative Colour Photography

by
Roger Hicks and Colin Glanfield

COLOUR LIBRARY BOOKS

Creative Colour Photography

We live in a colourful world. Not only strong, vibrant colours, although there are plenty of these to be seen, but also soft, subtle and gentle colours. Without light there are no colours and, indeed, colour changes in hue and intensity according to the level and angle of the light reflected from it. Photography, too, depends on light. A lens gathers and focuses light; a shutter allows a measured amount of light to pass – to a film which consists of a light-sensitive emulsion that, when processed, renders permanent the image we wish to capture.

The photographic image – particularly in colour – nowadays plays an important, accepted and established part in all our lives. We rely on it, whether in the form of cinematic or television film or still pictures, to provide us with information about places, people and events. We also rely on it, together with the printed or spoken word, to educate or inform us of subjects which, otherwise, we would have no way of seeing for ourselves. We can 'freeze' action and analyse it split second by split second, studying each small movement better to understand its working; we can send cameras to the bottom of the oceans to record and study what we find there, at seemingly impossible depths, and we can send them out to the edges of the solar system; we can record what can only be seen through the microscope, and we can make all this visual information available to millions of people all over the world. We now accept, and take for granted, all the photographic information with which we are surrounded every day, but, in addition to its primary function of supplying information, photography can appeal straight to the emotions, in much the same way as can painting, sculpture or music. We can be moved – emotionally affected – by the content or subject matter of a photograph, or – and this is what should interest us – by the way the photographer has seen and interpreted it. To a considerable extent, of course, photography is directed, or controlled, by someone other than the photographer, particularly for such purposes as advertising and fashion. Nevertheless, individual photographers still bring to such subjects their own style or interpretation; they may even become well known for it and influence the whole area of photography in which they are involved. But it is when photographers take pictures for themselves or are asked to work within very broad limits that we start to see, to a greater or lesser extent, interpretative involvement. If we were to ask three different, competent and involved photographers to present their interpretation of almost any subject we should probably find that they produced three quite different sets of pictures; the same subject seen from three different emotional, and visual, angles. Of course, the same thing would happen if we were to ask three painters to carry out the same task, and it is the similarities between the two mediums that have led, ever since the beginnings of photography, to controversy regarding its acceptance or rejection as an art form. 'Painting is art – photography is not' has long been the widely accepted view, and it may well be so, but it surely matters very little. There are good and bad painters just as there are good and bad photographers, and who is to say which is which? It depends very much on timing; yesterday's masterpiece can become today's cliché and a hitherto disregarded work can suddenly be attributed to a master and achieve immediate fame. This already happens with painting and, to a lesser extent because of the comparative newness of the medium, is happening with photography.

Pretentiousness exists in photography of course, but, again because of its relatively short history, not to the same extent as in some other art forms. It is very seldom that a photograph provokes a query as to the name of the photographer. We are far more likely to ask questions as to its content, such as 'who is it?' 'where was it taken?' or, maybe, 'what does it say, or mean, to me?' Perhaps this is one of the strengths of photography; the photograph has to stand on its own to a very large extent and no-one has any reason to be in awe of it. We may be interested, at some stage, to know the photographer's identity or we may not; we are familiar enough with photographs to be able to reject what we don't like and accept what we do on the basis of our own judgement and nothing else. Any 'art' there is in photography surely lies in seeing or visualising the picture to begin with; without that there can be no good pictures. Translating the original idea into a finished product can be put down to craft or expertise, both of which can be taught.

The term 'commercial photography' immediately suggests photography taken for a specific purpose, be it to advertise a product, appear on a package, adorn a calendar or magazine, or whatever. Whilst this is, of course, true for the bulk of the photography used in, particularly, advertising, it is also true to say that a considerable amount of photography that is used for a variety of purposes is obtained from stock sources. This was not always so, however, simply because there were no stocks of pictures to call on in the early days. A few specialised agencies were gradually set up over the years to syndicate, primarily, news and features, but, these apart, if photography was required it had to be commissioned. With the advent of colour films, allied to more sophisticated methods of reproduction, the demand for colour photography increased, not only in quantity but also in diversity of subject matter. How far we have travelled along this road may be judged from the enormous variety, in style and content, of the photographs in this present volume.

A fair question to ask is: 'When does a photograph become a commercial photograph?' It may be supposed that as soon as a photograph is sold for a particular product, be it a calendar, a book, an advertisement, a travel brochure, or for use in one of the many other ways in which we see colour pictures employed, then it becomes a commercial photograph. On the other hand, it could be argued that commercial photography is only that which is specifically commissioned for a stated purpose.

'Control' does not mean curbing any individuality that a photographer may bring to his work. It simply means that a photographer can be sent wherever he or she is needed, be it into the studio or to South America, to take pictures that are required for a special project or because they would provide a useful addition to a publisher's files. From then on, however, although the photographer will normally be provided with a brief, it is up to the individual how he or she interprets what is seen; after all, this is what they bring to the job; anyone can be taught, in a relatively short time, how to handle the controls of a camera, and whilst an ability to 'see' the telling picture can be developed and encouraged, something has to be there to start with; it is this that separates the technician from the 'creative' photographer.

Whilst it is obviously true to say that a 'bad' camera – i.e. one in which the lens gives poor definition and the shutter inaccurate exposure times – will deliver poor pictures, it is as incorrect to say that a 'good' camera will always produce good pictures as it is to say that a 'good' piano will always play good music. Both of them depend on the operator, performer, artist – call them what you will. It has been said so many times that it hardly bears repeating, but it is the man behind the camera who makes the picture; the camera only does his bidding. It never ceases to amaze; the assumption that the possession of an expensive, sophisticated camera should almost guarantee good pictures, and the disappointment when it is discovered that the camera has accurately recorded and exposed on film just what it has been pointed at and focused on – no more and no less!

As photographers, we have at our disposal a wealth of highly sophisticated equipment with which we can alter the 'straightforward' appearance of our subjects. We can use telephoto lenses or wide-angle lenses to alter the apparent perspective and introduce all sorts of distortions; we can throw backgrounds and foregrounds out of focus; we can use long shutter speeds to blur images, or very short ones to freeze movement; we can select unusual viewpoints from which to take ordinary pictures and render them less ordinary; with zoom lenses we can change the focal length during exposure; we can alter colours almost at will by using emulsions designed for light sources that are different from those under which we are photographing, or we can add coloured filters to change the overall colour. There are now available 'creative' kits that include just about every optical trick that can be used to make our pictures look 'different', and all these methods plus many others have their place, but if they are used indiscriminately they will simply result in gimmicky pictures; pictures with nothing to tell us; pictures which, without the gimmicks, we would throw away as worthless. No amount of technical manipulation can replace the ability to see and select; it can add a little 'something' to an already good picture but it should never be used as an end in itself. There seems to be far too much of a tendency, nowadays, to reach straight for the 'special effects' before we have fully considered and understood what it is about the subject that interested or excited us in the first place. There are exceptions, of course, and a considerable amount of commercial or commissioned photography comes into a category that demands a particular treatment. In many cases, however, if we stop and ask ourselves exactly what it is about the subject that has made us stop and look, and then try to translate those feelings onto film in order to share the experience, we will find that an honest and straightforward photograph that shows the light catching the subject in just that way, or at just that angle, with all our concentration on selecting the viewpoint and deciding what to include and, perhaps more important, what to exclude, that anything else is unnecessary; all that is required is our seeing eye and careful photographic technique.

The task of choosing the photographs for this volume has been both enjoyable and immensely difficult. For each picture that was selected there were many, many alternatives, and the overriding consideration has been variety: variety of pictures, of course, but also variety of technique. There are numerous ways in which a flower, a landscape or a girl can be photographed and no one way is necessarily the right way, or the best way. Despite what was written in the previous paragraph, there are photographs that display various forms of photographic tricks, indeed, a whole section of the book is devoted to them, for, if you are interested in using them, then it is as well to understand fully their effect.

Whether the desired aim of this volume – to present an informative collection of some of the best photography available today – has succeeded, is up to the reader to judge, but there is a wealth of written information here which, together with the photographs, will surely provide guidance and inspiration to both novice and experienced photographers.

Outdoor Photography

Contents

"Keep the sun over your left shoulder, and everything will be all right." This advice was given to generations of outdoor photographers, and it is true that it will ensure acceptable-to-good results with almost any camera, even the very simplest.

But our expectations have grown nowadays. We are bombarded with high-quality images in newspapers and magazines, on television and in the movies, and (especially) in advertisements in all media. We want to equal and even excel these professionally-produced images: how do we do it?

It is a good idea, before you embark upon anything, to decide exactly what it is that you want to do. What are the special problems of outdoor photography? The usual problem is one of *too much* space, of not being able to get close enough or of not being able to draw sufficient attention to the principal subject – the surroundings just dwarf the subject. This most certainly does not mean that you must always slavishly follow the advice to fill the frame with your subject, as immense effect can be gained by contrasting (for example) a tiny figure with the vastness of the landscape. What it does mean is that you must take very great care, when you look through the viewfinder, that the principal subject is not lost in a confusing jumble of shapes and textures.

Another difficulty, closely related to this one, is the temptation to take in too much. This can manifest itself in two ways. One is the picture with two or three or more conflicting principal subjects, and the other is the picture in which the scale and majesty of the subject is completely lost as it is compressed onto a tiny rectangle of paper or plastic: landscapes, and particularly seascapes, are very likely to suffer from this.

Once again, either of these effects can be turned to good use. A really crowded frame, with a great deal happening, can have the narrative fascination of a Breughel painting; some of the Victorian masters of composite printing demonstrate this perfectly. Equally, a vast expanse of azure sky, completely featureless save for the gentle gradation from the deep blue above to the pale blue of the horizon, has its own fascination and impact. But unless you deliberately strive for these effects, it is very easy to come unstuck and to produce a picture which is neither one thing nor the other.

Another thing which is, perhaps, more characteristic of outdoor photography than of any other is *action*. There is usually plenty of room for things to move, and move they often do. Getting close enough can be a problem once again – a problem often solved with the help of long-focus lenses – but so can the actual technique of expressing movement. You can do this in a hundred different ways, from freezing it with very high shutter speeds to letting it flow into a long sinuous blur; but again, you need to be aware beforehand.

Apart from these specific differences between (most) indoor and (most) outdoor photography, there are all the usual technicalities which are common to both. There is image sharpness; colour saturation; correct exposure; and 'accurate' (by which we mean pleasing) rendition of tones and colours. Lastly, and perhaps most importantly of all, there is the undefinable aesthetic question of what makes a 'good' picture.

*Shooting into the light, be it for landscapes or townscapes, is a way of adding impact to what might otherwise be an ordinary picture. By reducing objects, such as smoke stacks **below** or craggy mountain peaks **facing page,** to their basic outline form, the photographer has conveyed a mood in the simplest and most striking way possible. There is more to contre-jour than just pointing the camera to the light, however; think of what you wish to show and adjust exposure accordingly.*

When we talk of outdoor photography it is easy to forget the enormous number of subjects that fall into this very broad category. Presented with a diversity of choice, the photographer must beware of falling into the trap of trying to capture a multiplicity of scenes without actually doing justice to one. A far safer approach is the one adopted by many professionals who know, before setting out, what they need to shoot. A little forward planning will tell you what to expect, where best to set up the camera and what lenses and accessories you may need. You can even go to the extent of waiting for the appropriate light or weather conditions to arise before setting out.

OUTDOOR PHOTOGRAPHY

This has to come last, though, because there is no art which is not also a craft. A composer must learn to read and write music before he can start on his symphony; a writer must learn the craft of words; a painter must learn to draw, and paint; a sculptor must learn the ways of stone, or wood, or steel; and a photographer must know how to use not only his camera but the whole photographic process.

There is an old saw which says that it is not the camera which makes the picture, but the photographer. Whilst there is a certain amount of truth in this, in that the person with a good eye and a mediocre camera can often excel the person with a first-class camera and no imagination or creativity, it is basically bunk – and dangerous bunk at that.

It is bunk because a good camera extends the range in which we can work. With a box camera, we have no control over focus or image sharpness; we cannot take pictures in poor light; we cannot affix a telephoto lens to single out a piece of the scene which interests us, but which is otherwise inaccessible. It is bunk because a good camera is a pleasure to use, and because good art deserves good tools: the sculptor does not use blunt chisels, or the painter threadbare brushes.

It is dangerous bunk because it implies that picture-taking is merely an automatic process, and that the artist's essential purity of vision will somehow magically translate itself into the final image. It is a real something-for-nothing chimaera. A good photograph has to be worked for. Sure, there is the occasional lucky strike, the picture which comes out better than you ever expected, but if you rely on that miraculous happenstance you are unlikely ever to improve your work.

The biggest distinction between the experienced photographer, whether professional or amateur, and the beginner or casual photographer is that he (or she) can more-or-less guarantee to produce an image of a given subject: there is no question of 'if it comes out'. This image will meet certain minimum technical requirements of exposure, sharpness, and so forth: it will be readable.

An even bigger distinction exists between the photographer who will produce a pleasing image, and the photographer who will merely produce an image. The criteria for 'pleasing' will vary with the photographer and his audience: for example, there are no more than two or three of my own photographs each year which I consider first-rate, aesthetically delightful as well as generally competent, but there are many, many more which I know are perfectly successful for the purpose for which they were taken. They are what one might call commercial successes: they illustrate well what they are supposed to illustrate, and some of them are very attractive – but they are not the very best.

It is unrealistic to hope that every picture you take will be a masterpiece. Even the very greatest photographers – Bill Brandt, Margaret Bourke-White, Dorothea Lange, Ansel Adams, Yoshikazu Shirakawa – shot pictures which were 'also-rans', and no doubt they were (or are) greater critics of their own pictures than I would dream of being. What you can do is aim to take pictures which are always good, and which are sometimes superb.

Exotic, unfamiliar lands; their architecture, people and their way of life cannot fail to arouse the interest of the photographer. Rather than giving way to impulse and trying to encompass all the sights, *however, think of what sums up the essence of the place in your mind and try to capture that feeling. Whilst this may not be an establishing shot in the strictest sense, its personal significance may be greater.*

At this point, several words of warning are in order. The first is a caution against being too serious. You do not *have* to try for a masterpiece every time: there is a place for the snapshot. As you become more and more aware of the potential which can be realised in a picture, you may become more and more demanding in what you want of a snapshot – but that is no reason to stop taking them.

Secondly, remember that a photographer's greatest friend can be a waste-bin. Be a little ruthless with your pictures. Throw out any which exhibit technical flaws, unless of course the 'flaws' are attractive in their own right or the subject is so fascinating you can put up with the flaw. Then throw out, or at least reclassify as snapshots, those which do not come up to scratch aesthetically. There are no criteria for this, but you will know whether a picture moves you or not. Do not be too demanding; a good test is to ask yourself whether or not that picture is up to the kind of standard you would expect in a magazine. If it is not, then leave it out of the pictures you show around.

The 'shooting ratio' of exposures made to exposures shown can vary enormously. Most photographers I know would be delighted with 50%, and regard 25% as pretty good. Even 10% would not be unreasonable, though if you start going below one picture per roll you would do well to ask yourself why. A very useful side-effect of such 'pruning' is that it does wonders for your reputation, which in turn helps your self esteem, which in turn

*The opportunities for shooting found, rather than planned, pictures outdoors are all but endless. With such shots, technique is often of secondary importance; it is the photographer's eye, his powers of observation and ability to see the picture potential of a scene that makes the photograph. Sights such as those shown **facing page top and bottom left** are common enough in any* town, *but how often do we even think of capturing them on film? Pictures need not be representational of course; even the abstracted view of a skyscraper against a clear blue sky **bottom right facing page** can make an interesting composition. Sport, pageantry and everyday life – all will present their own, unique photographic opportunities.*

seems to result in more good pictures per roll.

The third and final word of warning is against confusing technical quality with aesthetic worth. Camera clubs used to be notorious for praising 20 x 24″ prints which were technically superb but artistically a complete yawn, just because they were difficult to produce. This attitude is not completely dead. There was a sad example of it in the Journal of the Royal Photographic

Society a while back. Someone had submitted a portfolio for consideration, and when he was not awarded his Licentiateship he complained that he was hard done by. The judges did not understand, he said: the pictures had been particularly hard to get; the viewpoint difficult of access; the selection of the lens critical; exposure and development meticulous; and printing extremely demanding. So what? If the picture was boring, who cares how hard it was to take.

Neither this book nor any other can turn you into a genius. If there were any such book, we would all have read it and we would all be geniuses. What it can do, though, is to show you the path to competence, perhaps even to excellence, and thereby provide you with the means to express yourself.

It does this in two ways. To begin with the more obvious one, the text is a distillation of a good few years of hard work, of experience, of mistakes and disappointments, of pleasant surprises and joyous discoveries. Although written by one person, it draws upon the experience of countless others – of friends who have been kind enough to comment upon my text, and of many whom I only know through reading their books and looking at their pictures.

And the pictures are the second point of this book. For years, I used to read photographic books mainly for the text; there, it seemed, lay the hard facts, and the technical secrets I was after. After a while, though, I began to realise that the theory which can be put into words is just that: theory. You need to know it – try explaining the basics of exposure or development without words – but unless you start looking at pictures, you are working in a vacuum. Look at the pictures in this book, at your own pictures, at every picture you can see. Then look at the world around you, and try to work out how to translate it into pictures. Do not be afraid to copy – it is a tried and tested way of learning – but equally, do not be afraid to experiment: that is a tried and tested path to becoming an artist.

After a while, both routes will begin to merge, to become one, and almost to fade away. You will have mastered all the basic techniques – they are not particularly difficult, but you have to want to learn them – and your learning will start to come from inside yourself: you will realise that you could have done it better like this, and that next time you should do that. The books will (I hope) always have something to tell you; but you will have more to tell yourself.

It is by no means unusual for a wealthy amateur to own equipment which would put many a professional to shame; and equally, it is not unusual for many dedicated photographers to struggle along with equipment which they know is not of the first rank, simply because they are not wealthy. Fortunately, photography is a field in which the wisdom with which you spend your money is at least as important as the amount you spend.

What Impressionism did for painting, fog, flare and a touch of imagination can do for the photograph; transforming it from a straightforward statement of fact into the realms of poetry. In the shot **top left** the vague shapes of the trees and fence posts, lit by a hazy sun, paint a far broader picture than might at first appear. In the shot of the fog-enshrouded Houses of Parliament **facing page,** note the effect created by the sun's reflection in the water, and how dead the picture would look without it.

EQUIPMENT AND TECHNIQUES

The first point, though, must be one which has often been made before in other fields: quality does not cost, it pays. It is far better to have a limited amount of sound and reliable equipment than to have a gadget-bag crammed with dubious gew-gaws and cut-price, cut-rate lenses and accessories.

Apart from cost, the selection of photographic equipment must always be based on three criteria: the quality of the results, versatility, and convenience in use. In a sense, these tend to quite an extent to be mutually exclusive. For example, a pocket snapshot camera like Kodak's Disc is very easy to use: but even Kodak would not pretend that it is as versatile as a system SLR, and next to a larger format the quality of the results is not very high. At the other extreme, something like my Linhof Technica 70 gives quite stunning quality and is extremely versatile, but is, to put it bluntly, very inconvenient to use. In between, there is something like a Mamiya M645 1000S. The results are excellent – better than any 35mm, because of the much larger negative – but not as good as the Technica 70, which is twice as large again. The versatility is at least on a par with the average 35mm camera, though it is not perhaps quite as good for action, and it lacks the extreme close focus facility and camera 'movements' (rising front, swings and tilts) of the Linhof. And for convenience? Well,

I would rather use a 35mm camera, but it is very little behind and the quality of the results is for me the decisive factor.

Of course, most people choose the 35mm SLR, which wins hands down for versatility and convenience but is, at least from a professional point of view, on the very border of acceptability for technical quality. There are some fields – sports photography, extreme close-ups, and so on – where 35mm's advantages are decisive, but otherwise one rather has to put up with the postage-stamp size negative in return for all the other advantages. The fact that the camera type is so popular also means that it is cheap, which can be a pretty decisive factor.

If money is limited, as it is for most people, then you have to decide what you are going to sacrifice. I suspect that almost all professionals would sacrifice a certain amount of versatility and convenience in order to keep quality, and that their choice would be a second-hand Rolleiflex or one of its imitators – Yashica still make an excellent TLR – which can be picked up very cheaply indeed. Almost everyone I know reckons he could earn a living with just a Rollei, though most admit it would come hard after what they are used to.

Whilst you may still want to stay with the convenience, lightness, and low running costs of your 35mm camera, this does

illustrate one fundamental point: in order to get the very best image quality, you may have to re-think your priorities at the drop of a hat. The same is true, as we shall see later, not only of other items of equipment but also of techniques such as exposure assessment.

What do we mean, though, by image quality? There are really three things which we assess as we look at a picture: contrast, resolution, and distortion.

Contrast is perhaps the most underrated of qualities, and the one which can make the greatest difference to an image. A picture which is lacking in contrast will have no black blacks (though it will almost certainly have white whites); even the smallest degradation, long before the picture begins to look muddy and flat, will detract from the crispness which we associate with the very best pictures.

Factors which lower contrast are numerous, but the most obvious ones are easy to spot: lenses with too many glass-air surfaces, poor coating, dirty lenses, and the lack of a lens-hood. Many wide-angles (especially ultrawides), many extreme-speed lenses, and many zooms exhibit the first fault, and in the absence of first-rate coating, the light bouncing about between the elements will eventually be reflected back to the film and flatten

Fast film, slow shutter speeds *and a sturdy tripod are indispensible aids for photography under subdued lighting conditions. Equally important is the photographer's ability to interpret the readings indicated by his exposure meter. These readings are only suggestions and our personal vision of a particular scene will determine whether we increase or decrease* *exposure; whether to expose for the highlights or shadow areas. For trick effects, such as in the picture **bottom left,** it is necessary to double-expose the film: once for the moon and again for the main scene. Some photographers go to the lengths of taking whole rolls of moon shots and keeping these handy for whenever a suitable view presents itself.*

EQUIPMENT AND TECHNIQUES

the contrast. The quality of coating is easily compared by looking at the 'catchlights' in the lens itself: the harder they are to see, the better. Modern multicoating is certainly a great improvement on the older techniques. Dirt on the lens is easy to spot, and almost as easy to clean. Lens-hoods are a vexed point: the advertising which would have you believe that multicoating does away with the need for them is dangerously misleading. Ideally, a lens-hood should have the same shaped aperture as the format of the camera on which it is used, and it should be as deep as possible without encroaching on the corners of the image – check at infinity and minimum aperture, as this is the easiest way to spot any darkening at the corners. The use of a lens hood is, perhaps, one of the clearest distinguishing marks between the serious photographer and the novice.

There are occasions, though, when a certain lack of contrast is not only unimportant, but actually beneficial. Portraits are a classic example, but there are many other occasions when soft, muted colours and highlights 'bleeding' into the shadows can be used to good effect.

Resolution is the quality most bruited about when talking about lenses, and it is scarcely less important than contrast. As with contrast, slight defects make their presence felt long before they become obvious: a slight mushiness in hair (especially beards), or foliage, or anywhere that there is fine detail. It is important to realise that resolution is a compound of many things: of the lens, of the film, and of the degree of magnification of the original negative or transparency used to get the final image. It is also very much influenced by contrast, and a contrasty lens with relatively low resolving power can appear sharper than one with much higher resolving power but low contrast.

This is one of the ways in which the larger formats score over 35mm. With the small negative, only quite modest enlargements are needed before the dye structure of the film (or the grain, in conventional black-and-whites) becomes obvious: the resolving power of the lens becomes almost irrelevant, especially when using fast films. There is also a certain luminosity, a 'seeing into the shadows', which is associated with the larger formats.

Once again, resolution is not everything. There are many pictures in which resolution is incredibly low, but which still work beautifully: but in others, such as snow scenes with plenty of foliage detail, there is no mistaking the advantage of having as much information as possible on the negative.

The last of our three criteria, distortion, is surprisingly rarely relevant. It is at its most obvious in pictures of buildings, especially brick buildings, where walls which are bulging (barrel distortion) or sucked-in (pincushion distortion) can look very distressing; but unless there are straight lines near the edge of the frame, you will never even notice if your lens suffers from it. Wide-angles commonly suffer from barrel distortion, compact telephotos from pincushion distortion, and zooms from both – one at one end of the zoom range, and the other at the other.

Although these three characteristics are vital in assessing the quality of a lens, they certainly do not tell the whole story.

*Choosing a lens to photograph a particular subject is a personal matter. In people photography, for example, there is no single ideal focal length – wide angle, standard and telephoto lenses are equally appropriate. The pictures **above** right and bottom left facing page were taken with standard lenses while the depth and slight leg distortion in the shot **right** indicates the use of a wide angle lens. A long-focus lens was considered suitable for the study **facing page top**.*

The other thing is much less definable, though: it is to do with the suitability of the lens for the subject, the selection of viewpoint, and the composition of the picture.

The suitability of the lens for the subject is a cumbersome way of saying that you need different lenses for different kinds of work. As a starter, I am a firm believer in the much-maligned 'standard' lens of about 50mm focal length (proportionately longer for larger formats). It is cheap; it delivers excellent image quality, according to the three criteria listed above; the angle of view is a reasonable compromise; and it is fast.

The last characteristic, speed, should not be neglected. There are some people who decry the fast standard lens as an unnecessary extravagance, and say that they do all their shooting at f/5.6 or below. Fine; but what happens when you are shooting in the fast-fading twilight, or before dawn, or even at night? Ever since I had my first fast lens – an f/1.8 Super Takumar on a Pentax SV – I have wanted something faster. At present I use both f/1.4 and f/1.2 lenses, and if I could afford it I should buy an f/1.

Only buy another lens when you find that your present equipment is limiting you; this is as true whether you own one lens or a dozen. For me, it would be a wide-angle, as (after speed) I find that I always want to get a bit more in. The focal length you choose will depend to a great extent on what you want to do, but most people would agree that there are three choices: 35mm, 28mm, and 24mm or 21mm. The first of these is sufficiently close to 50mm that many discount its value, but with an increase in the angle of view of 50% it is very useful; in addition, it does not give the dramatic perspective effects associated with the shorter focal lengths. The next, 28mm, is certainly quite spectacularly wider than 35mm; but for my taste, you might as well go to a 24mm and get something *really* dramatic.

Whilst there are many excellent 35mm lenses of around f/2.8 or so, and good 28mm and 24mm lenses of the same

aperture, anything significantly faster is going to be quite noticeably more expensive, or optically inferior, or (quite possibly) both. At 35mm, the extra stop (to f/2) will probably double the price: going to f/1.4 will probably double it again. It is probably no exaggeration to say that no 35mm f/1.4 is as good as the slower lenses from the same manufacturer, and indeed you have to spend a small fortune even to get tolerable quality. If speed is important to you, take note.

Going in the other direction, the traditional first accessory lens was a 135mm – to my mind, a terrible compromise. Something rather shorter, in the 85mm–105mm range, is a lot more use for candid shots of people, or nature photographs with an increased working distance; it is also likely to be faster and more compact. Alternatively, something like 200mm gives you real 'pulling power' to select details from a distant scene.

Nowadays, the first choice is as likely as not to be a zoom. I have very mixed feelings about zooms. I own two, both Vivitar Series I lenses, and they are very good indeed. On the other hand, they are heavy, expensive, and of limited maximum aperture. The ones I own are also fairly restricted in zoom range – 35-85mm and 90-180mm – which accounts in large part for their image quality. It is simply not possible to build small, light, compact, cheap zooms with a large maximum aperture and a long zoom range: something, namely image quality, has to go. I am just acutely aware of their optical limitations.

It is also demonstrably true that in even remotely critical applications, zooms cannot equal the best fixed-focal-length lenses. The best are very good indeed: but the best fixed lenses are even better. As far as I am concerned, I love the convenience of zooms – they are much more convenient than having to change lenses all the time – but otherwise, I only tolerate them.

Convenience, of course, is very relevant to selection of viewpoint. Whilst it is often possible to vary your viewpoint by taking a few steps forwards or backwards, it is equally often

Indoor locations are not the only ones where flash is useful. There can be many occasions, in nature photography for example, where, even in bright conditions, the ultra-fast shutter speed that the flash simulates is needed to freeze movement. The usual practice in bird photography is to arrange the guns near the nest or feeding spot and shoot from a distance using a long lens. Alternatively, the camera and lens can both be mounted near the subject's expected position and fired remotely. In close-up photography, where maximum depth, and hence small apertures, are invariably needed, flash can provide the obvious answer.

impossible: gaping chasms, crash barriers, or security police stop you getting any closer, or a brick wall stops you going any further back. With a zoom, or a battery of fixed-focal-length lenses, you can select an *effective* viewpoint much closer (or further away) than your *actual* viewpoint. This is why the selection of an additional lens must be a personal matter; only you know what you want to photograph, and how close (or far away) you can get. Sometimes, you may have to compromise, and that is why so many professionals carry a teleconverter in their gadget bags. It may degrade optical quality, but if it is that or nothing, you use it.

When we reach the 'that or nothing' stage we begin to get into the aesthetics and extrinsic qualities of the image; and as this section deals with equipment and techniques, we shall leave that topic until later.

A good meter is essential with modern colour transparency films, and will lead to very much better results with both black-and-white and colour negative films. There are two main types of meter, incident-light and reflected-light, and they differ quite widely in their use.

All meters make use of a curious but demonstrable fact: the vast majority of scenes reflect 18% of the light falling upon them. They read this reflected light, and recommend an exposure which will result in a picture which likewise integrates to an 18% grey.

If a scene – snow, for example – reflects much more than this 18%, the meter will still read it as if it were 'average', and recommend an exposure giving an 18% grey. Result: dark snow.

If altenatively it reflects far less – a black cat in a coal cellar, perhaps – the meter still faithfully recommends its 18% scene. Result: an overexposed coal-cellar.

With a reflected light meter, therefore, you need to give *more* exposure to light scenes and *less* exposure to dark scenes. You learn how much by experience: often one stop, sometimes two stops, very rarely more.

An incident-light meter, on the other hand, reads the light falling on the scene: it is unaffected by the reflectivity of the scene itself, so you need to make no allowances.

So far, so good; but you run into two problems. One is the tonal response of the film, and the other is the aesthetic requirements of the picture.

A sunny day can easily exceed a brightness range, from the brightest highlights to the darkest shadows, of 256:1 – nine stops. A colour film can only meaningfully record 8:1 – four stops – and even with black-and-white film it takes something of a genius to get more than 128:1 - eight stops.

With a colour film, the normal response is to expose for the highlights, and let the shadows 'block up'; with a black-and-white film, most would expose for the mid-shadows, so that only the very darkest shadows 'block up' and only the very brightest highlighs 'burn in.' But what if the detail you want is in those shadows, or those highlights?

The answer, of course, is that you will have to sacrifice one end of the tonal scale for the sake of the other. If you want detail in the shadows, you will need to overexpose to a certain degree; if you want highlight detail, you will have to underexpose.

The adjustments required are usually of the order of one stop, and are quite easy if you are using an incident-light meter. For the black cat, for example, you overexpose: for the snow you underexpose, both as compared with the meter reading. With a reflected light meter, though, they are in the *opposite* direction to the adjustments you are already making. For the black cat, you might subtract two stops and add one: for the snow scene, you might add two and subtract a half.

This seems mind-bendingly complicated, and I only know

one way to learn it. With this book shut, try and explain it to someone else – even an imaginary companion, if you have no long-suffering friends or family who will listen. When you have finished, check and see if you have got it right. If you work it out from first principles, you should have.

So much for the film's requirements: what about the aesthetics? There is a simple and oft-repeated example which illustrates this: a pretty girl in front of a sunset. Expose for the sunset, and the girl will be a silhouette: expose for the girl, and the sunset will be a wash-out. You can of course use supplementary lighting – fill-in flash or a reflector – to even up the lighting on the girl, but otherwise you have to choose.

Rather less obviously, different levels of exposure give different effects. Considerable underexposure can give a moonlit or twilit effect; slight underexposure saturates colours, and makes them more vivid; slight overexposure desaturates them; and considerable overexposure is usually useless, as it washes them out altogether. Almost all professionals aim for a slightly dark transparency – about ⅓ stop under the ideal projection density – as this is much better for reproduction, but it is worth remembering that there is no such thing as a 'correct' exposure – only an exposure which gives the effect which you want.

Which is, equally, the reason for using filters. This is an enormous subject, and whole books have been written about it – Colin Glanfield's excellent *Filters and Special Effects*, is one of the best. Basically, they are used for four reasons. The first is *correction* – they make the light look more the way we expect. 'Warming' filters make a bluish scene sunnier, whilst 'cooling' filters have the opposite effect. Powerful correction filters are used when ordinary daylight-type film is used in the yellowish light of tungsten lamps: their blue colour restores a semblance of normalcy to the scene.

The second is *protection*.Many so-called UV filters serve a slight effect, in that they make the bluish light at high altitudes rather less obvious (though modern lenses are so 'warm' in their colour rendition that this is not particularly important), but their main purpose is to keep dirt, sand and sticky fingers off the front element.

The third *effect*. There are all kinds of filters available which colour part or all of the scene, either to enhance an existing mood or to inject some life into an otherwise boring picture. These must be used with restraint – a funny-coloured boring picture is still boring – but in the right place they can be very effective. Numerous other lens attachments add starbursts, or streaks, or fog, or all kinds of other effects.

The last is the *suppression of reflections*. Most people are familiar with the effects of a pair of Polaroid sunglasses, and polarising filters have a similar effect. Their use is not limited to removing obvious glare, though. By removing white-light reflections, they allow colours to be seen much more clearly. They can also be used to darken a blue sky, but be careful with blue sea: they can remove the colour, as it is the reflection which is coloured.

The other accessory which should be seriously considered by all photographers, indoor or outdoor, is the tripod. Its first and most obvious use is that it provides a stable and shake-free camera platform. Even with a standard lens at 1/125 sec., it can make a significant difference to image sharpness in many cases, and at slower speeds or with longer lenses it is invaluable.

Almost equally important is the fact that it frees you from having to hold the camera. Before you chide me for being such a weakling, I would point out that the difference between a mediocre picture and a good one is often only a matter of waiting. Holding any camera in one position for a few minutes, or even a quarter of an hour, can be pretty fatiguing.

It also allows you to spend more time looking around, taking exposure readings, perhaps moving the odd piece of garbage which is in shot, and *thinking*. One of the greatest drawbacks of the 35mm camera is the way it encourages a 'machine-gun' approach: the tripod can slow you down (when it is appropriate) and give you time to make a better picture.

A depressing number of tripods designed for amateur use are so flimsy and wobbly as to be useless, and you will have to reconcile yourself to spending quite a lot of money if you want a good one. I can heartily recommend the Benbo tripod, made by Kennet Engineering in England, both for rigidity and versatility.

There are also all kinds of other alternative camera supports. My wife (who accompanies me as a photographer in her own right), supports her Mamiya 645 on a monopod, and swears by it; I can't stand them. A very useful and cheap little accessory is the bean-bag or sand-bag, which is just what its name suggests and is interposed between a solid surface such as a wall or tree and the camera, and allows it to be supported far more firmly than if it were just rested on the surface itself; it also removes the the risk of scratching. I often use a Leitz table-top tripod, a dinky little thing which doubles as a shoulder support; just look around, and read the accessory catalogues, and see what suits you.

Most other accessories range from the desirable to the convenient, though there are a few which are simply so much excess weight in your gadget bag. The first accessory is probably the gadget bag itself, in which you carry the camera. Like most professionals, I am a sucker for these, largely because the perfect one does not exist. For transit, a suitcase-type bag is best: I use Halliburton and Adapt-a-case. In the field, soft bags with dividers are generally best. I have one excellent device, by Camera Care Systems of Clevedon, called 'The Photographer's Workbench,'

which fits around the waist and makes carrying much easier: an alternative (which I also own), is a 'photographers' jerkin,' with lots of large pockets – both this and the Workbench spread the load better than a shoulder case and are better for you from an anatomical point of view. They are also much harder to steal from!

Motor drives and autowinders are as much a matter of fashion as anything else, unless you are a professional or very dedicated amateur sports photographer. They are undeniably fun, and nice things to have, but they are also expensive, heavy, and get through film at a frightening rate. They are discussed at greater length in the sections on sports and action photography.

Flash guns are not as useless out-of-doors as one might think, especially for fill-in flash; they are dealt with in the section on photography at night.

One luxury which rapidly becomes a necessity is a Polaroid Land back. Although these are only available to the users of large-format cameras, some rollfilm cameras, and (at great expense and difficulty) a few 35mm cameras, they are such a delight to use and such a staple of professional practice that they are mentioned here.

They allow you to check lighting, composition, and exposure, so that you know what the picture you take will look like: the sense of security which this gives is enormous. Although the cost per exposure is high, most people will gladly pay it for the peace of mind. Another use is when you are travelling: the prints make excellent presents.

Other accessories worth having include cleaning materials (blower brush, lens tissues, lens cleaning fluid); a set of small screwdrivers, for tightening up screws which work loose as a result of vibration; a Swiss Army Knife, one of the most useful single possessions in the world; a grease-pencil, for marking film ratings on canisters, and many other purposes; gaffer tape; a few feet of string; and some paper clips (an excellent source of wire). A cable release (and preferably a spare) is of course essential

Fast films are the natural choice for the sports or action photographer, despite the limited drawbacks of coarser grain and slightly lower resolution when compared with the standard emulsions. Where the action is fast, the more sensitive film will enable you to select a higher shutter speed, thereby freezing movement. Where considerable depth of field is required it will allow for a smaller aperture to be used, and when light levels start to drop it will give you that valuable extra edge. An incidental benefit of the faster emulsion is that it generally shows greater latitude to exposure error. There are occasions, of course, even in sports photography, when wide apertures and slow shutter speeds are required; should surplus film sensitivity become a problem then you can always call into use that almost forgotten neutral density, or even polarizing, filter.

there, 64 ASA Ektachrome is the leader, with Agfa close behind – many prefer its colour rendition.

With colour print, the wise 35mm user will restrict himself to 100 ASA, as the faster films will begin to show their grain structure in all but the most modest enlargements; in rollfilm, faster films are quite practical.

It is worth noting that the so-called 'professional' films, both colour slide and colour negative, are substantially a waste of money unless you refrigerate the film until a few hours before using it, expose the whole roll at once, and then have it processed immediately – circumstances which are rarely practical in outdoor photography. Unless they are treated in this way, these films – which are designed for studio use – can actually deliver worse quality than the ordinary variety.

As for black-and-white, few people who are not already reasonably familiar with photography will use it nowadays. It is well worth considering, for its graphic qualities, its capacity for abstraction, its long tonal range, and the inherent beauty of a well-made black-and-white print. The very slow emulsions of 32-50 ASA will give incredibly smooth gradation although they require critical exposure and development), even on 35mm; the medium emulsions of around 125 ASA are the usual standards; and the fast emulsions of 400 ASA can be 'pushed' to the most incredible effective speeds, such as 1600 or even 3200 ASA, for really fascinating reportage work at night.

Whilst black-and-white is best processed by the user, who can then exercise the enormous control which is available over the medium, colour film is best processed by a *good* lab. 'Snapshot'–type labs are fine for snapshots, but they will not process as carefully as the professional labs, and nor will they take such good care of the film. In a professional lab, scratches on the film are a reason for taking your business elsewhere: in some of the worse amateur labs, they seem to be the norm. Professional labs are a little more expensive, but after a while, you begin to see why.

Whilst there is no point in processing colour *film* at home – the labs can do it better, and frequently cheaper and faster too – colour *printing* is another matter. First-class colour prints cost a fortune from a lab, and whilst they are expensive at home, you can work for exactly the results you want and still save money.

Although the above recommendations are a fair general guide, there are three overriding considerations which should apply no matter what film you use.

The first is that the film which is right for you is the one which gives the results you want. If you need the speed, use a faster film (though it is notable that most serious photographers prefer Kodak's 200 ASA film 'pushed one' to 400 ASA to the 400 ASA material processed normally); if you like someone else's colour rather than Kodachrome, then use that.

The second is that you will get better results if you stick to one film. You get to learn what it will do in various conditions, and how it reacts to different degrees of over and under-exposure. If you are forever chopping and changing, you will never be really sure what you are going to get.

The third is that there is nothing sacred about the ASA (strictly ISO) film speed on the box. If, after a few rolls, you find that you would prefer something a whisker lighter or darker, them just re-rate the film: many a 64 ASA film is rated at 50 ASA (⅓ stop slower) in order to get a slightly brighter picture, or at 80 ASA (⅓ stop faster) in order to saturate the colours a bit more. Both cameras and meters exhibit a certain amount of variation, as do individual working methods: do not be afraid to make allowance for them.

when using a tripod – if you forget or lose yours, try using the self-timer for a vibration-free release.

All of this equipment is of course useless without film; and although you doubtless have your own favourite brands, a few general remarks may not come amiss.

The choice is between colour slide (transparency, reversal, positive), colour negative, and black-and-white. The first is essential if you want high-quality printed (photomechanical) reproductions from your colour photographs, and is the norm in professional photography. Colour print appeals principally to the happy-snap market, which is a shame; it is capable of very good results indeed, and is ideal where a display print is required. Alternatively, you can use one of the pos-to-pos processes (Cibachrome is generally agreed to be the best) and still shoot on colour slide. Black-and-white has a certain professional following, largely for newspaper and similar purposes, and a devoted following in the 'fine art' market. It is far more permanent than the conventional colour processes: a properly-processed black-and-white print measures its life in centuries, even millenia, whilst a well-stored transparency can last for decades. Colour prints range from decades (Ektaflex, Cibachrome) down to months.

In 35mm, most serious photographers using colour slide stick with Kodachrome: it is far and away the finest-grained, and an easy favourite with printers' blockmakers. It also lasts much longer than other films, and is extremely resistant to abuse, notably high temperatures – an important consideration in outdoor photography. Unfortunately, it is not available in rollfilm:

Most of us, whether we admit it or not, are people-watchers. Little scenes from everyday life are always attracting our attention: a pretty girl (or handsome man) walking past; a minor drama at the next table in a restaurant; a beggar, or an old tramp; a self-important businessman; a child playing.

Photographing them is another matter. We often feel that taking pictures of people is not quite a nice thing to do; it is a bit like pointing at them, which we were told when we were children is rude. It is undeniably true, though, that there are some marvellous pictures to be had, if only we were brave enough to take them.

An easy start is with people who actually want to be photographed. If you take your camera and go for a walk, sooner or later there is bound to be a request to 'take me photy, mister'. Most often, it will come from a child, but it can go as high as teenagers and even mature people: I remember being asked by one man to take his picture "Because I've just come up on the horses and I've never won anything before in my life." You can explain to them that they will never see the picture: it doesn't matter. A moment has been immortalised and that is what is important.

Because the people are strangers, the pictures will nearly always be 'grab shots'. This is not necessarily the case – I have been known to shoot two or three rolls of people I have met in the street – but it is nearly always so. As a result of this, you have to try to capture something immediate; there is no time to 'get inside' your subject.

Sometimes, your subjects will have their own ideas on poses; as often as not, these will be parodies of poses they have seen before, carried to grotesque limits, but even this can be interesting. At other times, they will let you choose: think quickly about what you want, select a suitable background and angle, and take the picture *fast* – no messing around with your equipment, changing lenses and taking exposure readings.

People are flattered that you are taking an interest in them – but they will soon become bored, and if you take too long a natural reserve may reassert itself and they will become self-conscious.

Do not expect many of these pictures, especially your first attempts, to be anything very worthwhile. Instead, think of them as a free lesson in photography, generously given by your subject. Sometimes, it may be possible to arrange to give them a copy of the picture: most of the time you will have to explain politely but firmly that it just is not practical. If you have an instant-picture camera, or a Polaroid Land back for a large camera, you may be able to give them a picture on the spot: this is dealt with at greater length in the section on travel and vacation photography.

From this, it is surprisingly easy to move into taking pictures which you initiate. There are some subjects which are fair game: 'hot gospellers' and soap-box orators, cheapjack street-vendors (though some do not take too kindly to it), and the obviously 'picturesque' people such as London's hot-chestnut vendors (yes, they still exist). Others simply seem to present themselves: it is usually sufficient to point the camera at them, without taking a picture, and smile in a way which is obviously asking, "May I take your picture?" Nine times out of ten you will get an answering smile: you may even get into a short conversation. It is as well to have a short speech prepared, nothing too grandiose, about how you are photographing people in Bristol or Milwaukee or whatever: tell them that people fascinate you, and that they looked like a person worth photographing.

Meeting people, whose customs and cultures are far removed from one's own, is one of the pleasures of visiting foreign lands. Many travellers, however, either through shyness or a belief that it might cause resentment, avoid adding human interest to their photographs. People are amenable, and as long as they are approached tactfully, will invariably agree to pose briefly for the photographer.

PEOPLE

The only real difficulties arise on that one occasion out of ten when you are not greeted with a smile. You may decide to take the picture anyway, or you may decide that discretion is the better part of valour. If you get a snarl, or a yell, a quick assessment of your chances is a good idea: you might get an excellent picture, but equally, you might get chased. If it is any consolation, I have been taking this sort of picture for about fifteen years, and only twice have I had any trouble. One was from a market trader who probably thought I was a spy from the Department of Health and Social Security, and the other was from a wino on a park bench. The former contented himself with hurling a few insults – he could hardly attack me in the middle of the market, and anyway I was bigger than he was – and the latter ran after me for a few paces, but I (being sober) was a great deal faster.

In practice, you can get away with an incredible amount unless you are downright foolhardy. If you are nice to people, you can work in the seediest areas of town, and make friends (especially if you hand out a few prints), and get pictures which you would not have dreamed possible.

Whilst you can use almost any camera for this sort of work, ther is no doubt that 35mm is far and away the most suitable. It is unobtrusive, easy to carry, and gives you plenty of shots at each loading. The classic reportage camera is the Leica, and the classic reportage lenses are 35mm, 50mm, and 90mm: the focal length you choose is up to you. Some people prefer the extra stand-off a 90mm lens gives, but the vast majority of professionals in the field prefer to get in among the action with a 50mm or even a 35mm; I use 35mm as a matter of course, with even wider lenses on occasion – I have been known to use a 21mm, because I thought that the violent perspective would suit the rough and violent area in which I was working. Short-focus lenses are also

less critical to focus and easier to hand-hold at low shutter speeds when the light is poor.

Black-and-white film is the traditional choice for reportage, though this may have a lot to do with the fact that most magazines and newspapers have always been in black-and-white. It does have the advantage, though, that exposure is not so critical as with colour film and that there is no danger of colour casts from odd lighting. It is faster, too.

Although in many people's minds (including mine), reportage tends to imply the seedier side of life – slums, whores, and the like – or war photography, there is absolutely no reason why this has to be so. It is equally possible to take reportage pictures of Boston drawing-rooms, of English public schools (speaking of slums . . .), or of playboy parties: the only difficulty lies in getting in!

For this aspect of photography, the ingredients are the same no matter what your field: brazen nerve, a smooth tongue, and an ability to exploit whatever leads or contacts you have. A certain amount of protective colouration is useful, too; not just wearing the right clothes, but speaking with the right accent and expressing the right views. You would not expect to dress or talk the same at a meeting of a Hell's Angels chapter as at a diplomatic garden party.

Reportage, though, is only one aspect of people photography. Another, equally important – probably more important for most people – is taking pictures of people you already know. At one extreme, this shades into reportage, and at the other it moves into formal portraiture.

The reportage end is really the snapshot – although, as I have already said, there is no reason why a snapshot should not be a worthwhile photograph in its own right. To my mind, what distinguishes a snapshot is that the picture is a response to a situation: it is not the primary aim. For example, when you are on the beach, or at the fairground, you take pictures for the fun of it. Admittedly, there are some people (me among them) for whom the pictures are the primary source of fun, and the fairground secondary; but this does not apply to most people, and it most

Whatever problems one may encounter when photographing people, lack of variety is surely not one of them. Apart from the individuals themselves all being different, in looks and in character, there are also their expressions and activities. Add to this the various ways in which they can be portrayed and the permutations become endless. With posed subjects, the photographer can generally pay considerable attention to technique and composition, *perhaps using a darkened interior as a background* **facing page top** *that helps focus attention on the sitter. For candid shots* **above and facing page bottom** *speed of operation and a longer than standard lens may be necessary if the subject is to remain unaware of your attentions. Action pictures* **top right** *may involve panning if you are to get the best results.*

PEOPLE

certainly does not apply to the subjects.

With these pictures, you have to be very careful that what you are doing does not simply shade into self-indulgence. If you are too engrossed in the fun of the fair (or whatever), you cease to be primarily concerned with the picture – and it shows. There is an old saying to the effect that eternal vigilance is the price of freedom; it would not be an exaggeration to say that the price of a good a picture is not far below.

Although it is essential to concentrate upon the picture on such occasions, moving around to get the best background, making sure that your subjects' faces are not obscured by heavy shadow, and so forth, you do not want to be too encumbered with equipment. This is partly for your own convenience, but also because you do not want to waste other people's time: few people are less welcome than the photographer who is forever fiddling with his camera, and asking them to 'hold it a minute' while he takes another exposure reading. If you use 35mm, stick with the 35mm-50mm-90mm trinity, or a zoom in the same sort of range: a 35-85mm f/2.8 is ideal. Alternatively, a fast-handling rollfilm camera such as the Mamiya 645 or Bronica ETR is worth considering.

A specialised but important subdivision of people photography is glamour photography: and for many amateurs, the idea of a couple of weeks in some tropical paradise in the company of two or three or more beautiful girls may seem to be the ultimate photographic assignment. In a way, so it is; but it is also very difficult indeed.

A low camera angle in the shot above helped remove a fussy background and used the plain sky to help focus attention on the subject's face. In the picture *below the eye is drawn by the silhouette figures in the foreground while maximum depth opposite has ensured a wealth of surface interest.*

The professional pictures you see are of unusually attractive girls in unusually attractive settings, and the pictures are taken by very experienced photographers on top-class equipment, usually medium-format. It is all very well to say that a good photographer can make any model in any setting look good, but this is only a part of the story. In the first place, there are some parts of the world which are so pretty, with just the right balance of sun, sand, and lush vegetation, that they form the perfect backdrop. There ar also some girls who are so lovely, so very nearly flawless, that you have to be fairly careless to make them look anything less than beautiful in a picture. Only with the perfect model and the perfect setting can you hope to get first-class pictures with any degree of certainty. Add in to this the fact that the whole trip costs several thousand pounds, and that you *have* to get first-rate pictures in order to justify it, and it is not hard to see that you are more inclined to think about the pictures than about the beautiful girls!

In a sense, this sort of picture is very close to other forms of portraiture. You are primarily concerned to represent the person clearly and (although no-one may admit it) flatteringly. Although portraiture is normally thought of as an indoor activity, there are in fact three clearly distinguishable types of portrait which are normally shot out-of-doors.

The first is the formal portrait of an individual. This is very rare, but it does exist: classic examples are a senior army officer taking the salute, a farmer with his prize bull or whatever, and the shipowner with his new ship. Such portraits are very close in both spirit and execution to indoor portraits, and may well involve quite a lot of supplementary lighting – at the very least, fill-in flash or reflectors. They are shot on medium or even large format, and may even be retouched afterwards. For the most part, such portraits only fall to photographers who specialise in this particular area. To take the example of the prize bull, the photography of prize animals is incredibly complicated as each different type has particular characteristics which must be clearly visible in the final picture, or the client will not be satisfied. From time to time, though, a totally novel approach pays dividends: a famous example is the Victorian portrait of the engineer Isambard Kingdom Brunel in front of a mass of enormous chains. It says very little explicitly, but it works on a much deeper level.

The second sort of out-of-door portrait is the (more-or-less) formal group portrait. There are several kinds of these, but the most usual is probably the wedding group, in which various permutations of the bride and her family, the groom and his family, and assorted friends and hangers-on are recorded for posterity. Another, almost as common, is the group picture of a football or other sporting team, a graduation or other class, or some other band of like-minded people.

The big problem with such pictures lies in getting a picture in which everyone is not only recognisable but also presentable. In a wedding group, for example, you might as well reconcile yourself to the fact that the picture which shows the bride's mother to the best advantage will show the groom's at her worst, and vice versa. In a sporting group, there will always be someone sneezing, or scratching, or looking in the wrong direction: but with any luck, they will carry their sportsmanship over into their reaction to the picture.

On closer examination, this resolves into two problems: the question of marshalling the people, and the question of technical quality. The first is partly a matter of personal presence – either you have it or you don't – and partly a matter of experience. It is very important, though, to be quick and decisive. The former means knowing your equipment, and being able to set it up quickly and confidently – a point which has been made before, and will be made again. The latter means having a clear idea of what you want, and ordering people about until you get it. If you are lacking in experience of a particular kind of shot, look at the work of some other photographers: there are whole books on wedding photography to tell you about the standard pictures, and you can always look in the display windows of professional photographers for further inspiration (or warning!).

Technical quality is another matter. Although you may be able to get away with 35mm, especially in black-and-white with fine-grain film, you are likely to run into resolution problems if you try to use colour print film (the natural choice for most people) for anything but the smallest groups. The vast majority of professionals use rollfilm, traditionally the old 12-on 6 x 6cm but increasingly the 15-on '645' format or the 10-on 6 x 7cm.

For this sort of work, the rectangular formats have a great deal to recommend them. For small groups, such as weddings, the 645 format can be more than adequate, but for larger groups the 6 x 7cm is much more useful. Not only is the image 25% bigger than 6 x 6cm, but the format corresponds much better to the typical shape of the picture: because no space is wasted above or below the picture, the effective area is twice that of the 12-on format, with a corresponding increase in quality.

An advantage of rollfilm which is seldom considered by amateurs is that it is much easier to 'pull up' an individual face out of the group. This is requested surprisingly often, for a variety of reasons. It may be that an individual is wanted by the police, or is missing, or has been murdered – though these are mercifully rare. More often, he (or she) is a celebrity, or becomes one at a later date, so that the picture has a certain news value. Finally, simple vanity plays a part: people want pictures of themselves, especially if (as is usually the case) their particular friends are

Frequently photogenic in itself, architecture can also play an important part in creating a stronger image in people photographs. This is a particularly common ploy in subjects such as weddings *facing page,* where arches and doorways may be used to 'frame' the figures. In the picture *far left* the arch helps establish the setting and adds symmetry and balance to the whole. There are occasions, of course, when the buildings, rather than the people, are of prime importance as in the picture *below.* Here, the figures have been introduced to emphasize the scale and solitude of the setting. The background pillar and arches in the picture *left* are incidental, and yet they add an indefinable appeal to the scene.

close beside them in the group. Of course, all the advantages of rollfilm thus far cited are even more true of larger formats, such as 5x4."

The final advantage of rollfilm (and to a lesser degree cut-film) is that you can take enough pictures for variety without going to excess. It is always a good policy to take several apparently identical pictures as insurance against yawns, scowls, nose-scratching, etc, and the more people there are in the group, the more this is true. With 35mm, there are simply too many pictures on the roll, and with cut film the temptation is to expose rather fewer than the dozen or so pictures available on rollfilm. Furthermore, most pro labs offer a wide range of package deals (process-and-proof) on 120 rollfilm, so there is a considerable financial advantage to the professional in using this format.

The third and last type of out-of-door portrait is the informal (or pseudo-informal) portrait of an individual. The degree to which these are set up varies widely, but it is probably true that the very best informal portraits are neither totally spontaneous nor totally contrived.

For practical purposes, such pictures can be divided into two groups: those in which the subject is actually doing something, whether it be woodwork or windsurfing, and those in which he or she is simply lounging about.

Although the first sort might seem to be easy, they do require quite a bit of forethought. The main dangers are either that you will not be able to see the subject clearly, or that it will not be sufficiently obvious what he is doing. A classic example of the former is the tiny speck on the horizon, which might be anyone windsurfing, and the latter might be represented by a person behind a few pipes which might be a motorcycle, a bicycle, a hang-glider, or an unusually futuristic set of tubular bells.

The secret, obviously, lies in showing enough of what the person is doing without showing so much of the surroundings that they overwhelm the main subject. An easy way of doing this, in many cases, is to use either a long-focus or a wide-angle lens.

The long-focus, used from a distance, will enable you to compress the perspective and 'stack up' the subject with whatever he or she is doing. You will have to choose some fairly readily

Even if your subject is immediately recognisable, you have to show enough of the surroundings to show the context. Here, careful framing shows just enough to make *clear the compassion, humanity, and sheer energy of the Holy Father as he dispenses a blessing with one hand whilst listening to another woman at the same time.*

Left: You can suggest more than you show. The hat and curls indicate an orthodox Jew; the wall must be the Wailing Wall. This is a picture of Jewry rather than of any particular Jew.

Careful framing pays dividends. In the picture top attention is concentrated on the flame; in the picture of the cricketer, tight framing shows the tension and energy; and in the picture of the girl, the inclusion of the shower shows where the water is coming from and makes a pleasing pattern in its own right. More background would result in a loss of impact; less would not show enough.

with petroleum jelly, things can get even more unpredictable. The effect of all these attachments will also vary in different ways with different apertures: with a true soft-focus lens, the image simply becomes sharper as it is stopped down. Experiment is the only way to check out the results; for personal choice, the very expensive Zeiss Softars made for the Hasselblad and a few other Zeiss-equipped cameras give the most pleasing results.

As for the choice of camera, there is little doubt that the best quality is obtained with medium-format equipment; but there are many occasions when this is outweighed by the greater immediacy of 35mm. If you use only 35mm, then it is simply decided – but if you are serious about portraiture, you may wish to consider rollfilm.

Whatever camera you use, and whether you choose the kind of picture where the subject is doing something or the kind where they are just relaxing, the golden rule is to think and to look around before you actually start shooting. Some photographers like to 'shoot towards' a picture, taking a sequence of shots in the knowledge that the first few are unlikely to be of much use, but knowing that they are improving as they go along; this method has the advantage that there is the occasional bonus among those early pictures, but it can also get expensive in film. With a bit of self-discipline, you can get results every bit as good in most cases by just wandering about first. The wandering period also has the advantage of getting the subject used to your being about with a camera.

Hard, sharp, saturated colours suit the picture of a New York taxi fire *below*, but a more muted approach, with a touch of soft focus, suits the romantic scene *right*. Would soft focus, and perhaps a warming filter, have improved the picture on the left?

identifiable part of the whole; but if you show a pole, and part of a sail, and some sea and sunny sky, it is fairly obvious what is going on.

Wide-angles, on the other hand, are used very close-up. You can even use fish-eye lenses if you are careful; I remember one particularly striking picture of someone working inside a wooden frame, where the wood and the joints of the table she was making loomed large around the edge, whilst the face in the middle of the picture did not seem distorted at all – although, of course, it would have been if compared with a 'straight' portrait.

For the second sort of picture, perhaps 'lounging about' conveys the wrong sort of impression, but it does have the connotation of relaxation which is the essential part of an informal portrait. There are innumerable poses which you can use: lying in a deckchair, leaning against the wall or reclining against a rock, sitting on the edge of the swimming pool . . . the important thing to decide is what sort of image you are trying to put over, whilst still retaining the character (real or assumed) of the subject.

To this end, you can vary not only viewpoint, but also technique. For example, hard bright colours, wide-angle lenses, and graphic simplicity might suit a Californian swimming-pool scene; but soft-focus, desaturated colours, and soft printed cotton dresses might be more appropriate to a countryside shot.

The techniques of soft-focus are extremely varied. The best soft-focus pictures are usually obtainable with special soft-focus lenses: they have a sort of luminous quality, with the shadows spreading into the highlights, which can be extremely attractive. The very best, such as the the SF-Fujinon, do not even lose contrast: there is just something faintly magical about them.

Failing this, most people will use some sort of front-of-lens attachment. The effect of these varies very widely indeed, and if you start introducing such home-made effects as a piece of nylon stocking stretched over the lens (with or without holes, inserted with a match-tip or cigarette end), or an old UV filter smeared

TRAVEL AND VACATION

For many people, perhaps most, travel is the most powerful stimulus of all for their photography. The big risk is that the novelty is overwhelming: the craft of picture-making is forgotten, and the camera is fired willy-nilly in all directions.

There is absolutely nothing wrong with 'holiday snaps', pictures which serve no other purpose than to remind you, and anyone you were with, of what a good time you had. On the other hand, they are not usually the sort of picture you would want to show around – just consider your own reaction to yet another stack of unsorted, out-of-sequence, frequently duplicated snapshots. If you want to take really good pictures, you are going to have to work at it.

To begin with, it is a mistake to assume that you can totally change your style just because you go abroad, or at least away from home. You will do best if you build on your existing interests in photography, whether people, landscape, sport, or whatever. If photographing plants is your thing, then make sure

'Establishing shots' can be done in a number of ways. Well-known landmarks are one obvious approach, and including a signpost in a picture is another; only rarely, though, will a signpost **on its own** be sufficient. In less well-known areas, a general shot which shows the **type** of surroundings is very useful; the beach picture could set the scene for pictures of the individuals, whilst the picture of the clapper bridge **facing page left** shows the mixture of wildness, serenity, and antiquity which makes Dartmoor so attractive.

you photograph plenty of plants abroad. Even if you then branch out into something totally different, you will have done two things: you will have broken the potential block, of not knowing where to begin, and you will have reminded yourself that the discipline of taking pictures has not mysteriously relaxed just because you are on holiday.

Be selective about where you go: if taking pictures while you are on holiday is something important to you, then go somewhere that you will want to take pictures. This is not something which can be readily defined; as much as anything else, it is a sort of inner yearning or conviction. You may well turn out to be wrong – but there are a few guidelines you can set yourself.

For example, is the architecture of a city important to you? If it is, you will do best to pick somewhere with plenty of character: for example, you might prefer San Francisco to Los Angeles. Do you want to go to the city? Perhaps the mountains or the sea are more for you. Or is it people that fascinate you? Go somewhere the people are friendly – Portugal, perhaps, rather than Spain, or Southern Germany rather than Northern. Of course, such generalisations are dangerous, but until you get to know a place, they are all you have to go on. Ask yourself what you really want to do; you will enjoy yourself far more, and get better pictures out of it.

Even if you cannot choose – for example, if you are going somewhere on business, but think you may have some time to yourself – your next step is the same: find out all that you can about the place. Read books; talk to people who have been there; and, whenever possible, look at pictures. Do not worry about

stunting your own creativity: you will have plenty of opportunity to exercise that when you get there. Think, react, and form a picture in your mind. You may have to change your mind when you get there, but at least you will have something to go on.

An important part of planning is getting your equipment together, and apart from the usual dictates of pocket and personal taste, there is one very simple rule to apply: just how much are you prepared to carry?

There is a strong temptation to take everything you have, especially if it is only a question of loading it into the back of the car, but the drawbacks of this approach become obvious when you reach your destination. You have the choice of carrying it

everywhere with you, which is tiring, boring, and frequently unnecessary, or leaving it behind in a hotel room or in the car where there is not only a constant worry about security but also a certain degree of pointlessness: if the gear is not with you, you can't use it.

Whilst the 'kitchen sink' approach does have its merits, the occasions on which it is justified are limited. I would only bother if photography were the primary purpose of the trip; if I had an assistant to carry and help set up the gear – and it must be a willing assistant, not (for example) a press-ganged member of the family; and (most important of all) if I had very little idea of exactly what I would be photographing, and under what conditions.

An example of this occurred on a trip to Northern India, when I was working on two books: a biography of His Holiness the Dalai Lama, and a book on the symbolism of Vajrayana Buddhism. I used three systems: Linhof for close-ups, architecture, and some hand-held reportage (though I was limited in the latter by the f/4.5 lens); Hasselblad, for those occasions when the extra speed of the f/2.8 Planar was necessary, but the quality of the larger format was still possible; and Nikon, for those occasions when fast lenses and speed of handling was more important than getting a big image. Nowadays, I would only need two systems: I have an f/2.8 lens for the Linhof, which obviates the need for the Hasselblad (and

leaves me with a bigger picture into the bargain), and I would probably use a brace of Leicas with four or even five lenses for the 35mm side. This would deprive me of my fast 200mm f/3 Vivitar Series 1 (for the Nikon), but would give me a much faster wide-angle, the 35mm f/1.4 Summilux, which I use much more.

I am also fortunate in that my wife would have her own camera, the excellent Mamiya M645. This is a particulary useful camera because of two lenses: the 80mm f/1.9, which is very fast indeed for a rollfilm lens, and the 35mm f/3.5 which is very wide – about the equivalent of 21mm on a 35mm camera. Although the M645 is not quite as versatile as the Linhof (and in any case I prefer rangefinder cameras for many applications), it is a lot smaller, lighter, and easier to use – and about a third of the price, too!

At the other extreme from this approach is what might be called the minimalist. At its very least, this means carrying just

*Although some famous landmarks, such as the Taj Mahal, can stand perfectly well on their own, a much better picture will often result if there is some strong foreground interest. The brightly robed ladies **below** provide a superb colour contrast, whilst the artist **facing page** gives a valuable 'second view' of the subject. The problem lies in getting enough depth of field and in balancing the foreground and background exposures – a particularly difficult thing to do in the picture on the left.*

one camera and one lens, though the extra versatility conferred by an extra lens usually far outweighs the minor inconveniences of weight and complication; the latter, incidentally, is exemplified by the old saying that if you have two lenses, you will always have the wrong one on the camera.

With the minimalist approach, a lot depends on the quality that you want. In many ways, the M645 (especially with the two lenses mentioned above) suits me perfectly; a low-cost alternative would be a second-hand TLR. In 35mm, a good choice is a really first-class zoom like the Vivitar Series 1 35-85mm f/2.8; if you back it up with something like an 80-200mm, you have a very versatile outfit indeed. The quality increase from using prime lenses will not be significant in the majority of cases, though you may find their extra speed useful.

Although the minimalist approach may seem to the well-equipped to be unnecessarily limiting, it is quite astonishing what you can do with a single lens, let alone two; you may even find that your photography improves as a result of this voluntary limitation, because you are free to concentrate on the picture rather than being distracted by having to decide what equipment to use.

If you only own one camera, you may think that this last statement is foolish, even patronising. One the one hand I agree with you: for years I was in the same position, and I must confess that the extra equipment I now own makes my photography both more pleasurable and easier. On the other hand, I know that I take better pictures if I select from my armoury the very minimum of equipment I am going to need, and take that. The rest stays at home.

In between the two extremes is what one might call the sensible approach. You can arrive at what to take in two ways. Either you can work out what you want to photograph, select the gear you need to do it, and leave the rest behind, or you can work from the opposite direction and leave out the stuff which you know you will not be using.

This sort of selection is one which really does depend very much on what your personal interests are, and of course it shades into the minimalist approach at one end and the kitchen-sink approach at the other. From a practical point of view, it is as well to carry two bodies, both as a precaution against mechanical failure and to allow you to use two film types, or two lenses with the same film type; a reasonable range of lenses; a flashgun if you normally use one; a tripod; and a number of the more useful accessories such as a polarising filter, an 81A (to 'warm up' dull days), and a teleconverter for use in emergencies.

A good way to choose a 'sensible' outfit is to start out with a gadget bag, and to carry only what will fit into it. The tripod and maybe the flash will have to live outside, but everything else should go in. This not only makes it easier to carry: it also makes it easier to check that you have got everything, and makes for greater security. If you pick the right bag, you can carry a staggering amount: one of my gadget bags is the very elegant leather Bach'o, into which I can fit two Nikons, five lenses plus all hoods, a teleconverter, a set of filters, a Weston Master, sundry

Minimalism triumphant: each of these pictures was taken with a standard lens. They are very different, yet each sums up a scene in its own way; careful selection of viewpoint, framing, and composition is far more important than having a bagfull of lenses to choose from, and *indeed too much choice can mean that you spend more time thinking about equipment than about the picture. Most people find that a standard lens, or a moderate wide-angle, or a 'standard zoom' is ideal for the vast majority of pictures.*

TRAVEL AND VACATION

accessories such as cable releases and flash couplers, a moderately powerful flashgun, some spare batteries, and even a few rolls of film. It only measures 10″ x 14″ x 5″, but with all that lot in it, the weight is alarming!

However much, or little, equipment you take, you have to realise that you are going to be away from home and away from your usual sources of supply. If you are somewhere reasonably civilised – most of Western Europe, for example, or a substantial part of the United States – this may not matter too much, in that you can always buy anything you may have forgotten. Even then, there are good reasons not to be so careless. It is galling to have to buy something you already own, merely because you were stupid enough to forget it: I own three 52mm polarising filters for that very reason. Unless you are very close to a camera store, you have the distraction of going to get it, and it can be quite an extensive journey if you are somewhere remote. It is likely to cost you more than it would at home, and you may have some difficulty in asking for it: I had Hell's own job getting some lens-cleaning tissues in Portugal, and was eventually given some as a present by a friendly professional in Braganza. And finally, there

is always the chance that you will not be able to get it at all – and the further off the beaten track you go, the likelier this becomes.

The most obvious consumable is film. Apart from variations in price from one country to another, there is the fact that you will not know the best place to go to buy it, and that if you are in a tourist area you will suffer both from increased prices and from dubious film freshness; if you want reasonable quantities, you may also find that you have cleaned out the local dealer.

After film, batteries are perhaps the most important. I like to use AA cells in everything possible, and to recharge them with a small multi-voltage charger; but unfortunately, cameras, motor-drives, and meters seldom run on AAs. If you only travel once a year, it is a good idea to replace all batteries before you go – but remember, even 'fresh' batteries can be exhausted. What I do, and what I advise anyone else to do if they travel reasonably regularly, is to take a *complete* spare set of *tested* batteries with you – a battery testing meter is not expensive, or the shop may do it for you, and it will considerably improve your peace of mind. It is also a good idea to be as independent of batteries as possible, and this is why so many travel photographers use

What is it that strikes you about a place? Spend a little time thinking about it, and then photograph it; this is a sure recipe for a good souvenir. Having a good idea of what you want also enables you to concentrate on composition and exposure; the boy in the palm tree was a tricky subject, but one well worth the effort.

mechanical cameras and Weston meters. The only equipment I use which goes dead without a battery is the Mamiya 645; and I *always* travel with a spare.

The other minor consumables include lens cleaning materials and such things as gaffer tape, but a 'consumable' of a different kind is anything which is breakable or capable of being lost. For example, I normally carry a spare ground-glass for the Linhof, a spare cable release (or two), a spare darkslide for the Linhof's interchangeable backs, and a spare flash-synch lead for the Metz. Check over your own gear: you will soon find the likely bits, if you have not already discovered them the hard way on a trip. Camera screws on some tripods are another favourite: in desperation, a bolt and wing-nut from a hardware store will do the job.

One last 'accessory' which I find invaluable is a Polaroid Land back for the Linhof or Mamiya RB67. I use the inverted commas because I do not use it primarily for its normal purpose, which is checking exposure, composition, and so forth, although it comes in handy for that. Instead, I use the pictures as presents.

It is astonishing how well they go down, with everyone in every culture. In a more sophisticated country, it is an amusing and friendly gesture to give someone a Polaroid: in a poor and backward country, you may be giving someone the only decent colour picture he will ever get of himself or his loved ones. What is really important is that you are not merely handing out *baksheesh;* you are really doing something for someone, and communicating as a human being. Furthermore, it is something which is acceptable to everyone, from the High Abbot of a monastery to the poorest slum-dweller. Sometimes, it is hard to feel that you are not making poor recompense for the hospitality that you are being shown; but the recipient of the picture does not see it that way.

It is also a useful gesture of involvement. Snatching pictures

is an old tradition, but there is an even older saying: 'poverty is picturesque – provided you aren't poor.' Having anyone poke his nose (let alone his camera lens) into your private life is bad enough: it is all the more galling if you know that he is laughing at you, or worse still pitying you, as he does so. Whenever possible, I greet someone (greetings are easy to learn in any language) and ask either in words (if I can) or in gesture (if I cannot) whether I can take a picture. I do not like to give a tip: I think it is demeaning to both sides. Far better just to say "Thank you" (another word easily learned), or if you get more involved to give a Polaroid picture. The only exception to tips is children: a small present, such as a pencil or a couple of sweets, is unlikely to upset anyone. Make sure the parents understand, though, or your motives could be misunderstood!

Some travel photographers carry a Polaroid Land camera just for this purpose; the only real risk is running out of film if you give in to all the demands for pictures. It may be hard, but you have to refuse some.

One last equipment recommendation is a simple one, oft-repeated and equally often ignored. NEVER take an untried camera (or any other piece of equipment) on a trip where the pictures are irreplaceable – which means most vacations for most people. Always put at least one roll of film through it, and preferably buy it sufficiently far in advance that you can familiarise yourself with it before you go. Even a minor meter malfunction can end up meaning your pictures are all hopelessly under- or over-exposed, and there is always the risk that through failing to read the instructions properly you will mess things up yourself: the collapsible lenses on old Leicas, which had to be pulled out and locked into position before they were used, were one favourite, and nowadays there is always the multi-exposure button or mirror lock to confuse you.

When it comes to actually taking the pictures, there are a few simple guidelines which should considerably increase your chances of taking good ones.

Take plenty of pictures. The increase in cost is not all that great, and it can make the difference between having (almost) all the pictures you wanted and having half of your beautiful memories unsupported by images.

Use establishing shots. These are the shots used in movies to show where you are. In New York, it's the Manhattan skyline; in Paris, it's the Eiffel Tower. Apart from these rather obvious establishing shots, there are others which are more intimate, but will evoke sighs of recognition from people who know the place and give some idea of its flavour to those who do not. London is (of course) the red double-decker buses and the black taxis, Portugal is the political slogans painted everywhere and the contrast of past and present, and so on.

Don't just shoot the obvious. As well as the establishing shots, photograph personal stuff or things which catch your eye. Photograph the bar where you had a drink; the street signs and advertisements; the people you met on the trip; the traffic jam on the way to the beach.

*Everyone takes pictures of guardsmen, but how many achieve this kind of graphic simplicity? It is partly a matter of coming in close, and partly a matter of exposure; that red really is **red**. A much less dramatic picture, but one which is equally typical, is that of the* *French schoolchildren in their smocks; 'crocodiles' like this are a familiar sight. Keep an eye open for the unusual, too; subjects like the signpost **left** may seem silly at the time, but memories fade fast, and long after the vacation is over it will continue to amuse you.*

TRAVEL AND VACATION

Decide what you are trying to show, and show it. If it's your girlfriend, show your girlfriend – not an anonymous and tiny figure lost in the middle of the picture. If it's the Eiffel Tower, show the Eiffel Tower – not a crowd of knick-knack vendors and fellow tourists. And if it's your girlfriend in front of the Eiffel Tower, then have your girlfriend close enough that you can see it is her and the Eiffel Tower far enough away that you can see it is the Eiffel Tower, and not just a jumble of girders that could be anywhere.

Take a bit of care. It is easy to be overwhelmed by the novelty of the situation, and not to pay attention to what you are doing. Beware of messy backgrounds, trees growing out of people's heads, tilting horizons, prominent signs indicating the nearest WC, and so on. Remember that your brain simply does not register a lot of information which the camera will faithfully record: and of course, Polaroid Land cameras are ideal for teaching you how to avoid this problem, but otherwise there is no substitute for just *looking* through the viewfinder. Sometimes, for a bit of variety, try taking really bad pictures: it may be an oversophisticated way of amusing yourself, but it sometimes works.

Shoot around the subject. Change angles. If you want a straightforward shot, then by all means take it – but then try something different. Some of my favourite shots of the Eiffel Tower, for instance, are semi-abstracts: the ironwork is lit gold by the setting sun against a clear deep blue (underexposed one stop) sky. Try reflections, unusual viewpoints, night shots, novel foregrounds and backgrounds; anything for variety.

Don't give up when the sun goes in. In colour, an 81C will remove the bluish cast of a rainy day, and if there is no sky or rainy foreground even the most overcast day can be made to look quite sunny. Alternatively, make the most of the bad weather. In black-and-white, rain-washed streets and damp moors can look doubly romantic, regardless of how cold and unpleasant they were in reality. Orange filters bring out dramatic clouds, and besides, there are some places which are more attractive in cold weather. In winter, beaches are deserted and clean, and parks are not infested with daytrippers: on a cold day in winter, you can get some real travel-brochure shots if the sun is shining.

Get plenty of people in. Crowds and locals provide local colour: people you met and talked to will fade from memory unless you record them on film. Either way, people are every bit as important as places.

Take pictures when you are enjoying yourself. A happy atmosphere is often evident in a picture, but in any case there is some magic in a photograph which enables you to recall the moment you took it. Sometimes you do not even need to look at the picture, because the memory of taking it is so vivid.

Unfortunately, there is a negative side to travel photography, too: a few do's and don'ts may be useful.

Be aware that some countries impose restrictions on the number of cameras or the amount of film you can import. This will seldom affect the bona-fide holidaymaker, though it can be awkward for professionals. Check before you go, especially to some 'third world' countries.

Respect local customs. In most countries, people are either indifferent to being photographed or actually enjoy it, but in some (especially Islamic countries) they may not be at all keen, particularly if you point your camera at a woman. Usually, smiling will get you out of a lot: but do not push your luck. Try to put yourself in their place: there is a story of one young lady who wanted to be photographed sitting in the lap of a Thai Buddha,

Cities as famous and *photogenic as Venice and Paris seem to provide opportunities for establishing shots at practically every turn. There is no reason, however, why these should be the boring, cliché shots that almost every visitor to these places might take. The inclusion of gondolas and statue in the photographs shown* ***facing page,*** *lifts these pictures out of the realms of the mundane. Rather more subtle is the information provided by the* picture ***above,*** *of a religious ceremony at the Wailing Wall. Travel photography need not be limited exclusively to the picturesque. Scenes of squalor and deprivation* ***top*** *are equally valid as subject material; they will, after all, provide a more complete, if somewhat less palatable, image of the country. You should, however, spare the feelings of those who have to live under these conditions, by avoiding the open-mouthed, voyeuristic approach.*

and who in the furtherance of this ambition found herself hurled in jail for a couple of days. This may seem a very un-Buddhist reaction (even from Theravadins), but how would you feel if a scantily-clad girl wanted to be photographed lying on the altar at your local church?

There is always the risk that you will be accused of spying. This is fairly standard practice in many Eastern European and African countries, though few take it as far as Tanzania where it is (or was – I don't know the current state of the law) illegal to take any photographs of anything without a permit. Generally, you will have little problem if you were acting in good faith; but you must realise that to many of the more paranoid governments 'military and strategic installations' can include bridges, dams, railways, airports, roads, public buildings, and even policemen and public servants.

You are very unlikely to run into such problems, though, and the only remaining question is one of how you are going to present the pictures when you get home. The following notes are particularly applicable to slide-shows, but they can be adapted to exhibitions, albums, or even just handing around prints. First, weed out the bad pictures and the duplicates. Next, put them in order: it need not correspond exactly with the order in which they were taken, but it should make sense. Use the pictures to tell a story with a beginning, a middle, and an end. When you have sorted them, decide what you are going to say about each: make it short, and make it informative. Finally, watch out for any signs of boredom in your audience: if you detect any, either speed up or stop, according to circumstances, and shorten the presentation next time.

*The speed of operation that results from a familiarity with equipment is a definite asset when photographing people. Be it in Central Park **above** or central Africa **facing page,** people going about their daily lives have more to concern them than posing for some eccentric* stranger's camera. If speed is of the essence in many people shots, then the reverse applies to landscapes and shots of inanimate objects. Here, a few moments spent considering composition, exposure and any other variable will pay dividends.

Whilst it might be going a little far to say that everyone loves a parade, it is certainly true that few can resist one. Even dedicated misanthropes have to admit that the colour, the emotion, and the theatricality of parades and similar spectacles can make for some good pictures, and less phlegmatic individuals can throw themselves into enjoying the occasion.

There are two ways of approaching such occasions. One is to do what the press does, and use long lenses in order to concentrate upon the principal players, and the other is to try to capture the general sweep and feeling of the thing by showing the crowds and the ordinary people enjoying themselves. Although the second approach is much less demanding of equipment, it does require considerably more originality and effort in finding pictures. This is one of the reasons, of course, that press photographers have to use the first approach: in the first place, they *have* to come home with identifiable pictures, and in the second, it is asking rather a lot of any photographer to be creative and original all the time, to order.

One thing which is essential is to keep equipment as simple as possible, so that the minimum of time is spent fiddling around and changing lenses. It is quite usual to carry two cameras,

loaded with the same film but with two different lenses, so that you can grab the one that is most appropriate for a particular picture and use it without further ado. There are two reasons for this. One is that the best pictures always seem to come up when you are reloading or changing lenses, and this approach minimises such a risk. The other, perhaps even more important, is that it is not a good idea to change lenses too often in a jostling crowd. You run the risk of dropping something, and there is also the possibility of theft from your gadget bag.

The standard format is 35mm, for four main reasons. The long 36-exposure load saves reloading too often; the handling is much faster and easier than with other formats; the light weight

Parades and marches, with their mass of colour and carefree atmosphere, are invariably photogenic. With jostling crowds to restrict your movements, however, you should be prepared to accept the shots that come your way. An early start may guarantee you a good vantage point, but failing this you can still achieve a great deal with a simple-to-use camera fitted with a wide angle lens. If there is no alternative, you could even do what some professionals do and shoot with the camera at arm's length above your head.

POMP AND CIRCUMSTANCE

As a participant at a festival, you may find that close-ups of the action are a possibility, and once again a wide-angle lens, perhaps as fitted to a compact, could prove the most suitable. The alternative onlooker's approach is to distance oneself from the proceedings and shoot through a telephoto lens. Several lenses or a long range zoom will allow you to be more selective in what you show. With longer lenses faster films become useful, as they will allow you to select the smaller aperture and higher shutter speed, thus maximising depth and minimising movement blur.

and lack of bulk is invaluable when you are trying to get through a crowd or to a vantage point; and there is a tremendous choice of lenses, especially telephotos.

The very long lenses of 500mm and above are best used with a tripod. The old rule is never to use a shutter speed lower than 1/focal length (in mm) if you want to avoid camera shake in hand-held shots: this means 1/500 second for a 500mm lens, and 1/1000 for an 800mm or 1000mm lens. With 64 ASA film, even a bright day means that you are working at f/5.6, which is beyond most 500mm lenses, let alone 1000mm. Consequently, you will have either to use a faster film (with consequent loss of quality) or a slower shutter speed.

With these long lenses, you can pick out not only the VIPs (if any), but also other individuals from the crowd – which can be quite fascinating. The difficulty, of course, lies in finding somewhere to set up the tripod.

A more realistic approach, therefore, relies on hand-held

POMP AND CIRCUMSTANCE

photography. For this, 200mm or at most 300mm lenses are advisable, and it is as well not to indulge in any violent exercise, such as running or climbing, immediately before taking a picture lest camera shake intrudes again. Except at the most crowded events, these focal lengths should be sufficient: and besides, if you are really keen, you can always arrive good and early, before anyone else, to secure your vantage point.

It is always well worth reconnoitring the terrain beforehand, for two reasons. It helps you to spot the best vantage point, and it also enables you to check out that vantage point without having to fight to get there. More than once, I have found that an apparently superb viewpoint is wrecked by something obvious, like a telegraph pole in the way, or by something.more subtle like the well-known prominent WC sign. If you have struggled through a crowd for ten minutes to reach the point, this can be something of a disappointment!

Whatever equipment you are armed with, you will invariably find that something is missing. Rather than dwell on these shortcomings, however, be positive and concentrate on achieving the possible. Try looking for pictures that others may fail to notice; the sideshows that others ignore simply because they appear so unremarkable at the time, but that can be so telling in a pictorial essay. Look around the scene through the camera's viewfinder – what you see in this way may be considerably different from what your eyes previously noted. Look not only at the objects and people that surround you, but also the colours and how they interact to create pleasing compositions. Above all, don't stint on the film as you may not get another chance.

POMP AND CIRCUMSTANCE

If you can secure a really good viewpoint, you may even be able to get away with a 105mm lens or something similar; but this is very much a matter of luck. One thing that these lenses may well be useful for, though, is showing the 'massed band' effect of a parade: not just the parade itself, but also the crowds. It is a curious fact that whenever you want to show how crowded a place is, the people melt away like the morning mist; but when you want to move, or to get a clear viewpoint, they are packed like sardines.

Standard and wide-angle lenses are of most use either when you can get in among the action or when you want to show the people near you enjoying themselves. They may be wearing extrovert clothes, waving flags, and shouting or cheering, and they may be in odd positions on peculiar vantage-points: you can get some very amusing and cheerful pictures this way. Many professional reportage photographers use rangefinder cameras (which essentially means Leicas) for the wide-angle shots with 21mm, 28mm, 35mm, or 50mm lenses and reflexes – traditionally Nikons, but also Canons – for the longer lenses, where reflex focusing comes into its own.

The question of getting press 'privileges' is a vexed one. For some occasions, all you need is a bit of nerve: you will be allowed anywhere. At other times, a letter beforehand to the organisers may give you a press pass, or at least admission to a reserved viewpoint. Quite often, though, you will need a press 'ticket' in order to get in – and unless this is issued by a recognised body, such as the National Union of Journalists, it is meaningless. The so-called press passes you can buy through the small ads may sometimes get you past someone gullible, but you could probably get past just by smooth talking. Even if you do have a genuine press ticket, it is no guarantee that you will get in. Although I am eligible for a press ticket, and indeed used to carry one, I decided that the advantages were not worth the subscription. I can, therefore, quite honestly say from experience of both sides of the fence that I have very rarely found a press ticket a clear advantage (let alone a decisive advantage) in getting a picture, and that unless you are in the position of a pressman (where you have to get a picture of the event, no matter what) you may well get better pictures and enjoy yourself more by mixing with the general public.

Before we leave the subject of photographing occasions, there is one other point which must unfortunately be made. We live in troubled times. A camera could easily conceal a bomb, and a long lens (especially when mounted on a shoulder stock) could be a disguise for a gun. On many state occasions, security will be tight. There are a few things you can do to emphasise your *bona fides* – I know of one photographer who painted the barrels of his long-focus lenses orange, so that they would be good and obvious, and not mistaken for guns – but if you are stopped, cooperate. It is a much better idea than getting your camera smashed, your film ruined, and possibly a dented head into the bargain.

Photographs of outdoor occasions, whether joyous or solemn, do not need to be brilliantly planned and executed to be successful. More often than not, what is important is to get a record of the happening, with whatever imperfections this may entail, and to transmit the overriding feelings and sentiments in the resultant image. The pictures on **these pages** leave the viewer in no doubt as to the mood of each occasion and while they may not communicate much more than this to the outsider, to the individual who took the shots, his or her own memory will fill in whatever is not shown. The photograph itself serves as a tangible link with the past.

SPORT AND ACTION

Sports and action photography covers an enormous range of events and conditions. It includes a school sports-day; a powerboat travelling at 70mph in a cloud of spray; a hang-glider floating in the air; and a Porsche going down the Mulsanne straight at two hundred miles an hour. Lighting can be anything from brilliant summer sun to lashing rain – at Le Mans, you can get both inside a single 24 hours. Despite this wide disparity, there are a number of general observations which are true of most sports.

The first concerns equipment. About the only use for large format is shooting something like the finish of a race, so that the winner can be 'pulled up' individually without too much loss of quality. Even then, anyone who knows the sport can usually get a better picture by anticipating the action.

Although there are a few events, such as a kindergarten

may have to resort from time to time to slower shutter speeds than he would like.

Opinions are divided on motor-drives. There is no doubt that if you learn to anticipate the action you will get very much better pictures than someone who simply keeps his finger on the button at five frames per second – look at some of the pictures taken before the war on Speed Graphics with slow film, slow lenses, and very slow film changing – but there are occasions when a motor-drive is handy or even indispensible. It can be used at full speed for a sequence such as a crash in a motor race, but it can also be set-up in an inaccessible spot and triggered remotely: if you look above the ring at a major boxing match, you may well see several motor-driven Nikons bolted to the ceiling.

The question of anticipation is fundamental, and brings us to the main non-equipment point: in order to get the best

footrace, where you can get in among the action, even the most undemanding sport will usually require something of the order of 85mm or 105mm. For sports such as powerboat racing and motor racing, there is virtually no limit: 300mm is commonplace, 500mm useful, and 800-1000mm not out of the way. Furthermore, because hand-holding is normal, you need fast lenses or fast films or both to offset the high shutter speeds needed. It is sports photographers who buy such alarmingly expensive lenses as 300mm f/2.8s and the like – and unless you have these lenses, you cannot compete on equal terms with the big boys. The poor man's alternative is, of course, ever-faster film; and even then, he

Panning, in sports and action photography, can be used to do more than simply freeze lateral movement and blur backgrounds as in the shot **above.** *Different effects can be achieved by varying the duration of the exposure as shown **facing page.** Here, slow shutter speeds were employed to create blur, and hence a feeling of speed, in*

*the backgrounds as well as the subjects themselves. Notice the effect that this has had on the appearance of the runners' and horses' legs. The elongation of the animals' bodies in the picture **bottom** is a characteristic of panning with cameras using horizontally running focal plane shutters.*

pictures, you have to know the sport. Ideally, you should have some experience of practising it, but at the very least you should be reasonably familiar with what is going on. You should also have some knowledge of the players, if at all possible, so that you can capture any particular tricks that they are known for.

There are three refinements to anticipation: panning, pre-focusing, and allowing for the delay between pressing the release and firing the shutter. The last simply has to be learned for each camera, but it is worth remembering that even a fast-acting camera like a Leica introduces a delay of about 15-20 milliseconds. A manual SLR can take 30 ms (the extra time is required to get the mirror out of the way), and automatic cameras or medium-format SLRs can double or even triple this.

Panning consists of following your subject with the camera so that it stays in (roughly) the same place on the film. This not only allows you to use a rather slower speed than you might otherwise need: it also increases the odds of the subject's being where you want it in the frame, and (if the shutter speed that you select is slow enough) it gives a blurred background and an excellent impression of speed. Incidentally, do not be afraid of a little blur (or even a lot) in the subject itself; it can also help to

give an impression of movement.

Pre-focusing means that you focus on a spot where the action will be, and press the button when it gets there. This is at its most useful in motor racing and the like, where there is a clearly defined track, but it can also be used (for example) in cricket, to focus on the bowler at the wicket; in baseball, to focus on the hitter; and in football, to focus on the goal-mouth.

The points about finding the best locations which were made earlier are equally applicable, and while you are at it, you may check out the WCs, the food and drink stands, etc; this can give you quite an advantage over the opposition later!

Unless we in some way *participate in such events, the photography of water sports such as these will depend greatly on the use of very long lenses, as well as the ability either to follow the action or* *predetermine its course. Where mountains of spray **facing page** feature as part of the picture, care should be taken to allow for this if subject underexposure is to be avoided.*

There is one more technical point: you should never, but never use flash. At best it is distracting, even when used as synchro-sun in daylight, but when used at night it can be dangerous or even deadly. Consider rally-driving: if you are driving fast, in pitch darkness, the last thing you need is some fool letting a flash-gun off in your face.

Whatever sport or activity you photograph, don't forget the spectators and ancillaries. At a kindergarten sports day there is a big hug from mummy for the winner (and the losers!), and at any event there is the anticipation of the participants before they start; the rapt attention of the spectators; and the concentration of the judges. There may be children wandering about eating ice-creams, and there are all sorts of little dramas being played out among the spectators: lover's tiffs, bored wives, sleeping fathers. At motor races, there are usually lots of pretty girls.

Look out for the mechanics, the marshalls, the stewards, the security men, the other photographers, the competitors' friends and family, the cheer-leaders, and all the other people you find at a sporting event: unless you are out to produce a strictly factual record of the race (or whatever) itself, you may well capture the feeling of the occasion much more effectively by concentrating on these seemingly incidental pictures. Do not completely neglect the main event, or the pictures may seem a little aimless, but try for an 'all-round' coverage.

The rest of this chapter looks at some individual sports, divided very roughly into four groups: races, field events and similar competitions, team games, and individual sports.

RACES

Motor racing, motorcycle racing, bicycle racing

Although many professional events keep you so far from the action that you can barely see anything, let alone photograph it, some amateur events allow quite terrifying access to the event itself; off-road motorcycle and automobile races, scrambles, etc., may well use only a bit of tape between stakes to mark off the course. In such cases, you must be very careful not to endanger yourself or the competitors, who have better things to do than to worry about avoiding half-witted photographers.

Corners usually afford the best pictures as drivers compete for the best 'line'; the stacked-up-perspective effect, obtainable with long lenses (200mm +), is also very effective especially if the cars are already 'bunched.' With motorcycle racing, dramatic angles of lean add still more to the cornering shots. In rallies and the like, the 'yumps' where the vehicles are airborne are often impressive, and if racing is on dirt-track or open countryside the showers of gravel and stones thrown up on corners and when accelerating can look good. This debris is travelling pretty fast, so make sure that it doesn't get you or your camera in the eye.

Ordinary bicycle racing can provide some great shots, too, and because it is a minority sport you may be able to gain access to the very best vantage points even at quite major competitions. Because the riders' faces are not obscured by helmets, you can get some remarkable pictures of the tension and strain as they struggle to win.

Powerboat racing, air races and displays

You will usually need *very* long lenses (500mm minimum) if you want to capture individual boats and the dramatic clouds of spray which can surround them at the turns. It is as well to use

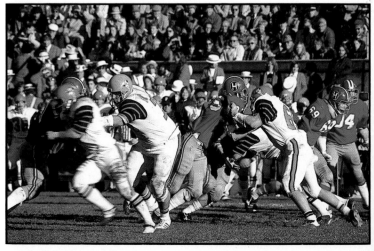

UV filters to protect the lens from flying spray, which can carry for a surprisingly long way.

With air displays, there is little hope of showing individual aircraft in the air unless they are flying very low indeed; most of the best shots are made air-to-air, or show several aircraft in the air at once, usually with smoke trails.

On the water and in the air, contrast is high and brightness ranges misleading. White spray and reflections from water will mean that you must open up at least one stop for most powerboat shots (or use an incident light meter); for aerial shots, the choice is normally between deep blue sky and silhouetted aircraft (meter the sky) or detail in the aircraft and white washed-out skies (open up two or three stops, or use an incident light meter).

Horse racing and equestrian events

At serious professional events, you are unlikely to be allowed close enough to take any very good photographs with anything less than a 200mm lens. Jumps generally provide better pictures than the flat, and the best shots are taken when the horse is just starting the jump or is about half-way over. A very long

lens (at least 500mm) can capture some fascinating expressions on the faces of both horse and rider.

Amateur events are usually much easier to get to: if you volunteer your services as jump steward (with duties no more onerous than replacing the poles knocked down in bad jumps) you can even get in among the action. You will have to stay at your post, and keep clear of the horse as it comes over, but you can get some very impressive shots.

At rodeos, an automatic camera with a lens of 200mm or so is usually ideal; you may need to reset the ASA dial to allow for light backgrounds (try doubling it). Even more than in other

One of the great strengths of *the professional sports photographer is his knowledge of the events he is covering, as well as the locations where they take place. By understanding the sport he can tell with some certainty when and where the action will reach a peak, and by knowing the location he can choose the best vantage point. In motor sport, for instance, this may be at the end of a straight, or on a bend where much jostling for position takes place, and in a ball game it could mean being in good view of the goalmouth.*

Exact timing and a long, tripod-mounted lens were responsible for the portrait of concentrated effort **left.** While such peak of action shots are invariably effective, there is no reason why you should ignore the temporary lulls that occur in any sport. Consider the moment when expectation, elation, fear or exhaustion may show on the faces of the competitors, and

how telling a study they too could make. Occasionally coupled with the peak of the action comes the moment when movement appears temporarily frozen, as in the picture **facing page left.** Such moments, although they require fairly exact timing, allow the photographer to freeze subject movement even without the benefit of a fast shutter speed.

types of sports photography, you will need to be able to handle your camera *very* fast – a motor drive can be a boon. An interesting shot is the apprehensive face of the rider just before the horse is released!

Other races

In foot races, concentrate on competition between individuals (first and second, last and next-to-last) or 'bunch' the runners with a long lens, showing the facial expressions.

Rowing and sculling are very hard to photograph; usually, close-ups of faces work best, or try long exposures to give blurred movement.

'Joke' races, such as three-legged, egg-and-spoon, pancake-tossing, and so forth are best shown by concentrating on individuals; otherwise, the picture just looks 'busy' and lacks a main subject. The same tends to be true of swimming.

FIELD EVENTS AND COMPETITIONS

Throwing events – discus and javelin – trace their ancestry back to weaponry, and the projectiles can hurt or kill. Stay out of the way. The same is true of caber-tossing and golf, though their aim was not to harm people.

Usually, tight close-ups work best, and selecting the right moment is a question of knowing the game. Personal asides are often worth-while, too: muffed shots, facial expressions before and after the action, and even relaxing at the nineteenth hole. With golf, a very quiet camera is desirable – a Rollei is just about perfect.

High jumps and pole vaults are best caught at take-off or at the zenith of the jump, when the jumper is almost motionless. Long-jumps, on the other hand, are best captured on landing: the kicked-up sand looks most impressive, but keep it out of your camera.

Bowls, boules, and petanque are chiefly noteworthy for the characters who play them: often elderly , frequently irascible, and

not uncommonly drunk. The small local game is usually vastly more fun and far more photogenic than the trumped-up tournament, and pictures are as much a matter of character study as sporting reportage. Once again, a very quiet camera is essential.

Tennis pictures almost invariably show one contestant, hair flying and teeth bared, in some improbable position as he or she hits the ball. This is because tennis is not actually very photogenic: if you can think of something new, then the very best of luck to you. Use as long a lens as you need to fill the frame, and watch out for under-exposure, especially on light-coloured hard courts.

TEAM GAMES

As a general rule, the best pictures of team games show individuals or small groups involved in specific plays: a football field, for example, is a big place, and if you try to show too much at once you will have mainly field with a few small figures on it.

Football, rugby, soccer, hockey, lacrosse

Unless you understand the game and can anticipate what is likely to happen, you are very unlikely to get good pictures. You have to show something *happening*: mere preparation, such as running to be in the right place at the right time, is rarely photogenic even if tactically brilliant. Far better to show the pass, the interception, the tackle, the save (or the failed save). Medium-long lenses (around 200mm) show the players in context, and long lenses (300mm+) show individuals and expressions . A *very* long-range zoom, like Nikon's 50-300, can cover just about everything from a single position.

Baseball, cricket

These are rather easier, as a lot of the action takes place at well-defined spots. As with football, etc., you want to show action

– and some kinds of action are more photogenic than others. Unless you are a real student of the game, for example, the pitcher is less interesting than the hitter (though in cricket the bowler can be rather fascinating), and powerful hits make the best pictures. Slides and catches (both successful and dropped) are also very worthwhile. Do not neglect the expressions of the players: anticipation, jubilation, or despair.

INDIVIDUAL SPORTS

Hang-gliding, windsurfing, sailing

Hang gliding is one of the few occasions when there is unlikely to be any shortage of light. With colour, underexpose a little (say ½ stop) for a deep-blue sky and saturated colours in the sails; consider a polarising filter as well. Lenses only slightly longer than standard, say 105mm, are often ideal.

Windsurfing has similar requirements, though you will usually need longer lenses and filters to protect them from spray. The same is true of dinghy sailing.

Sailing and yachting races are substantially similar to power-boat racing, save that even the very fastest yachts do not travel as fast as power boats, or change direction as quickly, or kick up the dramatic clouds of spray. Professional yachting photographers tend to use medium-format cameras with long-focus lenses – typically, 250mm or 500mm on a Hasselblad – for maximum quality and finest gradation.

Skiing

Skiers move alarmingly fast and can damage themselves, and you, in the event of a collision: only top-flight skiers are likely to have the skill needed to minimise the damage. There is usually plenty of light about, though on sunny days a lot of it is blue reflected from the sky: use a weak warming filter in addition to a polariser if this worries you. The best pictures are to be had at turns, where the snow is thrown up dramatically, and at jumps.

In terms of pure colour, you can have a field day: ski clothes are usually brightly coloured, and white snow and clear blue skies provide beautiful uncluttered backgrounds. Contrast is high, though, and exposure can be tricky: try 1-1½ stops extra exposure if you are using a reflected-light meter, and ½-1 stop less for incident light.

Hunting and fishing

You must be careful not to frighten off the game, unless of course you are against blood sports. With guns, the firing of the gun, the return of the gun-dog, the *coup de grace*, and the hunter with his kill are all popular.

In fishing, you can go for the casting of the rod, a fish rising to the fly, and the later stages of landing the fish – especially with 'big game' fish such as marlin and swordfish. There are also some very interesting pictures to be had of the fisherman patiently waiting for a bite.

Falconry is best pictured by concentrating on the bird. The stoop and the moment of impact with the kill are both difficult and rewarding to photograph.

Always remember that the sportsman is likely to be far more aware of his quarry than he is of you. Fish-hooks are bad enough, but guns are deadly. Many hunters are alarmingly trigger-happy: remember Tom Lehrer's cautionary tale of the man who shot 'two game wardens, seven hunters – and a cow.'

Given the appropriate viewpoint, shots such as those **above** present no real difficulties. Lens hoods should be used to ensure maximum detail and colour saturation, and a longer than standard lens will help you fill the frame for maximum impact. Avoid the use of ultra long lenses as these can make following, or even finding, the subject rather difficult. Shooting into the light for the picture **facing page** has resulted in the profusion of flare spots and general image degradation. Some lenses are more flare-prone than others, but the use of multi-coated lenses, and a good lens hood, will limit the problem. If, as in this shot, the effect is desired, then it can be induced artificially. The characteristic blue 'cast' that so often appears in pictures of snow scenes, simply a reflection of the sky, can be minimised by using a polarizing or warming filter.

Landscape photography is a curious occupation. It is in many ways akin to fishing, in that the pursuit of the activity is as important as the end. In both, the most successful practitioner will enter into an almost mystic communion with nature, and the picture on the wall or the fish on the plate are almost incidental results of this.

Equally, though, it is a field where very considerable technical expertise is called for in order to get the best picture. Selection of focal length, and emulsion, and exposure, and processing can be every bit as critical as choosing the right viewpoint, waiting for the correct lighting, and balancing the elements of the picture harmoniously.

The first and most important rule in landscape photography – I sometimes think, in every kind of photography – is not to be in too much of a hurry. Take time to get to know the place you want to photograph. Take time just to experience it before you try to get it on film. Smell the air; feel it on your skin. Look individually at things: at trees, at the sky, at clouds, at the earth. Wait, and see what happens in your chosen field of view. Does a cow wander across the field? Are there birds nesting in the trees? What are the sounds around you?

It is difficult to express this without sounding like some spaced-out hophead. When I first took up landscape photography, I was amazed and horrified at the length of time a landscape photographer would take just to get one picture. As far as I was concerned, it was a matter of pointing the camera, determining the exposure, and pressing the button: elapsed time perhaps one minute. Because I lived in Bermuda, which is an astonishingly easy place to photograph (at least in picture-postcard terms), I used to get quite a lot of acceptable results. But I knew that they were not what I wanted. I learned to wait.

Grafted onto this first and most important rule is another, inseparable from it. Do not underestimate the rational aspect of the creative process. It is all too easy to become contemptuous of the ultra-meticulous approach of Ansel Adams, but who could be contemptuous of his pictures? One of my biggest steps forward in landscape photography came from a chance meeting with Hideki Fujita, a Japanese master of the art. We were both eying the same

The haze encountered at high altitudes has been used to enhance the aerial perspective in the landscape picture **facing page,** reducing the shapes of the distant mountains to a series of receding planes that appear darkest in the foreground.

Shooting into a setting sun with a long lens has added to the effect and clear skies are ideal if this is the look you are aiming for. In landscapes composed largely of snow **below,** *beware of unintentional underexposure of the main subject.*

LANDSCAPE

scene; he took out a pocket compass and said, matter-of-factly, that the light would be better at six. At first, I thought that this was carrying ratiocination too far; then I realised that I would have to buy a compass.

The point is that it is a long way from saying that six would be a *good* time for taking the picture, to saying that six would be the *only* time. You do not despise the exposure meter for the information it gives you when you decide to give three stops more exposure or two stops less; you treat it as a guide.

I do not think that it is possible to make an excellent photograph of anything unless you care about the subject, and are striving to do it justice. You may be able to do it competently; you may even, if you are good enough, be able to do it well; but you will not do it superbly. And unless you are on a commercial assignment, there is no point in trying for anything less.

So: you must ask yourself: what do you care about? In common with many other aspirants to landscape photography, I find my greatest inspiration in mountains and sea. There are others, though, who see more in the gentle pastoral countryside of Sussex; or who rejoice in the bleak moors of Yorkshire or Scotland; or who are at their best in forest, desert, or marsh.

Beware of confusing love of the subject with love of other people's photographs, or worse still with love of a philosophy. It may be that another photographer's work shows you something about the subject which causes you to fall in love with it; but that

There is more to landscape photography than the mechanical process of capturing an attractive scene on film. The scene itself may consist of a number of different elements that vie for attention and while the eye, with its selectivity, can cope with this abundance of detail, the resultant picture may appear distracting. Take time to look at the landscape, analyse its appeal and try to convey the feelings that it inspires in you rather than sticking to the panoramic approach.

Photography should not be limited to fine, sunny days when light levels are high and colours strong. The soft, misty light of a cold winter's day can have an almost magical effect on even the blandest of landscapes and, by subduing colour and form, it can create a scene with a rich, painterly quality. This effect can be enhanced by using fast film, with its inherently larger grain size, while slow film will add to the contrast and show greatest detail. Like film choice,

exposure, too, is to a certain extent a subjective matter, and will depend on the effect you are aiming for in the final image.

Cold weather can play havoc with photographic equipment; batteries may cease to function and shutters can become sluggish. To avoid any undue problems, keep the camera warm under your coat when it is not being used, and remember to watch out for condensation on the lens when you go back into a warm atmosphere.

love is not consummated, as it were, until you have attempted the subject for yourself. I always wanted to try photographing New York, but when I did I found that I was at best duplicating other people's work, and at worst I was finding nothing to photograph. I didn't like my pictures, either. I still admire the work of many photographers who have portrayed New York; but I would prefer to try to capture the Pacific Coast Highway, the mountains and the sea again.

The French have an uncharitable and racist proverb which runs, 'Life is like a Spanish inn; you only get what you bring with

you'. Regardless of the accuracy or otherwise of this slur on the Spanish, most people would agree that the proverb holds good – and it certainly holds good in landscape photography. What you cannot hope to do is to hop out of your car, take a masterpiece with a single snapshot, and then hop right back in and drive off.

At the very least, you will have to put in a bit of legwork. Often, the best views are from high places; and roads do not habitually run to the edges of precipices. A four-wheel drive, or a trail motorcycle, may get you a bit closer, but eventually you are likely to have to walk.

Golf is sometimes defined as 'a good walk, spoiled', and unless you enjoy both the walk and the photography you will be able to level a similar criticism against landscape photography. This may seem still more true in view of my next piece of advice: always use a tripod, and preferably use medium or large format cameras.

There are several reasons for using the tripod. The first, and most mundane, is that it will help avoid camera shake. If you have been scrambling up some rocky path, or even just walking up a long hill on a hot day, you are unlikely to be as steady as you might be when sitting in an armchair or strolling along on the level.

The second is that it is somehow easier to level a camera, to examine the focusing screen carefully, and generally to take everything into account when you use a tripod. You may not find

*A wide angle lens, stopped down to its minimum aperture, resulted in the picture **facing page,** where the long, distorted shadows, the crisp, unspoilt snow and the considerable depth of field suggest a feeling of utter desolation. The star-burst effect in the sun resulted from shooting against the light using a small aperture rather than from any special effect*

*device. It may not be often that the sun and clouds conspire to create the effect shown **above right,** but when they do, make sure you are ready to take advantage. Winter weather can provide a surprisingly diverse range of moods and effects, and while colour content may be limited **top,** an intense blue sky **above** often serves as the perfect backcloth.*

It may sound like something of a contradiction to use colour film to achieve a monochromatic look and yet, as the **contre jour** *picture* **facing page** *shows, the result can certainly be appealing. Receding planes add to the flat, almost two-dimensional feeling of the shot.*

Contrasts invariably create impact, and the scene of the factory buildings, with their belching smoke stacks, set against a landscape backdrop, was designed to do just that. The pictures **left** *show contrast of another kind. Both pictures were taken from the same viewpoint, but under different conditions, to show the degree to which weather can alter the appearance of a landscape. There is no reason why the changing face of the land should not form the basis of a year-round project.*

LANDSCAPE

it so; but most do.

The third reason, which begins to encroach upon the mystical, is that a tripod lends a sense of occasion. Setting up the tripod is a sort of declaration of intent to take as good a picture as you possibly can; you cannot just 'snap' the view.

As for the format, there are two reasons. One is just this sense of occasion, which frees one from the machine-gun mentality so often associated with 35mm – the urge to get a picture and get away – and the other is the amount of detail the bigger negative can hold. A landscape is a mass of texture; and, obviously, the bigger the camera the easier it is to record all this texture. Furthermore, the texture you see in the final picture is that of the subject: in 35mm, it is all too usual for a flawless blue sky to exhibit the dye structure of the film, which completely ruins the effect of the sky itself. It can be a valid artistic interpretation, but it is very unlikely to conjure up the same feeling as the larger-format effect.

Which camera you use depends on your pocket, your circumstances, and your disposition. The limitations of pocket are obvious, with 36 Kodachromes costing about the same as 10-15 rollfilm shots and one or two 5 x 4″ pictures, but it is worth remembering that you will take far fewer pictures on the larger format; for some people, 8 x 10″ or even 11 x 14″ cameras are the ideal for landscape work.

The question of circumstances is a lot more complex. Because I travel a great deal, often by air or by motorcycle, I have decided that 6 x 7cm. rollfilm is an excellent compromise, the more so because it is commercially sensible. A close friend, on the other hand, who loves backpacking and has no commercial ties uses a lightweight wooden 5 x 4″ camera and Grafmatic magazines. Three of these magazines hold eighteen exposures, which can represent anything up to a week's photography for him. And if I am out in my Land-Rover, I may well consider my old whole-plate (6½ x 8½″) De Vere monorail, with a massive old Vinten tripod; every now and then, I dream of an 11 x 14″. . .

As for disposition, it is really a matter of how highly you value convenience and versatility in operation as against portability and simplicity. A favourite camera among some landscape photographers is the old Zeiss Super Ikonta, with its excellent Tessar lens, large 2¼ x 3¼″ format, and fold-away-to-nothing portability. Personally, I loathe the viewfinder and find that I am forever making accidental exposures whilst focusing; the lack of a ground-glass screen and a Polaroid back also annoys me. For me, the extra weight and bulk of a Linhof is a small price to pay for the triple extension, the camera movements, the interchangeable backs and lenses, and (to be fair) the increased strength.

On the subject of interchangeable lenses, it is instructive to work out just how often landscape pictures owe their excellence to the selectivity of a long-focus lens rather than to a wide-angle. The immediate reaction is often to feel that the ability of a wide-angle to get everthing in is essential, but in many cases the reverse is true: the magnificence of the original scene is diminished by lack of detail and focal point, but still more by the changes in apparent perspective which a wide-angle gives. A standard or long-focus lens is usually considerably better at preserving the feeling of what we saw.

Whilst there are some landscapes in which this is not true – a sweeping pastoral scene, shot from on high, might be an example – the landscape photographer is likely to find that his most useful lenses are one of 'normal' focal length – 50mm on 35mm, 90mm on 6 x 7cm, 150mm on 5 x 4″ – plus one of two or three times that focal length: on 35mm, anything from 100 to as

Those photographers who put away their cameras when the sun begins to set risk missing one of the most exciting and photogenic times of the day. Glowing, colour-streaked skies are invariably picturesque, and light levels generally high enough to achieve those moody night shots without any difficulty. In the picture ***above,*** flash, balanced with the ambient light, provided the required foreground detail. ***Facing page:*** ultra-wide lenses are as valid for landscapes as in any other branch of photography.

much as 200mm, 180/210/240mm on 6 x 7cm., and 300mm or more on 5 x 4″. The wide angle comes a poor third for most people – but examination of the pictures in this chapter will show that they can be used to very good effect, especially if there is very strong foreground interest.

If you consciously adopt a large-format approach when working with 35mm, you can still improve your pictures immensely. In colour, the automatic choice must be the incredibly high-resolution Kodachromes, whilst in black-and-white, Kodak Technical Pan plus its own special developer is hard to beat. If you get serious, though, I suspect that you will at least begin to hanker after something bigger.

*Contrary to popular belief, wide-angles are by no means the best choice for landscapes; in the picture **above,** a medium-long lens (250mm on* *Hasselblad) was used, and in the picture on the **right** a 200mm lens on a Nikon 'stacked' perspective.*

Thus far, I have said very little about the actual subject matter, and how to approach it. The captions to the pictures are intended to produce some guidelines, but most important are the pictures themselves. Look hard at them, and decide which ones please you most. Then, try to work out how they were taken. The captions will help, but unless you try to 'get inside' the picture yourself, you will not derive the full benefit.

NATURE PHOTOGRAPHY

To my mind, there are two subjects which are properly covered at the same time as landscape, namely nature photography and the urban landscape.

The dividing line between nature and landscape is not clear: a picture of a tree, for example, or a cottage, might be classed by one person as nature and by another as landscape. For convenience, one might use the old quiz-game categories of animal, vegetable, and mineral.

Can a spider's web be a *landscape? To a spider it can, and you can show it as one with the right treatment. Always have an idea of what you are after; let inspiration precede the picture, instead of just shooting* *wildly. Whether you capture an autumnal mist in a forest, or the blue sky and fresh foliage of spring, let the subject dictate the treatment – and never underestimate the importance of technique.*

It is not possible to do so vast a subject justice in a few words; it deserves a book to itself. What can be emphasised, though, is the old saying, 'Biologist first – photographer second'.

This is really only a restatement of the principle outlined before: you have to know about and care about your subject before you can hope to photograph it well. It is all very well to look at, say, some stunning pictures of insects or flowers, and to try to emulate them; but you have to realise that often, the person who took these pictures is likely to be a specialist who has taken many years to reach their present standard of excellence, and who is as familiar with taxonomy and anatomy as with apertures and film-stocks.

The techniques required, of course, vary as widely as the subjects. For big-game photography, the norm is 35mm cameras with long or very long lenses – usually 200-500mm, often longer. This is partly because you have to shoot for the percentages, and 35mm allows you to do this more easily and economically; partly because long lenses keep you out of the way of dangerous animals, and stop you frightening timid ones; and partly because if you are 'on safari', you have to carry your equipment with you, which gives small, light 35mm gear with easily-available long-focus lenses a considerable advantage. Some people use 6 x 6cm., notably Hasselblad, and possibly remote operation with a motor drive.

With any long lenses, particularly in bird photography where 600mm and above are frequently used, you have to be aware of the likelihood of image degradation as a result of the atmospheric dirt and turbulence between the camera and the subject. This takes many forms, including flattening of contrast, loss of definition due to heat-haze and suspended particles, and a blueness familiar to anyone who has looked at distant mountains; the latter is a result of differential light-scattering, and is again a consequence of atmospheric particles.

Flowers are always a popular subject, but they are not always easy to photograph well. Depth of field can be a problem, though this can be used creatively to isolate single blooms **left and top,** or to suggest an almost endless field, as in the picture of the poppies **above.** *The colour of the flowers usually contrasts well with the* green of the foliage; the grass in the foreground of the poppy picture is an elegant foil, both in colour and in shape. Unless they are really dense, massed flowers seldom make a good picture; here **right** they work well, and the sign adds a touch of humour – or an ecological message?

NATURE PHOTOGRAPHY

Animal photography often does require long lenses; no-one (except other hippopotamuses) wants to get close to a hippopotamus! Most people, though, are content merely to get a picture; as can be seen here, it is possible to do much more than that. Never neglect the pictorial possibilities of domestic animals, either. As well as sharpening your stalking skills, they can provide some very attractive pictures in their own right.

These various defects can be reduced by using contrasty lenses, such as the two-glass Leitz designs, instead of flare-prone zooms; shooting at dawn, when the air is cooler and cleaner; and, of course, by getting closer. The last is one place where remote operation can prove safer and easier, though you will have to give some thought to protecting your cameras from climate, attack, and possibly theft.

Pet, domestic, and farm animals present few technical problems, apart from the difficulties of exposing fur properly: dark coats absorb far more light than you may expect, whilst light ones can be even more deceptive with some brighter than you think and others darker. If you think of these pictures as portraits, and apply broadly the same rules as you would for humans, you will not go far wrong.

Bird photography is not a single skill; rather, it is a whole range of related skills. Some, such as the familiar urban pigeon or the zoo flamingo, can be photographed with comparatively short lenses (135mm – 200mm on 35mm), and domestic pets such as this rather splendid parrot **top right** *can be taken with a standard lens and on-camera flash.*

Others, particularly birds of prey, will require the longest lens (and the stoutest tripod!) that you can muster, whilst pictures of birds at their nests will usually require specialised ornithological knowledge and, perhaps, remote-release cameras. Unless you know what you are doing, do not try for such pictures, as the parent may abandon the nest.

NATURE PHOTOGRAPHY

Close-ups are another matter. The first difficulty lies in getting close enough. Close-up lenses are a cheap and very effective solution, especially when used with lenses of modest speed; stop down two or three stops from maximum aperture for optimum results. Otherwise, there are many specialised lenses, which are far more convenient in use and allow continuous focusing down to 1:2 (half life size) or even 1:1 (life size). Those of close to standard focal length, such as the 55mm f/2.8 Micro Nikkor, are best for inanimate subjects; for insects and the like, something in the 90mm or 105mm bracket is likely to prove easier to use, because of the increased stand-off. Some even like to go to 200mm, and both Canon and Nikon provide superb close-focusing lenses of this nominal length. A word of warning:

The lichens on the tombstone below have an almost tactile quality; shot about ¼ life size on film, they are about 50% bigger than life size here. The use of flash **right** has isolated the dandelion clocks dramatically from their background, whereas natural backlighting has brought out a magnificent range of greens in the leaves on the **opposite page**. Both the dandelion picture and the leaves show clearly that 'correct' exposure is whatever conveys the effect that the photographer intended.

whilst there are a few zoom lenses capable of delivering superb close-up quality, there are many more which are simply dire in their so-called 'macro' mode.

Once you have managed to get close enough, you are afflicted with the twin problems of depth-of-field and lighting. Normally, the only way to get enough light onto the subject is to use electronic flash, though some sorts of insect photography are practicable using available light. A particularly useful device is the 'praying mantis' from Kennett Engineering.

Its proper name is the Kennett Macroflash, and it is an ingenious double flash bracket which can be used to position a main light and a fill almost anywhere within a couple of feet of the camera: even backlighting is possible in some cases. Because two lights are used, lighting can be very much more natural than if a single on-camera flash is used, and its only drawback is its size – it can be a bit embarrassing in the undergrowth.

It might seem that plant photography was less demanding than animal photography and to a certain extent this is true; but

it is not as easy as it looks. For a start, plants do not move from A to B – excepting, perhaps, triffids and tumbleweed – and unless you are very patient indeed it is not usually possible to wait for them to present themselves more attractively. You can choose the time of year and the time of day, which will affect both the state of the plant and the state of the lighting, but apart from that you will simply have to wander around until you find the best viewpoint.

Although plants rarely locomote, they do move. The wind is the usual culprit, and if you are shooting close-ups even the slightest breath of wind can cause the most spectacular movement of the subject in the view-finder. Even with trees, a windy day can cause notable blurring of leaves during a long exposure. With small plants, it is sometimes practical to build a windbreak using transparent plastic (so as not to obscure the light; transparent plastics also 'disappear' quite conveniently when out of focus), but otherwise you will need patience or a high shutter speed or both.

Urban photography is a blend of landscape, reportage, art, and social comment. It has many guises. One of the easiest, and also the most popular, is the Dark Satanic Mills school, which shows the city as an all-devouring monster. This is most easily achieved in black-and-white, with orange filtration to give the lowering doom-laden skies and a deadly pallor to the passers-by, and a wide angle lens (28mm or wider) to give a vertiginous nightmare perspective. Using grainy film and printing both high-key and low-contrast rounds it off nicely.

This is rather more difficult in colour, as the warm red brick and mellow stone of so many cities – even in slum areas – has connotations of working-class comfort, of warm coal fires and hot tea, and of a closeness lost in much modern living. A shift of emphasis is required, and this is normally done by showing modern ticky-tacky boxes of houses, tastelessly decorated and festooned with the detritus of the consumer society: plastic Christmas decorations, outmoded motor-cars, and (ideally) broken toys. Alternatively, spray-painted graffiti, damaged amenities, and rubbish are always popular.

If this sounds like an unusually vitriolic attack, it is because there is so much of this sort of thing, and so much of it is so badly done. There is a beauty in decay, if you must show decay, and irony too; and there is much that is good in cities. Cities are composed of people, and there is much that is good in people; if you do not agree, perhaps you should look inside yourself.

One can, however, go too far the other way. There is a saccharine brand of photography which might be called the Prospectus, or Chamber of Commerce, variety. It uses colour film in medium-format cameras, and 81-series filters, to show clean, wide streets populated with happy, smiling people some of whom are driving late-model cars.

I like cities: they fascinate me. And, like anything fascinating, they are hard to photograph. To a large extent, I tend to concentrate on people, as described earlier. There are, however, many specifically urban landscapes which I also try to photograph.

There are skylines, surely one of the most characteristic parts of any city. Some skylines are internationally recognisable:

*The most famous skyline in the world **above** is made more dramatic by a golden evening sky; and the same light, plus an autumnal mist supplemented by traffic pollution, conveys the fall of day at the side of the Thames **facing page**. Small details can catch the eye, too: how about the windmills in the window display **far left,** or the oblivious dish washer in the Chinese restaurant **left?***

parts of Paris, or downtown San Francisco or Manhattan. Others are more private; I lived in Bristol for many years, and the proliferation of churches (built with money derived from the slave trade!) is immediately recognisable to anyone who knows the city. Skylines can be particularly effective if combined with striking cloud-scapes, and some photographers go to the lengths of montage or combination printing to achieve this – though there is always a temptation to have the sun setting in the North or East when you do this!

There are individual buildings. The crazy baroque of San Francisco's older houses immediately springs to mind, or the mediaeval jumble of much of Southern Germany, but there are also the 'glass palace' offices of insurance companies, beautiful Georgian and Colonial terraces, nineteenth-century skyscrapers, castles, inns . . .

There are roads. These may seem unusually soulless, but

F.D. . . . N.Y. says the proud legend on the front of the fire truck, and we have no doubt where we are. The yellow cab is less identifiably New York (though look at the littering sign), but as a colour composition it is quite something. Antique/junk shops facing page often capture the spirit of a place or neighbourhood, too.

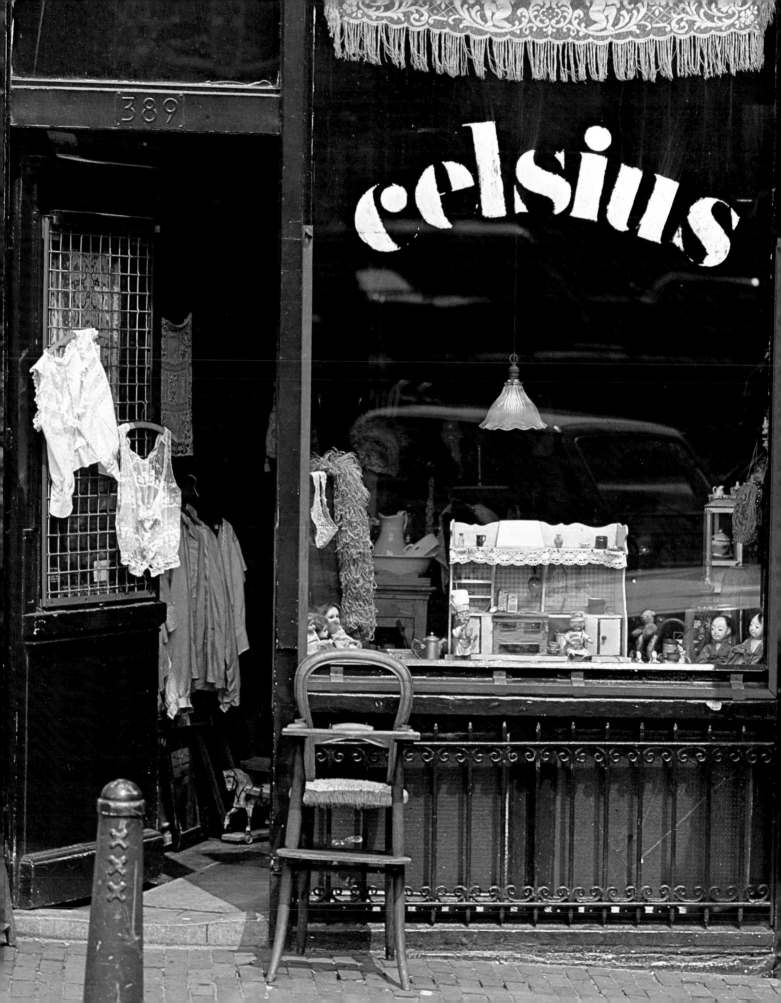

Popular gathering places often make for interesting pictures, whether of individuals or crowds, as in Central Park facing page.

Jumbled street markets, whether the ethnic food variety as in Chinatown above, or European-style 'flea markets' right, are always full of interest and activity; they make fascinating 'narrative' pictures in the tradition of Breughel. Street signs are always fun, too: Chinatown in almost any major city can furnish some spectacular ones. Fast-handling equipment with a modest wide-angle lens – say 35mm on a 35mm camera – is ideal for getting pictures like this.

URBAN PHOTOGRAPHY

People: people at work, people *relaxing, people reacting to their environment, or just people for their own sake – they are all fascinating. Many photographers are afraid to take such pictures for fear of adverse reaction from their subjects, but most people either ignore you or are actually pleased to be photographed. A 35mm camera with 35mm or 50mm lens – preferably fast – is all that you need; in a decade and a half of taking this sort of picture, I have had adverse reactions on fewer than half a dozen occasions.*

the freeways are in many ways more the heart of Los Angeles than the buildings. How can you show this in a picture? On a winter's night, jammed with cars, the air thick with exhaust? Or a sunny morning, with impressionistic blurs of colour? It is up to you.

There is the abstraction of the city, the interplay of line and form (and sometimes colour), the light upon the planes of modern architecture. Set this off with people, and you can show either the grossness of architecture too large for human scale or a dramatic artfulness.

At some points, the urban landscape must shade into reportage; if you try to convey a sense of community, for example, you are likely to do best with a 35mm camera and a reporter's eye – though there are some who use large-format even for this. Within reason, I prefer large-format (or at least 6 x 7cm rollfilm) for urban photography, both for the reasons already given under landscape and because of the camera movements.

The rising and falling front, and to a lesser extent the swings and tilts, available on a monorail or technical camera can be invaluable in architectural photography. We are all familiar with the 'falling over backwards' effect which results from pointing a camera upwards at a building. The old trick of raising your viewpoint by taking the picture from half-way up a neighbouring building is not always practical – first, there has to be a neighbouring building, and secondly, you have to get in to it – and in any case, it does not afford you the same freedom as the use of camera movements.

If you raise the front panel of a technical or view camera, the image rises with it; and as the image is upside-down, this means that the foreground is eliminated and the top of the building comes into view. The lens will have to have an unusually wide circle of good definition, but this is a characteristic of view-camera lenses such as the Symmar. On aesthetic grounds, you must also take care not to eliminate too much of the foreground, or the picture will look odd.

A similar trick can be done with a cross front, which is invaluable when you want an apparently head-on picture but cannot stand in the right place to get it, either because of an obstruction at the camera position or because of some awkward foreground item such as a street-stall, tree, or utility post.

Gasometers, power pylons, *refineries, cooling towers, and the like are seldom seen as attractive, but the photographer can uncover their beauty. A great deal of the secret lies in the colour of the sky, and all kinds of filtration can be used if the natural colours are not dramatic enough. Long lenses and wide angles also alter apparent perspective and size relationships, and even double exposure can be used, if this gives us the feeling we are trying to achieve. With the appropriate techniques, the photographer can convey gracefulness, power, dirt or decay; the statement you wish to make is up to you.*

URBAN PHOTOGRAPHY

Although it is possible to get 'perspective control' lenses for 35mm and some rollfilm SLRs, they are nearly as expensive as a second-hand technical camera and in any case do not give anything like as much movement. Most also lack the swings and tilts, which are sometimes used in architectural photography in order to hold a receding plane in focus.

They do this in accordance with the Scheimpflug Rule: if object plane, lens panel plane, and image plane all coincide at a single line, then everything will be in focus. This can be achieved without undue stopping-down, so allowing reasonably brief exposures, and (still more usefully) it is not limited as is depth of field: literally *everything*, from as near as you can see to as far, will be equally sharp.

By manipulation of the various movements, you can also achieve such tricks as showing both front and side elevation of a building – a 'three-quarter view', in photographic parlance – with the front apparently square; I find this a rather disturbing effect, but it is one sometimes sought by architects.

The beauty of the city is always there for those who are willing to see it. The picture **facing page** is perhaps the most obvious, with its brick sidewalk, soft colours, cherry blossom, and antique lamp; but a huge park of cars awaiting export has its own slightly surreal charm, and you can almost smell the clean air in the picture of the gable-end window, despite the fact that it is actually in the heart of San Francisco. The old shed with the decaying galvanised-iron roof could equally well be in the country, but in fact it was a shed on a piece of waste land, used as a den by children.

NIGHT PHOTOGRAPHY

Not so long ago, night photography was a real technical problem. Getting any sort of image was regarded as praiseworthy, and people used to show with pride pictures whose only detectable merit was that you could just about recognise the subject.

Although it is still very difficult to get night pictures with the wrong film and equipment, the right films and equipment are now so readily available – one might say commonplace – that one is spoiled for choice. Instead of being a specialised field for the few, it now offers both a new way of looking at old subjects – many street scenes are far more interesting after dark – and a new way of extending your vision, of seeing subjects which are uniquely characteristic of the night.

There are two ways of going about night photography. One is to use the existing light, and the other is to add your own. Whilst the latter has its uses, and is briefly discussed later, it normally destroys precisely the feeling we are trying to capture.

The most useful single weapon in the night photographer's armoury is fast film. Fast black-and-white films such as Ilford's excellent HP5 are normally rated at 400-650 ASA (depending on developer), and with some loss of shadow detail can be 'pushed' to 1000-1600 ASA (strictly, E.I., as ASA development standards no longer apply) or even 2000-3000 ASA if highlight detail is all that is needed. Specialist films, such as Kodak 2475 and 2485 Recording film, or the long-established Royal-X Pan, start at about 1250 ASA and can run to 5000-10,000 ASA within the same limitations.

Even in colour, there are ultra-fast films. At the time of writing, the fastest was Kodak's 1000 ASA colour print film; but it looked as if a slide film of similar speed would not be far behind. In any case, 800 ASA is fairly easily obtainable by 'pushing' 400 ASA slide films by one stop, or 200 ASA films by two stops (the quality is similar in both cases), whilst 3M's tungsten-light film is very acceptable at its 640 ASA base rating, quite usable at 1280 ASA when 'pushing one,' and tolerable at 2000-2500 ASA if there is no other way of getting an image.

In practice, film speeds are all but meaningless in most night photography. Because of the vast range of brightness in the subject, we can accept quite a wide range of exposures as 'correct.' The minimum exposure, for example, might show us the highlights and the streetlights, the shop windows, the moon, and a few reflections. Everything else may be in silhouette or even completely lost, but our brains will supply the missing information. At the other extreme, the maximum exposure is the one which lets us see the scene as if it were daylight. The light sources and highlights may be completely burned out and featureless, but because we see so many everyday details we can still accept that exposure is 'correct'. In between these two extremes are many other 'correct' exposures, notably those in which the people (or other principal subjects) are clearly visible but where we have both washed-out highlights *and* inky shadows. We can cheerfully accept all this, and the relationship between any of the 'correct' exposures and a meter reading is pretty much a matter of chance.

True night shots, like this dramatic, mercury-lit picture **right,** *are characterised by extreme contrast and often weird colours; two alternatives are marked underexposure* **top,** *or twilight pictures* **facing page,** *when daylight is fading but not gone and the lamps are lit: with the latter, effects ranging from* almost daylight to almost night *can be achieved by lengthening or shortening the exposure appropriately. Using a blue filter (or artificial light film) and underexposing considerably gives night-time effects even in broad daylight: cinematographers call it 'day for night' or 'la nuite Americaine.'*

NIGHT PHOTOGRAPHY

The only way to work out exposures accurately is to experiment a lot. Make exposures that you know are roughly correct, and note the meter reading; check the results to see how they correlate. The best way to make sure that your exposure is at least in the right parish is to use the manufacturers' published guides; Kodak's is reproduced here by permission, and other manufacturers are likely to prove equally helpful.

Note that some of the exposures quoted are a little eccentric by modern standards, and seem to assume that you will be using very slow lenses. Of course, faster lenses will allow shorter exposure times, and this is not just important for avoiding camera shake: it is also relevant to the film's performance. In the first place, longer-than-usual exposures may well require extra exposure – typically half a stop extra at one second – and secondly, colour films may exhibit a certain loss of colour balance, which is usually restorable with the appropriate filtration (normally CC filters in the 5-15 range; the colour depends on the film stock – ask the manufacturer). As already mentioned, exposure is not critical in many cases, and with a mixture of tungsten and discharge lighting, the same may well be true of colour rendition.

Exposures for lights and other night subjects with some 'Kodak' Colour Films

Film	Subject		
	Lights at night (no shadow detail)	Subjects lit by lights at night (some shadow detail)	Moonlit landscapes
KODACHROME 25 (Daylight)	1/15 sec at f/2.8	1/15 sec at f/2	45 sec at f/2
KODACHROME 64 (Daylight) EKTACHROME 64 Professional 6117 (Daylight) EKTACHROME 64 and 64 Professional (Daylight)	1/15 sec at f/4	1/30 sec at f/2	35 sec at f/2.8
EKTACHROME Professional 6118 (Tungsten) EKTACHROME 50 Professional (Tungsten)	1/15 sec at f/2.8	1/15 sec at f/2.8	20 sec at f/2
EKTACHROME 200 and 200 Professional (Daylight)	1/15 sec at f/5.6	1/30 sec at f/4	10 sec at f/2.8
EKTACHROME 160 and 160 Professional (Tungsten)	1/15 sec at f/5.6	1/30 sec at f/3.5	15 sec at f/2.8
EKTACHROME 400 (Daylight) KODACOLOR 400	1/15 sec at f/8	1/30 sec at f/4.5	12 sec at f/4
VERICOLOR II Professional, Type S and Professional 4107, Type S	1/15 sec at f/4.5	1/30 sec at f/2.8	Not recommended, but try 20 sec at f/2.8
VERICOLOR II Professional, Type L and Professional 4108, Type L VERICOLOR II Commercial, Type S and Commercial 4119, Type S KODACOLOR II	1/15 sec at f/4	1/15 sec at f/2.8	12 sec at f/2

The French call it l'heure bleu, *the blue hour; such pictures as the one **below** are often more attractive than true night pictures. The picture opposite is particularly interesting; the upper version was taken in daylight, and the lower one by moonlight. The exposure for the moonlight shot was about 100,000x as long as for the daylight picture! Note the faint star tracks in the sky.*

On the topic of lens speed, it is worth noting that it is possible to get too enthusiastic. With fast films, you can get away with f/2.8, and f/2 (or f/1.8, which is only ⅓ stop faster) is normally fine. A really high-quality f/1.4 lens can be a worthwhile investment if you are intending to do a lot of night photography, but you may still have to face some loss of image quality. Extreme speed lenses, such as f/1.2 and even fl, are so expensive that it is doubtful whether you will ever justify the cost for the sake of an extra half-stop or so. Unless they are first-rate, you may also run into flare and resolution problems, though (like anything else) these can be turned to advantage. I have a 50mm f/1.2 Canon screw lens (from the old Canon 7 rangefinder camera) which is perfectly acceptable – indeed, astonishingly good – in normal use, but which when used wide-open at night gives the most amazingly flary and soft images. I like the effect.

Because of the need for speed, the use of lenses other than standard may pose problems. To a certain extent, these are self-solving with wide-angles, because you can hand-hold them for that much longer: if you can hold a 50mm lens still at 1/30, then 1/15 should be just about safe with 24mm. Fast wide-angles for reflexes are frequently either very expensive or of inferior quality – and they may well be both. You may be safe with an f/2, but it is generally agreed that if you want to go to a 35mm f/1.4 the best way to do it is with a (proper, rangefinder) Leica. With longer lenses, anything much longer or slower than a 105mm f/2.5 is likely to prove an embarrassment, though I have on occasion used a 200mm f/3.

With rollfilm cameras, you are usually stuck with much slower lenses, which means increased film speeds. It is arguable, though, that 400 ASA on 6 x 7cm with an f/2.8 lens delivers better quality than 64 ASA at f/1.2 on 35mm: the only problem comes when you need 400 ASA at f/1.2!

After fast film and fast lenses, your last resort is a steady hand. What you can manage unaided will depend both on your physique and on your standards, but the old rule of never hand-holding a camera when using a shutter speed longer than 1/focal length holds good in 35mm. You can extend this by one or two steps by bracing yourself carefully, but after this you ought really to consider some form of additional camera support.

The simplest is the 'bean bag,' which is pretty much what its name suggests: a bag, or even an old sock, filled with dried beans or peas, which is interposed between the camera and a convenient wall, lamp-post, tree, or whatever. It allows a much larger contact area than just resting the camera on a hard surface, and reduces the risk of scratching.

Next comes the 'pocket tripod,' which can also double as a shoulder brace. The Leitz design is particularly simple and stable, and not particularly expensive despite its origins. The same regrettably cannot be said of the ball-and-socket head from the same source: it is undoubtedly one of the best (if not *the* best) of its size, but it is very expensive.

*When the sun is low in the sky, and much less intense than in full day, it can often be included in a picture. Sunset over water is almost a cliché, but it can be turned to good effect, as in the attractive semi-silhouette **facing page**. When night has fallen, there are other opportunities for experiment. A very long exposure gives a 'flow diagram' of the traffic, as headlamps and tail lights leave a trail. Note the flare around the street lights, caused by the small aperture, and around the HILTON sign, caused by atmospheric haze and lens flare. Moving the camera with the shutter open gives interesting abstract and semi-abstract patterns **left and centre left.***

NIGHT PHOTOGRAPHY

Finally, there is the full-sized tripod. This is moving into rather a different sort of photography, but it is still worth considering for many applications: all the observations made earlier about tripods apply. Two notes are first never to leave it where it could be kicked over – some people can be very careless as they stagger out of a bar at night – and secondly to remember that it often gets cold at night, and you may find the tripod's bare metal very cold to the touch, so use a bag or gloves.

Alternatively, as already described, you can use supplementary lighting. Movie companies set up huge generators, and can turn night into day, but for most people the likeliest approach is the use of electronic flash.

Simple on-camera flash can be used if your only aim is a record of the subject, or if you want dramatic effects with inky-black backgrounds, but even then you must be aware that the published guide number for most flash guns makes allowance for light reflected back from the walls and ceiling in an interior: indeed, one suspects that some guide numbers are determined in white tiled bathrooms. With no walls or ceiling to reflect back the light, the effective guide number out-of-doors may be around half of the indoor number, so make the appropriate allowance by opening up a stop or two.

Multiple flash is normally only practicable for immobile subjects, and can be achieved either by using a number of flashguns (preferably fired by optical slave cells rather than by a tangle of wires) or by 'painting' with a single gun.

The latter technique is best done with an assistant, who opens the shutter before the first flash and keeps it open until you have finished: a sheet of black matte paper held in front of the lens between flashes may be desirable if there is much ambient light. You will need to work out the angle for each flash carefully, so that there is no flashback from windows or the like and so that you do not register as a dark ghost in front of a light-coloured wall (you should, of course, wear dark clothing).

Exposure calculation is extremely difficult. The mathematically inclined can work it out by working out the appropriate aperture for each individual flash (using the normal guide-number method), squaring each aperture, adding all the squares together, and then taking the square root. Alternatively, if all distances are the same (from flash to subject), then the simple rule is that for each extra stop you close down you need to double the number of flashes: one flash at f/1.4 is two at f/2, four at f/2.8, or eight at f/4.

The simplest ways of doing it are either to use a flash meter or a Polaroid test print; but remember, all that extra flashing will weaken the batteries, possibly to extinction, and will extend recycling times.

*Here, we see the effects of taking pictures in early twilight (the palm trees and the moon), late twilight (the Houses of Parliament and York Minster), and at night (the fireworks). Pictures of the moon will show movement unless the exposure is shorter than a very few seconds, or an equatorial telescope drive is used; a common technique is to take a picture **without** the moon, and then double-expose it in afterwards. Incidentally, a* *tripod and a still night were needed in order to avoid blurring in the palm-fronds. Fireworks have their own requirements: the usual technique is to set the camera up on a tripod, with the lens stopped down to f/8 or so and then leave the shutter open until several bursts have recorded. Exposure is surprisingly uncritical; good results can be obtained with exposures of anything from five seconds to a minute or more.*

NATURE PHOTOGRAPHY

*Night can have many moods, and night photography can reflect them. The fire is an archetypal symbol of humanity and comfort, and by focusing attention on its glow **left** the photographer has evoked something very deep. The winter evening in London, by contrast, is eerily deserted – partly because it is a Sunday, but partly because the photographer waited until the very minimum of traffic was in shot. Then again, the picture opposite conveys all the energy of a big city; the dockside lights, the traffic on the freeway, the advertising signs – the whole image of the unsleeping city.*

THE GREAT OUTDOORS

If you have read every word of the book so far, including the captions, you have been through something over thirty thousand words. Have they said everything that there is to be said about outdoor photography? Absolutely not!

So, where do you go from here? I suggest a threefold approach. First, keep reading the books. I don't say this just because it keeps me out of the poor-house; I've been on your side of the page for far longer than I have been writing, and I know that I have learned a vast amount from books. Of course, it is a matter of diminishing returns, and some books are very much better than others, but I cannot recall a single book from which I did not learn something. In extreme cases, it may have been how *not* to do it – but that is still a lesson.

Do not confine yourself only to photographic books, either. Read detective stories, westerns, science fiction, to see how characters are described and how places are sketched. How do

The ways in which the elements of a picture can be tied together are myriad; strong shapes and bright colours **right,** a whole **ambiance below,** or a few simple elements carefully considered **opposite.** Perfection is rare: the picture opposite, for example, would be better without the cables on the street-lamps and the two white cars in the background – but the overall effect is what you are after. When you look at a picture, try to imagine that you had taken it; what would you have liked added, and what taken away?

Some pictures are narrative, and tell stories; others are graphic, and owe their appeal to shape, colour, tone, and form. The best pictures are both. Most people come from one direction or the other; work with what you have, and try to improve the other side of your picture-taking. The mere act of analysis can work wonders. Begin with these pictures.

you visualise them? Read comic-books, to see how the visuals are handled and how a story is built up out of a sequence of pictures; to see a master of the art, try to find Druillet's *Loane Sloane, Delirius, Yragaël,* or *Vuzz.*

Read books of poetry, of drama, of love, of war. Read the Bible: let it all mix together. Read the newspapers, the scandal-sheets, the memoirs, the girlie magazines. Learn about how to repair motorcycles, about Greek classical architecture, about

All four of the pictures on these two pages have a strong human content, even though two of them contain no people at all and the people by Mont St. Michel are insignificantly small. What is important is that all of these pictures show the work of man, and his reaction to his fellow man. Look at the steps, opposite. Whoever built them was helping people to make that arduous climb; but equally, it is difficult not to look at the picture and feel daunted, or even tired, at the prospect of going up those steps. Again, look at Mont St. Michel **top left**. It was ostensibly built **ad majoram gloria dei,** to the greater glory of God; but there is more than a touch of the fortress about it, which reminds us of the troubled times of the past. Those gates **above,** silhouetted by the sunset, were built to keep people out. Why? Where are they? What was so important that no-one should be allowed in? Perhaps the lady looking out from the window over the gateway **left** is the most immediately human picture, but it is enigmatic; is she waiting in hope, or looking back in sorrow?

*React to what you see. How would the pioneer who is carved in stone **below** relate to all those road signs? Could he have foreseen that one day the whole brand-new continent would have been criss-crossed with mighty highways?*

***Don't try to fake reactions.** If the gnarled tree on the Pacific coast moves you, photograph it to the best of your ability; if the carpet of autumn leaves stirs something in you, photograph that – but never feel that you **have** to photograph anything. Sometimes, use your camera to write notes to yourself; signs like the one above can jog your memory.*

navigation and archery. You will gain a better understanding of the people and things you want to photograph, perhaps some insight into how to go around problems rather than running up against them, and very likely some inspiration.

Secondly, look at the pictures. Every day, you are bombarded with them: look at the television, the newspapers, the posters, the magazines, the books, the box your breakfast cereal comes in. Ask yourself: how was that effect achieved? What went wrong with that picture? Why do I like this picture, but dislike that one? What do I mean by dislike – am I simply indifferent, or revolted, or bored, or shocked, or what?

Whilst this introspection may seem a little self-conscious at first, an easy way to get into it is on a boring train or bus journey, or when you are waiting somewhere – perhaps at the dentist's! You can 'see the joins' after a while, how a particular effect has been carefully contrived but still manages to look natural, or what the photographer was aiming at, and how he has failed. It will permanently change your way of looking at images – I used to drive one girlfriend mad at the movies with my analysis – but it should do wonders for your photography.

Once again, do not restrict yourself solely to photographs. Look at paintings, at cartoons, even at sculptures and architecture. What you are aiming to do is to extend your visual awareness. Even if this means looking at some truly disastrous paintings, remember that you are always learning: *why* are they disastrous? Even if you cannot answer in words, you will have added something to your unspoken visual vocabulary.

Does nature imitate art, as *Wilde said, or does art imitate nature? To the photographer, the question is almost meaningless. The picnic spread is obviously contrived for the camera, but the other two pictures are equally obviously 'found.' What the photographer has brought to them is a way of seeing.*

Notwithstanding the cries of its detractors, photography is not a mere matter of mechanical representation: the viewpoint is not selected, the moment of firing the shutter not chosen by pure chance. Photography is a medium of communication: what do you want to communicate?

THE GREAT OUTDOORS

This is the second source of your inspiration: the first taught you to look at subjects, and this teaches you to look at execution.

Thirdly, and finally, look at the world around you, and at how you could turn it into a picture. Even if you do not have your camera with you, you can still do this with your 'mental camera': a blink, and the scene is recorded. You are in the market: how do you show the produce on the stalls, the stallholder arguing with the housewife about the quality of the goods, the old sweeper slowly sweeping the dead cabbage leaves?

Best of all, look at what pleases you. Not in your mind's eye, not fantasising, but what there is in the world around you that gives you pleasure. Look at pretty girls, or handsome men: how could you best picture them? Look at an attractive building, at a sleek car, at a powerful motorcycle. Look at a child, look at your friends, look at your lover. How could a photograph express the way you feel?

Ultimately, that is what photography is about: not getting a representation of a scene or a subject, but of a feeling. And that is your third and greatest inspiration.

Vale; farewell. Frost-touched grasses in a Kentish meadow, a rainbow in a New England sky, broken ice on the pavement, trees reflected in a river. Pictures are everywhere, though we may sometimes have to wait for them, and through our pictures we can both explore ourselves and communicate with other people. Choose your audience – no-one has to love your pictures – and see what they give back to you when you show them your photographs. Live in growth; grow in perception.

The Creative Art

Contents

INTRODUCTION

*Creativity is an approach as well as a way of seeing. Two of the pictures: **right and below**, were taken with tripod-mounted medium format cameras to preserve richness of detail and gradation: one concentrates on the profusion of nature, and the other on its variety-in-repetition. The picture **far right** was inspired by the contrast in scale between the mountainside and the buildings; it was shot across the valley using a hand-held 35mm camera with standard lens. A larger camera would have been much harder work to carry – but the difference in quality is visible even in reproduction.*

Nowadays, colour photography is arguably the easiest type of photography available – at least, from the user's point of view. The immense and complex technology behind the image need hardly affect the photographer at all: George Eastman's old boast, "You press the button and we do the rest," has never been more true.

What, then, is the need for this book? The answer is twofold. First, there is a world of difference between a photograph which is a thing of beauty in its own right and a simple record shot. The difference may be a matter of luck, but more often it is a matter of creativity. Secondly, the photographer who understands the photographic process has the creative edge over one who blindly follows the meter's settings and the manufacturers' instructions.

Consequently, this book functions on two levels. The pictures are examples of creative photography – of making something more than just a record. The text tells you how to achieve these effects. Of course, some of the pictures could have been taken with the simplest equipment, because there is no substitute for the creative eye. Equally, all the technical expertise in the world can be insufficient to lift a really boring shot into the realms of creativity, but it is a fair comment that more potentially beautiful pictures are spoilt by a lack of technical ability than by an excess.

Before we go on, though, there is another very important point to remember. <u>Not every picture needs to be creative.</u>

Some people spend so much time agonising about creativity that they never take any pictures. Photography is fun. Simply enjoy it, and you will probably find that creativity will come even when you are not looking for it.

A good place to start on the technicalities of colour photography is a brief history; this not only introduces some of the terms you will hear used but also shows the diversity of processes available.

The first colour picture, taken in 1861, involved exposing three separate plates through three separate filters, one for each of the primary colours. The resulting lantern slides were projected (using three projectors) through the same three filters. When all three were in register, the red, green, and blue light combined to recreate the original colours. Because the process involved adding together the different colours, it was known as <u>additive</u> colour.

<u>Subtractive</u> processes, on the other hand, start off with white light and filter out the colours that are <u>not</u> wanted. All conventional modern methods are of this type. For example, a green field is represented by an area which transmits (on a transparency) or reflects (on a print) green, but absorbs all other colours. A white cloud is shown by an area which absorbs no light, and a black doorway by an area which absorbs all light equally.

The theoretical groundwork for these processes was laid in

In colour photography, restraint is often more effective than prodigality. In each of these three pictures, a single predominant hue sets the mood. On the far left, the yellowish green of the grass suggests spring or early summer; the water and the pine trees echo the look of cool freshness. On the left, the bluish tint (typical of high altitudes on an overcast day) emphasises the coldness of the water and the mountains: the impression is definitely cold and bleak rather than fresh and welcoming. The blue of the mist in the picture **below** suggests scale, by means of aerial perspective, and captures the rainswept grandeur of the Scottish coast; the grey-blue cloud also balances the mass of the land, adding interest to what would otherwise be a blank grey sky.

INTRODUCTION

the late 19th century, but it was not until 1907 that the Lumière brothers introduced the Autochrome, the first commercial application of the process. They used dyed potato starch grains as filters, and (hardly surprisingly) a lot of light was lost just trying to get through the *kartoffelsuppe* on the surface: the same objection also applied to the Finlay and Dufaycolor processes, which used mechanically ruled masks. In addition, the mask (or grain) structure became embarrassingly obvious at any more than the most modest magnifications.

In the second decade of the twentieth century, various people were working on the possibility of using dyes instead of masks to filter the colours, and of combining the three dye layers (again, one for each primary colour) in an 'integral tripack'. The technical difficulties were enormous, and they were not solved until the 1930s by Godowski and Mannes; even then, they had to rely on an enormously complex processing sequence in which, in effect, each of the three layers was processed separately one after the other. Their film, Kodachrome, was known as a non-substantive integral tripack, because the dyes were added during processing.

This approach has several advantages, though. The layers can be thinner than in films incorporating the dye couplers in the emulsion, which makes for increased sharpness; there is no danger of the dye couplers migrating to other layers before processing (which is what accounts for colour casts in badly-stored substantive films); and because user-processing is impossible, the manufacturer's quality control can be top-notch. These are the main reasons why Kodachrome continues to be the favourite of most professional photographers working in 35mm. It is also more stable than other slide films; modern Kodachromes will not exhibit detectable fading for 90 years or more, whilst some substantive films will begin to fade in as little as twenty years.

On the other hand, ease of processing means faster access to the finished image, and this is why such films as Agfa's Agfachrome (derived from the 1936 Agfacolor) and Kodak's Ektachrome (1946) are now so popular. Furthermore, because of processing difficulties, Kodachrome is not made in sizes wider than 35mm, so rollfilm and large-format users have to use substantive films. A good processing laboratory can deliver high-quality processed Ektachromes within two hours, and if the film has been properly stored before and after exposure results will be very nearly as good as Kodachrome; in the larger formats, the slight loss of sharpness is more than outweighed by the increased size.

At this point, a note on user-processing is very relevant. Professional processing is so cheap and fast (provided you have access to a laboratory) that it is scarcely ever worth considering doing your own processing. Furthermore, a good processing laboratory may make the occasional mistake, but you will probably make far more. In any case, their quality control and solution monitoring is vastly better than is readily attainable in any part-time set-up.

Choosing a lab is usually a matter of finding who the local professionals use; after all, their livelihood depends upon the quality of the processing. A few professional labs refuse to accept amateur work; some say that it is because they do not like to lower their standards (which is meaningless) but others do have a valid reason. If a professional's films exhibit some fault, he usually knows why. If an amateur's films have something wrong with them, he is less likely to accept that it is his own fault, and may want to argue with the lab. After a couple of bad experiences of this kind, the lab will refuse to accept any more amateur work.

These five pictures illustrate the effect of film choice on subject rendition. Some films deliver more saturated colours than others, and each reacts differently to over- and under-exposure; in the picture **right**, the underexposure chosen to saturate the colours has turned the water blue-black. Each, too, has its own colour cast – though the red of the picture **above centre** is a result of the creative use of filtration.

INTRODUCTION

Some cheap, amateur-only labs may scratch films (the cardinal sin) or deliver off-colour results as a consequence of less-careful solution monitoring, so the small amount you save compared with professional processing is hardly worth the effort.

So far, we have only looked at slide (reversal or transparency) films. Negative films are a more recent development (Agfa, 1940: Kodak, 1942) and use a similar dye technology to slide films. Tones are reversed (as in a black-and-white negative) and colours are also complementary: a green field reproduces as orange. A similar emulsion (or rather, set of emulsions – once again, the films are integral tripacks) is coated onto a paper base to make prints.

Although colour negative film can produce results of very high quality, the vast majority of colour negative users are snapshotters – and it shows. Machine printing varies from the acceptable to the horrendous, and high-quality hand printing costs the earth. Furthermore, for reproduction (in books, etc.) slide film delivers vastly better quality. The only professionals who use much colour negative film are those whose customers want a print as the final result; essentially, wedding photographers and portrait photographers. For amateur use, you will either have to reconcile yourself to variable quality or do your own printing (though for <u>film</u> processing the professional labs are fine). Life really gets interesting when the subject varies much from the standard which automatic printing machines are designed to handle; black backgrounds go a vile mouldering green, colours are washed out, whites go yellow . . . .

On the other hand, prints do have the advantage of being easily displayed, so it may be unrealistic to urge all serious photographers to use only slide film. One solution, as already mentioned, is to do your own printing. Another is to shoot reversal film, and to have an internegative made (or make it yourself) for printing; this is only feasible if you very rarely want prints. A third possibility, and the one which I use myself, is to use reversal printing materials.

These allow prints to be made direct from slides, with the

Colour saturation, or purity of *hue, is a very important aspect of creative colour photography. Polarising filters reduce white-light glare, and contrasty lenses reduce flare. A lens hood is of* course essential. The picture ***right*** *was taken with a long telephoto lens without polariser or hood; the difference is obvious.*

great advantage that you can use slide film and keep the benefits of cheapness, easy judging of results, and suitability for reproduction, whilst retaining the option of having prints. Commercial reversal prints are no worse than machine colour prints, and the best of them are at least as good as the best neg/pos prints. If in addition they are made using dye-destruction materials (notably Cibachrome) they are also considerably more permanent than other types of prints, with a life several <u>times</u> as long. In the dye-destruction process, the dyes are already present in the tripack and are destroyed during development in proportion to their exposure, which allows the use of very much more stable dyes than are found in most colour processes.

These are not the only colour processes. One of the most commonly encountered is the Land system used in Polaroid colour films. This involves migratory dyes that also act as developers, but are immobilised in so doing. The <u>unexposed</u> dyes continue to migrate until they reach the print surface, so the result is a positive (reversal) image.

Others, less frequently met with, include <u>dye transfer</u> (which involves separation negatives and three-colour matrices), trichrome carbro (a similar process), and Fresson (another offshoot of the same process).

Two other contenders, which were relatively new at the time of writing, are <u>Ektaflex</u> and <u>Lasercolor</u>. Ektaflex (from Kodak) is a simple-to-use system which can work with either negative or positive film; it involves an intermediate stage, something between positive and negative, in which a sheet of transfer film is exposed in the enlarger and then squeegeed into close contact with a piece of paper which will become the final print. It owes quite a lot to instant-picture technology, and results seem to be very good. It is especially convenient if used in association with slides, as mentioned above.

Lasercolor is the very antithesis of simplicity, requiring an enormous capital outlay on equipment and thus (for obvious reasons) is not suitable for the amateur. The transparency is laser-scanned to produce a 70mm negative and then printed conventionally. The quality is very high indeed, as is the permanence, and once again it works from transparencies – perhaps the ideal approach for someone who only wants the occasional print.

When it comes to choosing a colour film, a lot will depend on personal preferences and on the trade-offs you are prepared to make. Slide film is the accepted choice if you want to reproduce the picture in a book or something similar, but if you want prints you can choose the neg/pos or pos/pos routes.

Choosing between brands is even more personal. Kodachrome is the standard professional choice in 35mm, as mentioned, but you might also choose to use Ektachrome 200 or 400 ASA when the 25 or 64 ASA of Kodachrome is insufficient; ORWO, for its contrasty and saturated colours; Agfa 50S for its neutrality and absence of colour bias; and so forth. The choice in larger formats is similar, though (unfortunately) Kodachrome is not available.

Some manufacturers offer special 'professional' films. These can offer fractionally better (and more predictable) results than the standard variety, but they must be stored in a refrigerator and processed as soon as possible after exposure; if they are treated like 'ordinary' films, results may actually be worse than usual.

Finally, remember that just as there is no need for every picture to be creative, there is no need for every picture to be of the utmost quality. For snapshots, an ordinary amateur-only lab can be fine. It may not deliver the quality of the professional lab, but it is so much cheaper that you may decide that you are not worried. Keep a sense of proportion – and enjoy yourself.

I am not of that school which argues that everyone would do better if they were restricted to using Box Brownies. I firmly believe that in order to get the very best results, you need not only to know your equipment but also to have the <u>right</u> equipment.

The question of what <u>is</u> the right equipment is a vexed one, and in any case depends as much upon the user as on the type of photography he or she want to undertake.

The first and most important thing is always to use good fresh film and have it processed by a reputable laboratory (or, of course, process it yourself). Only fresh film will behave predictably: outdated film varies in speed and colour balance, and poor processing can make even fresh film behave like the worst old stock. Experiment if you like, but for serious work choose a single film and stick with it – or at least, work with a set of films matched to the conditions. I use Kodachrome for quality and its ability to withstand appalling conditions, and Kodak's

*Once again, attention to colour saturation is vital. These pictures also show how to use the tonal range of the film creatively: 'correct' exposure for the white doves and doors means that the blue sky records as indigo. The soft light on the horse and foal **facing page bottom right** allows the photographer to record all the tones present; a white wall furnished the reflector which was needed to stop the two white horses **bottom left** from recording as white blobs in a black hole, whilst in the other two pictures **facing page** the exposure was determined for the subject of principal interest. The picture of the dovecote shows the effect of not using an adequate lens hood: the flare, sharp-edged from the edge of a lens element, draws the eye away from the subject. Flare can be used, however, to soften the image if desired.*

EL 400 when I need the speed. On rollfilm, I use Agfa's R100S E6-compatible film instead.

Whilst it is possible to get great colour pictures using the simplest of cameras, it does make life appreciably more difficult. There is no doubt that 35mm is the best all-rounder, though you will need full manual control if you want to get the very best pictures in anything but ideal conditions; this effectively means buying an SLR or a system rangefinder camera. There is equally no doubt that rollfilm, or even larger formats, will *ceteris paribus* deliver better quality – at a price, in size, weight, versatility, and convenience as well as in money. It is quite possible, though, to use old Rolleiflexes and similar TLRs (available at very low prices second-hand) to give superb results.

Interchangeable lenses are desirable, but bring their own problems. Complex lenses with lots of glasses, like wide-angles of retrofocus design and zooms, can lead to contrast problems as well as reduced definition and increased distortion when compared with the standard lens. Even with standard lenses, the contrast and 'bite' is less on the faster lenses: to choose examples

from three formats, I use a 55/3.5 Micro Nikkor unless I need the speed of the f/1.2; a 100/3.5 Planar (Hasselblad) instead of the 80/2.8; and a 105/4.5 Apo Lanthar (Linhof) instead of a 100/2.8 Planar.

Whatever the lens, an efficient lenshood is essential for maximum colour saturation: I would rather use a normally-coated lens with a good lenshood than a multi-coated one without (though, of course, the best choice is multi-coating <u>and</u> a lens-hood). For maximum saturation, a polarising filter can bring surprising benefits by cutting out the white reflected light which scatters off any coloured surface and hence degrades the colour. Of course, if you <u>want</u> soft, degraded colour, leave the hood and filter off, and make sure that the front of the lens is covered with a good layer of dust: if you are after this effect deliberately, a dirty filter on the front of the lens is easier to clean (and less traumatic to smear with petroleum jelly!) than the front element.

With slow lenses and polarising filters, possibly combined with Kodachrome, exposure times are going to be long – so a tripod is a worth-while investment. The sort that extends to five feet from one is uselessly spindly: a good solid tripod is extremely unlikely to weigh less than 5lb, and twice that is not out of the way.

Accurate and controllable metering is essential, and you may wish to consider using a separate hand-held meter, even if you already have a built-in meter in the camera. There are some circumstances in which a built-in meter is far better – close-ups being an example – but there are also many where the ability to measure specific areas of the subject, or the light falling upon it (incident light), is a boon.

The two standard professional meters are the Gossen Lunasix (in both its incarnations) and the Weston Master (in all its avatars). The Lunasix allows you to measure ludicrously low light levels, such as 1 sec. at f/1.4 with 64 ASA film, with ease; with add-on accessories, such as the TELE semi-spot attachment which allows you to target a 15° or 7½° area in the meter's own viewfinder and measure that, it is even more versatile. The

Weston Master is more favoured for incident light metering, using the Invercone; this, together with an understanding of the admittedly complicated dial, allows you to place exposures exactly as you wish. Even if used with no understanding whatsoever, the incident light method will lead to a higher percentage of correct exposures than almost any other.

One thing which you must do is establish a personal rating for films. If your results are consistently a little lighter or darker than you would like, simply reset the ASA dial on your meter. Both meters and cameras vary: with a Hasselblad and a Weston Master, I find that my ratings agree exactly with the makers', but with Nikon and Lunasix they come out ⅓ stop darker than I like – so I rate Kodachrome 25 at 20 ASA. For reproduction, a slightly dark transparency is in any case desirable, so I suppose that for many people's taste I am rating it at 16 ASA; but it works for me, which is all that matters.

For really critical work, some people also use a <u>colour</u>

<u>temperature meter</u>. This indicates which filters to use to match the colour sensitivity of the film to the colour of the prevailing light; the filters in question are usually gelatine sheets, very easily marked, which come in tiny colour correction (CC) steps in both primary colours (red, green, blue), and subtractive primaries (yellow, magenta, cyan). They are distinguished by their initials

and a number which indicated their density: thus, a CC05Y is a very faint (barely perceptible) yellow, and a CC50M is very magenta indeed.

The question of correcting for lighting is further considered later but the so-called 'effects filters' can properly be mentioned here.

First, they are no substitute for real creativity. Use them to get a previsualised effect, or experiment with them until you get an effect that you like – but do not confuse the unusual with the attractive.

Having said that, there are literally millions of ways you can use these filters, either singly or in combination. For example, I once wanted to emphasise both the sparkle and the grossness of a commercial Christmas, so I photographed an illuminated city shopping centre at night with a 5-face prism and a 6-point star filter. The effect was at once excessive and magical – exactly what I was trying to achieve.

You need not restrict yourself to commercial filters, either. Pieces of lighting gel, old-fashioned multi-coloured cellophane sweet wrappers, nylon stockings with holes in them (produced with a hot matchtip or cigarette) – all can be grist to your mill.

In creative colour photography, there is no doubt that equipment has its place. Indeed, there are some things which simply cannot be attempted without more-or-less sophisticated attachments: creative darkroom techniques are an example. But in the majority of cases, it is the photographer's eye – <u>your</u> eye – that makes the picture.

'Straight' pictures of the right subjects are always more successful than attempts to liven up basically dull pictures with technical pizzaz. It is a fair comment on these pictures that not everyone has access to this sort of scenery, but the same is certainly not true of many of the other pictures in this book; the secret is in looking, not in travelling.

SEEING COLOUR

Some people see colour and black and white photography as rivals; but they are the same sort of people who see men and women as rivals, which is about as realistic as considering a knife and a fork as rivals, or a pair of chopsticks. There are some things which colour suits better, and others which black and white suits better – and yet others which may be photographed in either medium, equally well, but differently.

It is a matter for speculation what sort of conditioning makes us react to different pictures in different ways. It is probably as old as Man himself to associate blue with cold and reds and yellows with heat, but the association of coarse grain with immediacy and news is a much more recent phenomenon. 'Reading' blur as action is probably learned, too, from the cartoon movies of our childhood. Whatever the origins of our reactions, they exist, and the wise photographer will be able to use a little psychology (and even a little physiology) in creating a colour picture.

As with much of the rest of this book, you cannot learn from words alone; you have to look at the pictures. The secret of learning is simple: look, and think.

Whilst you are looking at a picture, consider the emotions and associations it conjures up in you. Ask how it achieves that effect. Could you duplicate that effect? Not necessarily the literal effect, by standing in the same place and pressing the same button on the same camera, but the same feeling, the same atmosphere? It is very tempting to say, 'of course', but have you tried it? I always thought that it would be easy to imitate a

It is interesting to consider how the pictures on these two pages might be treated in black and white. In the three flower pictures you would need a very different approach: the subject would blend in with the background and the soft-focus would merely look muddy. With the other three pictures, the range of tones and textures would allow you to treat the subjects in a similar way in black and white, though you might use more directional lighting to emphasise form and surface texture. Most photographers find that sometimes they 'see' subjects in colour, and other times in black and white. What you 'see' – line, tone, colour, broad shapes, fine detail – also varies. By being alive to this variation, you can make the best use of your perception; you can also learn to cultivate a way of seeing which produces the results you like.

SEEING COLOUR

Weston picture of a pepper – until I tried it. Unfortunately, armchair expertise is all too easy to acquire in photography: if you read the right books, and back up your opinions with an armoury of expensive equipment, many people forget the fact that they have never seen one of your pictures and tend to believe that what you say is true.

Of course, there are warm and cold colours. There are also 'advancing' colours, like most of the reds, which fairly leap out at you from the page, and 'retreating' colours (such as blue, with its suggestions of haze and distance) which suggest recession and expansiveness. Bright, vivid colours promote a feeling of liveliness: soft, pastel colours are often restful. Brighter colours in

the foreground, fading with distance, give the effect of aerial perspective. Vivid backgrounds with dull foregrounds, on the other hand, can promote a feeling of safety and security, as if the viewer is inside a room looking out on the big bright dangerous world.

Some of the most effective colour pictures are almost monochromatic – a dusty hot yellow landscape, for example, or the cool blue of a lakeside evening. Others rely on vivid contrasts

Snow is blue; this simple but often unpalatable fact is a result of its reflecting the blue of the sky. It can also (and simultaneously) be pink, as illustrated by the river scene, when the rays of the dawning or setting sun strike it. By looking at colours as they are, instead of as we expect them to be, we can take very much better pictures. Technical expertise, such as using a polarising filter or underexposing slightly, adds another layer of perception.

– instead of matching hues, jarring combinations of brilliant colours grab the attention. Whilst it can be very effective to introduce a colour 'note' into a picture – an orange jacket in a green-grey moor, for example – a picture which tries to get everything in is often unsuccessful; this is why so many garden and flower pictures fail to work; they are a jazzy mess of small areas of colour, none of them important enough to capture the eye. By contrast, a small patch of bright colour can draw the attention in quite a disproportionate manner compared with its size.

There are also some visual elements which are stronger than others. For example, a tiny figure in a huge landscape will catch the eye much quicker than anything else, such as a tree or motor-car, even if that is much bigger: again, one could cite evolutionary reasons, or simply accept it.

At this point, we are beginning to move into the realms of composition. In many circles, this is a rude word because of the sterile academicism which used to surround it. An example was the 'rule of thirds': divide a picture into thirds, vertically and horizontally, and the 'centre of interest' must lie on the intersection of a pair of dividing lines. Another was the S-curve, to 'lead the eye into the picture'. A lot of nonsense was talked and written about these and many other rules, until club photography became like the Chinese eight-legged essay: as long as it was

formally correct, the fact that it was utterly tedious or even completely meaningless was politely ignored.

In practice, if you analyse successful pictures, quite a lot of them accord with these so-called 'rules' – even more if you permit yourself the kind of freedom of interpretation arrogated by some judges – but quite a lot do not.

The best approach to learning about composition that I have ever heard came from a painter, Senggye Tombs Curtis. Take a piece of blue paper about 20 x 30." Cut out a number of pieces of orange card, in various shapes – circles, rectangles, irregular, smooth, jagged. Just sit down and play with them. See which combinations of shapes and placings please you. Carry on until you lose interest, then stop. Repeat the process a few times, and it will do wonders for your sense of composition. His other piece of advice was to consider the main subject, and to ask if that pleased you; and then to blank it out, either mentally or by putting your hand over it, and ask if the background pleased you. Move things around (or change your viewpoint) until the answer to both questions is yes.

Although it may seem at first that such a considered approach is too long-winded for most types of photography, it very rapidly becomes second nature, and you do it automatically; you just don't take pictures which aren't pleasing.

Alternatively, you may care to try Henri Cartier-Bresson's

SEEING COLOUR

approach. He looks through the viewfinder for a pattern; and when the <u>shape</u> is right (not the subject's expression, or any other detail, but the general shape) he presses the button. In lesser mortals than HCB, this may lead at first to a higher rejection rate of pictures which are unsharp, or in which the people are not doing anything very interesting, but (as with the Senggye system outlined above), it can rapidly grow on you.

The last approach I will suggest comes via David Gibbon, a photographer whose work I hold in the highest regard; he in turn heard it from another painter. It goes like this:

Imagine that you are wearing four pairs of sunglasses at once. With them all on, all you can see is the vaguest outlines. Sketch those. Take off the first pair: a little more detail is visible. <u>This</u> has a line running <u>that</u> way; <u>this</u> is much darker than <u>that</u>. Sketch that in. Take off another pair, and repeat the process; by the time you have taken off the last pair; you will have correctly observed all the details of the original.

Admittedly there is no parallel to sketches in photography (unless it be Polaroid test pictures!), but the application is obvious: as I said at the beginning of the chapter, look, and think.

*If we appreciate the photographic process, we can use camera and film to see colour in ways which are alien to us. The blue underwater scene is far more blue than we would remember it – our brain automatically compensates for the blueness, which the film cannot – and the slithering, sliding mass of fish waiting to be fed is frozen by a fast shutter speed. In all of the photographs on this page, a polarising filter has cut glare and saturated colours, either in a way we can readily recognise **left and below** or in strange and fascinating ways **bottom.***

ABSTRACTS

The classical analysis of a painting or photograph breaks it down into four components: line, tone, colour, and form. The four are fairly self-explanatory, though 'form' is sometimes called 'modelling' or 'chiaroscuro', and is to do with the play of light and shade which gives something its roundness or three-dimensionality.

In black-and-white photography, abstraction begins with line and tone; in colour, colour itself precedes tone. It is easy to see why, considering the composition exercise described in the last chapter; the cut-outs could be made of identical <u>tones</u>, but they would still be readily distinguishable by <u>colour</u>.

It is instructive to analyse the relationship of line, tone, colour, and form in each of the six pictures on this page. In a sense, they are very intellectual pictures: it is possible to work out how each one achieves its impact. Nevertheless, it is also impossible to deny their emotional effect. All of these pictures were taken with 35mm

cameras: the lack of detail, particularly in the three figures (figures always draw the eye) is noticeable. It is also substantially irrelevant, as the viewer supplies his own details. Only in the two abstract pictures, in which there is no sign of humanity, do we look more closely at the textures and shapes.

Alternatively, the abstract can work in different tones of the same colour – though now, we have introduced the third variable. Finally, we introduce form; but unless the picture is cleverly composed so that we do not immediately recognise the subject (or rather, so that subject is subjugated to the abstracted elements), it can scarcely be called an abstract. After all, 'abstraction' is by definition the art of taking a part, not all; and a recognisable picture can cease to be an 'abstraction'.

In practice, any one or more of the analytical categories can be the subject of the abstraction. In a picture consisting of a monochrome and black, it is almost possible to reduce it to pure line, and even taking so palpably real a subject as a nude, we can use very flat lighting to reduce the colour to a series of barely separated tones, so that the composition is again reduced almost to pure line.

Abstraction is a way of seeing, and it varies from person to person. Because of the posturings of some *avant-garde* artists, the word 'abstract' has become synonymous in some circles with incompetence; in others, there is the reverent attitude which holds: 'I don't understand it, so it must be art'. But think back to Senggye's lesson on composition: some ways of arranging things are pleasing, some are not. You would not expect everything

157

which pleased you to please everyone else, so do not expect their abstractions to please you, or yours to please them. Rather, please yourself – and if your inward eye is good enough, you will please yourself more and more, as well as finding that you can please other people.

Throughout our experience there are examples of abstractions: abstract nudes, abstract still-lifes, abstract landscapes, abstracts culled from city life, to name but a few. The reason for according them a separate chapter here, though, is that they are in many ways the purest form of colour photography, colour for its own sake.

Although the golden rule for understanding the abstract compositions of others, and for spotting your own, is still the same 'look and think', there are a couple of techniques – tricks, if you like – for seeing them. One is to select unfamiliar parts of the whole; a good way of doing this is to move in close, to around eighteen inches or so, or even closer if your lens can manage it.

By isolating things in this way, you can see them for themselves instead of in their everyday functional terms. Another good trick is to look for bright colours; at the intersection of two bright colours, you can get some really vivid colour abstracts.

Motor cars are a particularly good source of brilliant colour, and so is plastic kitchen ware. It sometimes helps to put your eyes slightly out of focus; that way, colours seem to become much, much more vivid in contrast with dull backgrounds.

Although anything can provide the inspiration for an abstract picture, there is often a lot to be gained from rubbish and decay. The higgledy-piggledy juxtaposition of discarded wrappings, toys, fruit peel, and so forth can furnish some excellent abstracts, though it is as well to use a slightly longer than usual lens to keep from getting too close! Cracked and peeling paint, on the other hand, is a lot more hygienic, and I find that I often prefer the aleatory hand of nature to the allegedly more skilled hand of Jackson Pollock.

Closely related to the abstract from a photographic point of view (though the artistic connection is more arguable) is the unfamiliar picture. 'Trick' pictures, from unusual angles, are not uncommon, but we can go beyond this and show something in a genuinely novel way. This is particularly true of close-ups; a common electronic circuit board can look like a surreal science-fiction landscape when carefully photographed. Close-up techniques are further described later.

These pictures are all exercises in tone. Colour variation and colour contrast have been almost entirely removed, and the use of silhouette techniques minimises modelling, so that form becomes line. The effects which result from using strong monochrome filters on colour film are hard to previsualise, because our eyes can compensate for colour casts to quite an extraordinary degree. The only way to learn about them is to use up some film. Try for strong, clear shapes, and underexpose quite dramatically: try two stops as a starting point (or quadruple your ASA setting). It may seem that reducing colour to monochrome removes the point of using colour film, but the simple question is whether the results justify the means.

Light is the basis of photography; the word <u>photography</u> comes from the Greek words for light and writing. Despite its pre-eminence, however, few photographers bother to study it that much, or even to think about it at all.

From a photographic point of view, the first important distinction is between <u>available light</u> and <u>controlled light</u>. Available light is the light as we find it. It is free, it requires no setting-up on our part, and most important of all it preserves the atmosphere of a place. Its drawbacks, though, are that it may not be as strong as we would like, it may come from the wrong direction, and it may be of the wrong colour. Controlled light comes from supplementary lamps under our control.

For some kinds of photography, the atmosphere is everything; to change the lighting in any way would ruin the picture. Admittedly, there is a kind of half-way house in which the available light is recreated (and modified) using studio lighting. There are also a couple of useful tricks such as using reflectors out of shot to get a bit more light where you need it, or even

We can, perhaps, best appreciate the changing nature of light by watching clouds in the sky – especially if there is blue sky and sunlight to set them off. The way in which brightness and shadow, modelling and silhouette, tone and line vary as we watch, is enormously instructive. If we look at a sunset as well, we can see the incredible range of colours contained in an apparently monochrome subject. Even without taking a single picture, cloud-watching is time well spent; and if we can capture the clouds, we have really accomplished something.

Always be on the lookout for lighting effects: if you cannot find them by moving around, **top right and top left,** then try waiting, **left and top centre.** A patch of sun breaking through clouds often makes for an attractive landscape, whether in Arizona or Hampshire.

LIGHT

replacing domestic 100 watt bulbs with 275 watt photofloods (which increases heat output as well as light, so watch out for lampshades and furnishings). Generally, though, controlled lighting implies a fairly significant change to the existing light; and it can be achieved in a number of ways.

The quality of light can vary in three main ways, <u>direction</u>, <u>harshness</u>, and <u>colour</u>. Each of these can be controlled.

<u>Direction</u> is the most obvious; the only physical difficulty in controlling it lies in getting the lamp to stay where we want it, and solutions to this range from having assistants to hold each lamp to buying various forms of lamp-stand. Accustomed as we are to the light of the sun, we expect the light to come from more-or-less above and from a single source. Apart from this, we have a free hand.

<u>Harshness</u> is more subtle. Basically, a point source (like the sun in a cloudless sky) casts very clear sharp shadows, whereas a diffuse source (like a cloudy sky) casts no shadows and gives a much softer effect. A small flashgun, or an unshielded bulb, casts strong shadows: for diffusion we can 'bounce' the light off a wall or ceiling or other flat surface, or diffuse it <u>through</u> some translucent material – one photographer of my acquaintance swears by stapling a huge sheet of tracing paper across a doorway and shining a light through that.

<u>Colour</u> is the trickiest of all. We can accept daylight as white, or the light of an electric lamp as white; but if we compare the two side-by-side, we see that the electric lamp is much yellower. Still worse are fluorescent lamps: we may see them as 'white', but on film they often record a sickly green. The problem is that we can adapt mentally; the film cannot.

The consequence of this is that if we use film in illumination for which it was not designed, we must either put up with colour casts or use filters. The easiest way to understand this is via a brief excursion into the theory of colour temperature.

If a perfectly black body is heated, it begins to glow as it gets hot. The hotter it gets, the more blue the light; this is illustrated by the fact that 'white-hot' iron is hotter than 'red-hot'.

Although perfect black bodies are rare, the behaviour of most things when they are heated gets pretty close; a candle, burning at about 1500°C, is redder than a domestic lamp running at about 2500°C and this in turn is redder than the sun (say 5000°C). Furthermore, even light which is not obviously produced by heating (such as the light from a discharge tube in an electronic flashgun) can be assigned a colour temperature. In practice, colour temperatures are given in <u>degrees Kelvin</u> (°K), which represent the same temperature increments as °C but start from 'absolute zero', about −273°C. Typical colour temperatures are, therefore:

Candle	1750°K
Domestic lamp	2600-2800°K (depending on wattage)
Nitraphot lamp	3200°K
Clear flashbulb	4000°K
Sunlight	5000°K
Overcast daylight	7500°K
Blue north sky	10,000-20,000°K

Small differences are more easily visible further down the scale, with a 3200°K lamp detectably different from a 3400°K lamp, and a domestic lamp noticeably much yellower than either. In the higher regions, beyond about 6000°K, it takes about a 500°K difference to be really noticeable.

Films may in theory be sensitised to suit any colour temperature, but they are usually 'Daylight type' (5800 or 6000°K) or 'Artificial Light' (3400°K or more rarely 3200°K). Light source and film can be matched by using warming (brown-orange) or cooling (blue) filters, either according to tables or

Haze, sun on water, the darkening sky: each kind of light has its own flavour, its own feeling. Do not be afraid to emphasise the feeling of the light, either by using filters or by colour contrasts within the picture, but be wary of changing it dramatically unless you want a deliberately unnatural or contrived picture. Even if you do want special effects, an awareness of the existing light is essential. Open-awareness – looking, and seeing – must remain the core of successful photography.

Colour temperature conversions

To obtain 3200 K from:	To obtain 3400 K from:	WRATTEN Filter	Exposure Increase in stops*	Filter Colour
2490 K	2610 K	82C+82C	1⅓	
2570 K	2700 K	82C+82B	1⅓	
2650 K	2780 K	82C+82A	1	
2720 K	2870 K	82C+82	1	**Bluish**
2800 K	2950 K	82C	⅔	
2900 K	3060 K	82B	⅔	
3000 K	3180 K	82A	⅓	
3100 K	3290 K	82	⅓	
3200 K	3400 K	*No filter necessary*		
3300 K	3510 K	81	⅓	
3400 K	3630 K	81A	⅓	
3500 K	3740 K	81B	⅓	**Yellowish**
3600 K	3850 K	81C	⅔	
3850 K	4140 K	81EF	⅔	

with the use of a colour temperature meter.

Whilst it does not much matter what sort of film and light we use, provided they match (or can be made to match), the difficulty comes when light from two different kinds of sources are mixed. Daylight and electronic flash are of the same colour temperature, and can be mixed with impunity, but daylight and tungsten light, or electronic flash and tungsten light, cannot. Electronic flash can be made to match tungsten by filtering the flash head itself with a piece of gel or acetate filter; if used in front of tungsten lamps these will often melt, and the only

practical approach is to use expensive dichroic glass filters – or to exclude all other light. Fluorescent tubes are in a class by themselves, as they do not emit a continuous spectrum and thus cannot be assigned a colour temperature; the best you can do is to try a CC20M filter and hope for the best.

In unavoidably mixed lighting, such as an office lit partly by daylight, partly by fluorescents, and partly by tungsten-filament draughtsman's lamps, it is flatly impossible to accommodate everything on one film. The best bet is to use Ektachrome 400, which appears to handle this sort of thing acceptably.

Given the three variables of direction, harshness, and colour, we can begin to choose types of supplementary lighting. Once again, there are three divisions: the small on-camera flashgun, tungsten lighting, and studio electronic flash.

The small on-camera flashgun is normally only suitable for snapshots; the harsh shadows behind the subject, the fixed and rather unnatural direction, and the danger of 'flashback' or direct reflection of the light back into the camera ensure this. The dreaded 'red-eye' is a variation of the last, and is caused by the light being reflected straight back from the eyes; the blood vessels of the eye give the characteristic demonic look. In addition, burned-out foregrounds frequently result either from miscalculation or from trusting an automatic flashgun against a dark background.

A certain amount can be achieved by 'bouncing' the light, as described before, but this relies on a powerful gun and a handy reflective surface; low-powered guns often lose too much light by absorption at the reflective surface, and in any case the flash-to-subject distance is the distance from the gun to the reflector and then on to the subject, which may be out of the gun's range. Coloured reflectors add their own tinge to the light as well as absorbing still more of what is available.

One other point which has already been made is that additional lighting can destroy the atmosphere, but there is one

case in which the atmosphere (literally) has its revenge and destroys the picture. A thick, smoky, hazy atmosphere reflects on-camera flash straight back into the lens, giving a flat and degraded picture – and the effect with bounce flash is not much better. 'Snooting' the flash to give a spotlight effect (use a cone of black paper) improves matters, but drastically cuts down on the amount of light available.

On-camera flashguns have other uses than providing straight-forward illumination, though. Fill-in flash, also known as 'synchro-sunlight', is used to fill shadows or to illuminate a subject against a bright background – a simple example is a girl against a sunset. The film cannot handle the contrast range involved, so normally the choice would be between a correctly-exposed sunset (and a silhouette of the girl) or a correctly-exposed girl (and a washed-out sunset). With the flash, you can expose for the sunset (with conventional metering) and light the girl to even things up.

Automatic flashguns are usually useless for fill-in flash, as you need to know the amount of light being emitted. Set them on manual, and use a guide number 50-100% higher than normal: for example, with a gun rated at GN 100 (feet) at 100 ASA, use a GN of 150-200. If the available light exposure is (say) 1/60 at f/8 (and you must remember to use a shutter speed at which your camera can synchronise), then you would need to be about twenty feet away (180 ÷ 8 = 22.5). If you want to be closer, try a folded handkerchief over the flash head: you can gauge how much light it is likely to absorb by metering 'through' it with a conventional meter. Alternatively, if you have a gun with switchable power, turn it down. You may even wish to consider a cheap small gun if you already own a large one, merely to use for

Pictures incorporating light *sources (including windows) require extreme care if these are not to 'burn in' to featureless areas of white. If in addition there is both daylight and artificial light, the problems are even more acute. Three* *possibilities are (1) multiple electronic flash fired simultaneously, (2) 'painting' dark areas with multiple flashes, and (3) relying on existing lighting as in the interiors on these pages.*

fill-in. By playing with the balance between the flash and the available light, you can achieve a variety of effects, including *'nuite Americaine,'* in which the daylight is underexposed and gives the effect of twilight or even moonlight.

You can also filter the light passing through a flash-head. Used out of doors, as balance flash, the filtration will only affect foreground objects: this gives some weird effects. Alternatively, by using filters of complementary colours over the flash head and the camera lens, you can get some quite extraordinary effects. Something similar is sold as 'Color Back' by Cokin.

Most amateurs who want something more versatile than a single flash-head buy lighting stands which accept photofloods. Whilst these have the drawbacks already mentioned of being of a low colour temperature (and furthermore of not being compatible with daylight), they are much less expensive and much less complicated than big studio flash units. They run very hot, and can get through bulbs at quite a rate: because the bulbs are 'overrun' for maximum light, their life is only a few hours, though gas-filled bulbs of the Argophot or Nitrophot type last longer at the expense of lower efficiency (less light for a given wattage) and a slightly lower colour temperature (3200°K instead of 3400°K).

LIGHT

Daylight is often rather bluish, especially at twilight: in the picture of the trees **right** the photographer has emphasised this with a weak blue filter. In the small picture **below,** the blue tinge is due to an overcast sky. A brown graduated filter was used to add 'interest' to the sky.

On the opposite page, the picture on the **top left** shows an intelligent use of a tobacco graduated filter. Combined with the very red light of the setting sun, the effect is surreal and fascinating. Frequently, of course, the sky produces even more fascinating effects quite naturally. When you look at a picture, try to work out whether the pre-dominant colour cast adds to or detracts from the overall effect. **Opposite page: lower left,** the misty blue is emphasised; the grass is almost cyan. On the **lower right,** the warm light complements the brown of the wood. If you have time, it is often worth trying three pictures of one subject: one without filtration, one with a filter which accentuates the colour of the light, and one which is complementary and so reduces it. An 81A (brownish) and an 82 (light blue) are all that is normally required.

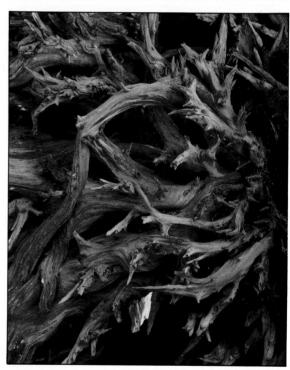

The advantages of tungsten lighting are its relative cheapness (apart from the bulb and power bills) and the fact that no special metering techniques are needed; the cheapest flash meter is about the same price as an expensive ordinary meter. In professional use, tungsten is only considered where other light can be excluded entirely, and where a tremendous amount of light is required. An example is car photography in a studio, where I have seen 28Kw in use – the equivalent, perhaps, of a thousand 100w domestic lamps.

A very much more useful and versatile approach is to adopt the third option and use studio electronic flash. This runs cool, uses little power, does not 'eat' bulbs, and matches daylight in colour temperature. On the other hand, it has three main drawbacks. First, it is expensive – up to ten times as much as comparable tungsten lighting. Secondly, although it is reliable it cannot be repaired by an amateur, especially in view of the lethal voltages stored in the capacitor. Thirdly, a flash meter is a virtual necessity.

All professional units use modelling lights, which are usually switched in proportion to the flash tube, so that you can gauge the lighting without strenuous previsualisation or Polaroid tests. They offer 'system' adaptability with 'brollies' or umbrellas for soft lighting, snoots for spot effects, and (with the bigger packs) a range of large diffuse sources ranging from the 'swimming pool' or 'northlight' (up to 6 x 4') down to the 18" square 'fish fryer'.

Whether you use flash or continuous lighting, or even if you rely on available light, you can greatly increase your scope by using reflectors and 'flags'. Reflectors can be anything from a sheet of white paper to an 8 x 4' 'flat' made of painted wood or (light but bulky) expanded polystyrene. Flags, also known as 'donkeys', are pieces of black card, wood, or metal attached to stands and used to shade or mask the subject from direct lighting; by having them bright on one side and dark on the other you can also use them as small reflectors.

People are one of the trickiest subjects to photograph creatively. Over millions of years, we have evolved to recognise people, to wonder what they are doing, and generally to take an interest in them. The drawing power of a figure in a landscape is well known; everything operates on the level of monkey curiosity. If we are to get beyond this, we need more than a sharp, well-exposed picture.

One school of thought maintains that any picture tells us more about the photographer than about the subject, and this is perhaps more true when photographing people than when photographing any other subject. For instance, one girl might be photographed in many different ways.

One photographer might see her as a classical nude, de-personalised and reduced to abstraction. Another might want to

Fantasy pictures can be tremendous fun for both photographer and model. These were set up as part of a set of pictures for a book on cocktails, but the choice of costumes, *props, and lighting is a textbook in its own right. You can use these pictures in two ways: either try to duplicate them, or devise other ways of illustrating the same theme.*

photograph her as a pin-up – no less depersonalised, but changed from an abstraction into a symbol, a focus. An advertising photographer might direct her like an actress, until she behaved the way he wanted in order to convey (say) a typical clothes-buying teenager. Yet a fourth might attempt an 'in-depth' picture, trying to show something of her feelings or emotions (at least as he perceived them), whilst a fifth might say that he was a passive mirror and photograph her without preconceptions.

Because all these techniques are essentially different, and employ different aspects of creativity, they are worth considering separately. Before that, though, there are a few observations about general techniques which may be useful.

Equipment is not critical. You can use whatever you have – although inevitably some types are going to be more useful than others. The 35mm SLR is (as usual) the best all-rounder, but for candid and unplanned work the rangefinder camera may be more appropriate. For better image quality, a larger format is obviously desirable – anything from an old Rollei through a Hasselblad to a 10 x 8″ studio monorail (some people use them for photographing nudes).

Exposure and colour, on the other hand, are extremely critical. We can judge flesh tones better than anything else, and pictures which are too light or too dark or exhibit colour casts (unless any of these effects is obviously deliberate) will be extremely obvious. Use fresh material, correctly exposed, and

PEOPLE

processed as soon as possible after exposure. If you <u>know</u> that the film has a slight colour bias, use a colour correcting gel. Professionals usually buy film in batches, and test the first roll both for effective speed and for colour balance; this is worth considering for the utmost in quality.

Special effects, such as trick filters, split-field filters, and so forth, should be used with great reserve; in this kind of photography in particular, funny colours can often be a substitute for creativity. Novelty is not enough: ask yourself what the picture gains from the use of the special effect. The answer may well be 'everything', but often it will be 'nothing'.

Finally, you will need to be able to handle people, in the style of photography which you have chosen. Taking candid pictures at a beer festival is different from directing a glamour session, which is in turn different from a portrait that is attempting to get under the model's skin. Too many photographers tend to hide behind their cameras: unless you really like people, and are able to get on with them, this may well be a branch of photography to avoid.

CLASSICAL NUDES

These may be either abstracts, as previously discussed, or what might unkindly be called old-fashioned pin-ups. The former requires girls of impeccable form and complexion if it is to be at all successful; abstracts generally have an almost tactile quality, and the sagging breast or wobbly bottom will not project this type of image.

The old fashioned pin-up is generally posed either in the fashion of a Greek statue, or to portray some activity carried to extremes; examples include the girl warming herself in front of the fire, the girl combing her tresses, or sitting on a rock and staring soulfully into the distance. When done well, these photographs can be very beautiful; they have a sort of innocence and purity of line which distinguishes them from lesser nudes. When done badly, though, they resemble Victorian cheesecake or worse. 'Worse' in this case includes those hideous goose-pimpled nudes, lit with three lamps which cast contrasting shadows and in any case are coloured with gels to cast violent smears of colour (usually deep blue, red, and magenta) all over the poor girl's

The one 'trick' which is often appropriate to photographing people is some form of soft-focus or diffusion. It is very much a question of fashion, of course: the undiffused picture on the **facing page bottom left,** dates from the 1960s. Since the overall effect is deliberately romantic, it is important to choose props, locations, clothes, poses, and lighting which are appropriate. Note the use of soft pastel colours and overexposure to desaturate even the stronger colours, and the generous use of backlighting. As diffusers (such as fog filters) diffuse some skylight into the picture, they often give it a bluish cast. A warming filter, such as an 81A or even something stronger, is appropriate: a scratched 81A combines both effects admirably!

A conventional flashgun, carefully hidden behind rubber balloons was the secret technique used in creating the particularly strong, almost unearthly images shown **top right and right.** Fill-in flash was used to provide the necessary detail as well as to reinforce the feeling of unreality. Most of the other pictures rely on saturated colour and a purity of line which is in itself attractive, quite apart from the attractions of the models; they also illustrate the importance of the background, and of separating the subject from the background visually. The use of medium format (Hasselblad) gives superb gradation.

body. This repulsive type of picture has neither the attractive innocence of the old-fashioned nude nor the honest sexiness of the more modern type: instead, it has a certain sleaziness which results from the photographer's refusal to face honestly how he would like to portray the girl, and his inability to do so even if he knew.

This, incidentally, is a fundamental problem when dealing with attractive models. If you fancy the girl, either have the guts to say so (directly or by flirting) or keep it totally professional: innuendo and uncertainty is no fun for either party.

GLAMOUR

The only spark of creativity exhibited in most magazines is in the contriving of story-lines to match the pictures. The girls are usually beautiful, well photographed from a technical point of view, and utterly predictable: the expensive flat, the lacy boudoir, or the well-padded sofa. Devising new surroundings is no mean feat; taking original pictures is nothing short of heroic.

Of course, the average reader does not want 'arty' pictures; he wants good sharp pictures of girls he can fantasise about.

Even when a really masterful photographer in this *genre* finds something new to say, the magazines prefer to run something in the same old mould.

Of late, a certain degree of departure from the super-sharp fantasy babies of the 1950s and 1960s has been seen in a return to romanticism, with soft focus, desaturated colours, and a sort of impressionist 'veil of light' over the pictures; this is further explored in the next chapter, 'The Romantic Image'.

DIRECTING MODELS

In this style of photography, you call upon the model to portray some person who is real only in your mind. Some photographers prefer to be totally autocratic, and to order the model to do this and that, but this only works at all well (if at all) if the photographer is very experienced and sure of himself and the model is a professional who can do as she is told. With amateur (or less martinet-like professional) photographers, and amateur models, it is much better to work together towards the kind of picture you want. Much of what is said here also holds true for the previous two categories (nude and glamour).

Always have the highest regard for your models' feelings; pretty girls in particular can be extremely insecure and easily offended, so offer a constant stream of praise and encouragement. A musician being tonguelashed by a conductor can set his jaw and play his heart out, 'just to show him'; a model does not really have this option. Few people look good (or respond well to directions, or have many ideas they are prepared to communicate) if they are at all upset.

Be reasonably sure of what you want, and that the model can provide it. If you are after flashing eyes and sultry *machismo* don't use a clean-limbed blue-eyed blond-haired Englishman. Work <u>towards</u> what you want; don't expect to get it first time, unless your model is psychic. In the same vein, make sure that

Truly successful pin-ups need not be very revealing. In all but one of these pictures the impact comes mainly from eye-contact and the model's expression; the bath shot succeeds by old-fashioned innocence and romantic prurience.

you have any props you need, that the surroundings are right, and so forth.

Finally, don't get too carried away on a tide of *simpatico* for the model; it is all too easy to get some fantastic shots, which suffer only from the slight drawback that they are totally unsuitable for the purpose for which they were taken. To an amateur, this may not matter too much (though it could be a warning for future sessions); the professional makes a shot list.

Merely because your subject is *a beautiful girl, there is no need to fill the frame with her. She can be an element in a larger picture – the jetty,* ***above centre and left,*** *or the sea and sky,* ***top left and right.*** *Slight underexposure accentuates a tan and saturates colours.*

The problems of exposure can *be considerable on the beach. In the small picture* ***above,*** *correct exposure for the model has led to a washed-out background; in the picture* ***facing page bottom right,*** *the underexposure necessary to capture the deep blue of the sky and the lighter blue of the water has meant that the girl's face is very dark. The other three pictures on the opposite page show the use of fill-in flash. On the* ***top left,*** *the aim was a balance: in the pictures on the* ***top right and bottom left,*** *the background is slightly underexposed for extra saturation and impact. All pictures: Hasselblad with underwater housing and tripod.*

Girls, sun, sea, and sand may sound like paradise – but they are a nightmare for equipment. Ideally, you should use underwater cameras or housings; at least, tape over all cracks and take great care to avoid splashing. Unless you use a sealed-leg tripod such as the Benbo, always rinse the tripod legs in fresh water after immersion; salt water can corrode light alloys beyond repair in a few hours.

Unusual lighting effects are as important in glamour photo-graphy as anywhere. In the picture **below** the red light of sunset and the darkening sky produce interesting colour contrasts; in the bottom picture, simple underexposure against the sun's reflection is used.

The big picture on the left is deceptively simple; have you ever **tried** to get a kite where you wanted it? Exposing for the sky has meant that the girl is reduced to a semi-silhouette, but 'fill' comes from light reflected from the sea and sand; mentally, we supply more detail than there is. Two flare spots, one above the kite and one on the girl's back, are slightly distracting, but that they are not worse is a tribute to the design and multi-coating of modern lenses.

PEOPLE

THE MASK BEHIND THE MASK

Some maintain that it is arrogant even to pretend that you can say anything which is truly about another person; they say that every statement you make, in word, deed, or picture, reflects only you. Whilst there must be a certain amount of truth in what they say, I distrust so extreme a posture. If you can really get to know someone, you may be able to get close enough to capture something of the way they see themselves, or at least of that underlying something which most people agree is the character or nature of the subject.

Some people can do this very rapidly; they are the great reportage photographers like Bert Hardy. Others take a few hours; the best thing to do is to get your subject to talk about himself (or herself) and just listen. Study the gestures, try to work out what is important in this person's life (you may be able to use an appropriate setting) and generally intrude as little as possible. Of course, you can bend the rules a little and interact with the subject to a greater extent; the picture will then reveal a little of him and a little of you. Some subjects only come to life in this way, and (infuriatingly enough) they tend to be the ones who present the most faces to the most people. I do not mean this unkindly, as I myself have significantly different faces for my drinking friends, my publishers, my Buddhist teacher, and so forth. With luck, the face that you get will be one which is recognisable to other people.

THE MIRROR

The mirror reflects whatever is put in front of it: it does not direct, or interact, or record. For obvious reasons, a photographer cannot be a perfect mirror (if only because he does record). It is possible, though, to get some interesting pictures by telling people that you will photograph whatever pose or aspect of their personality they choose to show to the camera.

The drawback with this approach is that most people are either self-conscious or over-inclined to intellectualise: they put on so carefully considered a face that it is hardly worth seeing. There are half a dozen standard pictures – hand behind the head, body grotesquely bent in a bow, teeth-bared smile, head thrown back, and obscene or aggressive gesture – which recur time after time.

The most successful way to employ it is to direct the photographs at first (no matter how lightly) and then gradually withdraw direction; once the subject gets some idea of what you are after, they may get some ideas of their own. I have always found that the best pictures of this kind are of children: they are unselfconscious and original, and they are so seldom asked how they would like to do something that they react extremely well. The other type of person who responds well is the creative artist or writer, who usually needs a very strong self-image in order to survive, but does not have the repertoire of stock gestures which actors so often fall back upon.

The carefully constructed public face of a pop-singer is a good place to start trying to capture what is 'typical' in a person; because all actions are carefully considered to support the image, you do not need to hunt very much. The only real difficulties are technical: All these pictures are by available light and make use of the rapidly- changing stage lighting. For this sort of picture, there can be no real substitute for using a lot of film. All of these were shot on 35mm, where the low cost per frame and fast action are essential. Be prepared to reject up to 90% of your pictures, but do not reject blur and odd colours out-of-hand.

PEOPLE

There is a recognisable style of romantic or nostalgic photography which gained ground in the 1970s. It eschews bright saturated colours and razor-sharp definition, and it is suitable (or has been adapted) for everything from portraits via erotica to recreations of scenes gone by. A number of different techniques are used, singly or in combination, and they are considered below.

Soft focus, the oldest of all the old-fashioned tricks, can be achieved in a number of ways. The best is the use of a special soft-focus lens, which gives a sharp image surrounded by an unsharp penumbra or corona (depending on whether you are using negative or positive film): it thereby differs from an out-of-focus image, which has no sharp central image, but renders a point as a blur of more-or-less equal intensity.

But soft-focus lenses are expensive, and in any case rare in 35mm, and so a variety of diffusion discs is available which give a similar (though not identical) effect. The best are probably the Zeiss Softars, with their little embossed lenticles, but these are extremely expensive and are only available for a limited number of cameras; of all the others, the only way to see if there is one which suits you is to read through the filter manufacturers' catalogues, and then to try the filter out on your own camera, at a variety of apertures. Almost all soft-focus lenses and attachments vary in their effects with aperture, and what is perfect at one aperture (usually wide open, or close thereto) may be a disaster at another.

After soft focus, there are a number of different ways of affecting the colour. A simple one is to overexpose the film, so that there is an atmosphere of lightness and ethereality: this has been done so often with ballet dancers that it has almost become a cliché. Because the overexposure required can be quite considerable – often two stops – fast films are the norm for this sort of treatment: after all, with a 2-stop overexposure, even 400 ASA is effectively only 100 ASA, Kodachrome 25 would be down to 6 ASA!

A rather more ingenious effect, which can only be done in two stages, is to <u>underexpose</u> the film quite severely – again, by anything up to two stops – and then to lighten it by duplication, either by recopying onto slide or by printing: this gives the kind of flat, faded colour which characterises David Hamilton's work, which has proved so successful (and commercial) for his beautiful photographs of young girls.

Another technique uses the granular structure of the film itself. The pioneer of this technique, and certainly one of its greatest exponents, was Sarah Moon, who used (and still uses, if

Bicycles and swans both have an image which conjures up the past; soft-focus, **below,** increases the effect. There is a vocabulary of 'instant nostalgia' which derives as much from the media as from reality; we have a conditioned response to some things we have never experienced except at second-hand. Whilst it may sound cynical and manipulative, an awareness of such popular imagery may often be used creatively.

The man and boy fishing left and the golden littoral *below* are both beautiful pictures which through their use of colour and light transcend their subjects. The other three are much more calculated and contrived. The monochrome filtration on the two bottom pictures concentrates attention on the subject by removing distracting colour contrasts: the picture *top left* romanticises farming.

THE ROMANTIC IMAGE

she can get it) GAF's 500 ASA colour film, an outrageously grainy material which nevertheless gave superb effects when correctly used – as it was in her hands. Others have carried it to extremes, composing the picture in the very centre of the film and then duplicating it up to full-frame again so that the dye structure gives a 'pointilliste' effect reminiscent of Seurat.

Almost by definition, the romantic image is a set-piece, not a reportage picture. In general, there are four categories of such pictures, and by applying the techniques described below, these can be extended to whatever ideas the photographer has in mind.

The pictures on these two pages illustrate the fine line between creativity and cliché; in any case, the distinction must be a personal one, based on whether a picture 'works' for you or not. The shot through the rain-streaked window **left** is truly creative, as it not only finds a way of surmounting a difficulty (the rain) but even manages to turn it to advantage. At the other extreme, the couple running through the flowers **facing page top left** is blatantly a 'formula' shot, but nevertheless successful in its appeal to publishers. It is nonsensical, however, to dismiss all fashionable or special-effects shots out of hand: often they will be extremely acceptable to the subjects, and sometimes they can be very attractive.

185

and the mood of the picture may be varied from 'high key' (with few or no dark tones) to 'low key' (in which dark tones predominate).

The third type of lighting is the effect light. Effect lights are used to add highlights to the picture, but great care must be taken that they do not throw shadows which conflict with the key. Typical uses of effects lights include backlighting, or rimlighting, which is particularly effective on hair or fur, and lights used to give sparkle to jewellery.

Finally, there is the background light. This is thrown not upon the subject but upon the background, and may make it uniformly lighter than the subject, uniformly darker than the subject (in extreme cases the background is left unlit, or lit only by the spill from the other lights), or with some sort of shading or modelling to give the background an unobtrusive shape which (usually) concentrates attention on the subject.

Such a lighting set-up may be used with or without soft focus; traditionally, there was always at least a trace of diffusion, but after a long period in which all soft-focus was disdained, quite intense diffusion is returning. The SF-Fujinon lenses for view cameras are probably the best available at the moment, though Rodenstock Imagon users would (with a strong case)

All of these pictures are unashamedly posed versions of something which really happened. They were all shot on medium-format cameras, with lenses from 80mm to 150mm; a touch of soft focus has been used in some. Getting a natural effect in such pictures is not as difficult as it might seem, as all you have to do is to get the parties believing in what they are doing. The little girl **facing page, top right** really is listening to her father reading a story, and the piano lesson on this page is genuine. The photographer must be unobtrusive, and fully in control of his equipment: clattering about changing lights, and taking meter readings, and constant false starts are all disastrous.

PORTRAITURE

Although available light may be used, far more convincing effects are obtainable with fully controlled lighting.

The classic lighting for a portrait makes use of four types of lighting: each may consist of a single lamp, though it is by no means unusual to use more. First, there is the main or key light: this is the one which establishes the shadows, and (except for special effects) comes from above camera level to strike the subject obliquely. It must be the <u>only</u> light which casts shadows on the subject (because split or double shadows are very distracting) but these may be more or less sharp: at one extreme, a spotlight is used, and at the other, a powerful 'trough' or 'northlight'.

The next lamp is the fill, a flat soft light from the direction of the camera, which lightens the shadows cast by the key. By manipulating this light, the dramatic effect of the key is altered,

dispute this; in 35mm there are a couple of proprietary soft-focus lenses which are no more than an achromat in a focusing mount, but are capable of quite excellent results. One slight problem with these lenses is their very cool colour rendition, caused by their simplicity and rather old-fashioned coating: an 81-series filter may be advisable to warm the image up a little. Mamiya also offer soft-focus lenses for their rollfilm reflexes: the days are now long gone when unkind wags could assert that the entire range of Mamiya mid-format lenses were soft-focus, but it is true that for cheap soft-focus effects a Mamiya C3 with the oldest possible lenses, used at full aperture, is superb and gives some substance to the old gibes – and, of course, they can always be stopped down for critical sharpness.

The props used with portraits depend very much on the character of the person you are portraying and on the effect you want to create, but unless you are very confident and very skilled,

THE ROMANTIC IMAGE

simplicity is generally better than complexity. Plain backgrounds, a simple chair, perhaps a desk or table, are all that you need. It is often very rewarding to try for a formal portrait of a child; children can have immense natural dignity, and a portrait which captures this can be very successful.

Whether photographing children or adults, it is always a good idea to have them bring along some prop or possession of their own which they feel happy with. This has two major uses: one is that it acts as a sort of pacifier, and gives the subject something familiar to play with during the essentially unfamiliar activity of having their picture taken, and the other is that it can be a very telling feature of the portrait. Many people have something which is always associated with them – a piece of jewellery, a pair of spectacles, a pipe, or whatever – and if this is included in the portrait it can be a powerful recognition aid, the kind of thing which makes people say, 'Oh, it's just like her.'

PASTORAL

It was the fashion at Versailles to ape the country life: jaded noblemen dressed as honest shepherds pursued their giggling consorts, who were similarly disguised as shepherdesses. There is a similar branch of photography, which dwells upon the pastoral: golden cornfields, sunny days, wild flowers, and so forth.

The first, and most essential, thing is to put the right girl in the right setting: rosy-cheeked blondes are the ideal, surrounded by the kind of landscape described above. Sultry brunettes, or fragile sylphs, are not really on, and nor are overcast days.

Because this is so arrantly a put-up job, the technical approach is usually utterly over-the-top, with lashings of soft focus, and anything up to a stop's over-exposure to give the right airy feel. Given the reflectivity of corn, even two or two and a half stops may not be unrealistic; the single stop applies when using an incident light meter, the higher figures when using reflected-light (especially built-in or TTL) meters.

Props are important, and must again be pastoral. Light-coloured clothes, with or without tiny floral prints, and even white, Alice-in-Wonderland aprons, are the thing; and uncomplicated hairstyles supported by Alice bands will further the illusion.

Grassy banks are ideal, especially if a tree is available for background, but steer clear of hedgerows (which are often visually interesting in their own right, and distract the eye from the subject) and beware of dappled sunlight unless you are using fill-in flash: the differences in light intensity between the shaded bits and the unshaded bits is such that the film cannot satisfactorily record it. The dark parts come out inky, or the light parts burn out – or in severe cases, both. Furthermore, the light is likely to be very green, and a CC10M filter will probably make the model look somewhat choleric.

A filter which is useful, though, is an 81-series warming type: an 81A, or even the stronger ones (81B, 81C, 81EF), will make the sun appear still warmer – unless you are photographing at dawn or in the late afternoon, in which case the effect may be excessive.

One other technical point is that deep focus is usually more effective than the time-honoured approach of throwing the background out of focus, because this type of picture is somewhat painterly, and few painters employ out-of-focus backgrounds.

Although the sheer drama of *the landscapes opposite might seem to be the very antithesis of 'romantic,' they could be regarded as the 'macho* *romanticism' of Jack London and Ernest Hemingway, in which harshness and grandeur replace mere prettiness.*

THE ROMANTIC IMAGE

The girl with the cart, facing page bottom left, is a sort of modern version of the eighteenth century pastoral look in Versailles, and so (arguably) is the picture on the bottom left of this page. The girl in the doorway, the tennis player, and the nymphet in the green stockings are all manifestations of the modern dream-girl: young, hard-seeming, careless. There is an old Tibetan Buddhist teaching: 'If someone I know does something I do not like, may he be my best teacher.' These pictures are an illustration of the need to stay open, and not to place things too rigidly in categories. Romanticism is as closely allied to fantasy as great wits to madness; recognising what it is in a picture which appeals to us is a major step towards being able to recreate that appeal. Some may cavil that any romantic interpretation placed upon a picture of a girl is nothing but a male fantasy, but the depressing logical consequence of that is that we should forswear all romance, and look at pictures of slums and wrecking-yards; better, surely, to stick to romanticism!

THE ROMANTIC IMAGE

EROTIC

These fall into two camps, the pictures suggesting innocence (or mock-innocence), and the pin-up type. The former is essentially a variation on the pastoral theme, and owes much of its appeal to the fantasy of perfection: if the model showed her awareness of being photographed, the picture would lose its appeal. Instead, they present a unique blend of innocence and availability, and pander to the Cider with Rosie myth of youthful sexual experience in idyllic surroundings – a myth so widely propagated that many people forget the terrors and delights of their own actual experience.

The pin-ups are equally concerned with perfection, but here the settings are much more explicit: luxurious boudoirs, fur rugs, velvet sofas. Here, it is not so much the sexual experience which is fantasised as the beauty of the partner and the luxury of the surroundings.

Either type relies heavily on everything being right, with no dissonant elements. The innocent-looking girl, for example, may be permitted an attractive scratch as if from a thorn – but a spot, a much likelier phenomenon on the average adolescent girl,

would be anathema. Again, her clothes must be fitting for a young girl: we do not expect to see her in satin underwear, but in cotton or something similar. Similarly, the adult pin-up must be free from bodily blemish (and the air-brush may be called in to ensure this, as described later) and the surroundings must be free from the paraphernalia which might well be found in real life – empty coffee cups, tissues, etc. Failure to observe these conventions can turn an attractive and more-or-less erotic picture into something little better than pornography.

Hammocks; picnics; rustic *bridges; riverside scenes; pavement cafes; bicycles. In a sense the very subjects are clichés – but they represent something we can all relate to, and if photographed with impeccable attention to detail are almost always attractive.*

NOSTALGIC

The past which these pictures purport to recreate is more often imaginary than real; it shares this characteristic with both the pastoral and the erotic picture. This has the inevitable implication that the whole effect is carefully considered: once again, no untoward elements are allowed to intrude – and the photographer must also be on his guard for anachronisms, such as a modern wristwatch, or a car or power pylon in the background. When such pictures are produced professionally, it is usual to hire models who look the part; each era has its own standards of beauty, and the girl who is attractive today would not necessarily make an Edwardian beauty or even a 1920s flapper. The same, of course, applies to men – though people are often a lot less careful to be accurate in this case.

Although both technique (usually soft, faded colours) and subject must be right, there is a third matter which must be considered: composition and posing. People nowadays sit in a different way from the past – we are more relaxed, more used to soft furnishings and warm rooms, and less inhibited. Similarly, we are much more open to unusual composition in a photograph, whereas a real Edwardian photographer would have been more accustomed to shooting to a set formula. The only way to get a feeling for pose and composition is to look through old pictures, in books and magazines, as much as possible. Of course, there will be little colour (though Autochromes were available in 1907), but surprisingly enough we can get away with more latitude here, provided we stick to the conventions which seem to have grown up of their own accord – principally, little contrast and rather faded colours, easily achieved by means of slight (half-stop) overexposure and perhaps a fog filter – or in any case, no lens-hood and a flare-prone lens. An old zoom, the worst available, can be very suitable, and a further note of realism can be injected by using very long exposures – at least ⅛ second – with the camera on a tripod. Needless to say, slow films are the most useful here, or you can use an ND (neutral density) filter, or even a polarising filter carefully set <u>not</u> to reduce reflections.

LANDSCAPES

Landscapes are an extremely traditional and extremely personal type of photography. Depending on the location, the scale, and the time of year, the range of colour can be almost monochromatic, or downright riotous. The mood can be massive, looming, and foreboding; sunny, summery, and airy; sun-baked and oppressive; soft, rain-soaked and romantic; or a succession of receding planes, like a Chinese painting.

Landscapes are also extremely difficult. Less than any other subject do they lend themselves to the casual snapshot or the record shot. That vast panorama, which looked so impressive in real life, is nothing but a grey-blue smudge topped with a vast amount of sky when it is reduced to the size of a transparency; and that beautiful shoreline is recorded as a thin, uninteresting line between the grey-blue of the water and the white of the sky.

With the exception of deep blue skies or massively spectacular cloud formations, skies on colour print film are pretty much a disaster unless you print them yourself or have them custom-printed. The averaging system used in machine printing reduces them to nothingness. The serious colour landscape photographer will, therefore, normally use colour slide film.

Furthermore, because landscape photography is something of a contemplative pastime (as fishing is alleged to be by its adherents), it is often as well to use a camera which promotes a contemplative frame of mind; most people find that the ground-glass of a reflex (without a pentaprism) or even a view camera has this effect. To be sure, there are masters like Yoshikazu Shirakawa who work quickly with big Pentaxes and the like, but whilst one is still apprenticed to the craft it is generally true to say

Almost all serious landscape photographers gravitate sooner or later to medium or large format, with 4 x 5" the acknowledged leader. It is not a question of the equipment making them better photographers; rather, it is that the best landscape photographers, the ones who care the most about landscape, buy the most suitable tools. It is possible, though, to get similar results by using 35mm like a large format camera. First, use fine-grained film: Kodachrome for preference. Secondly, always use a tripod. Thirdly, make each exposure count. Walk around until you have exactly the right viewpoint: select the right lens: meter carefully: compose unhurriedly. 'Machine gunning' very rarely works. As may be seen from these pictures and those which follow, the noonday sun is best left to mad dogs and Englishmen. Here, mist, dawn, and frost have all been used for their own special contribution.

that an ounce of forethought is worth a pound of snapshots.

Big transparencies also have their advantages. It is easier to study the relatively expansive screen of a medium- or large-format camera rather than the tiny jewel-like image of a 35mm camera. Even more important, the bigger picture seems better able to capture the subtle gradations which characterise some landscapes, and the vivid interactions and interfaces of colour which characterise others. Some landscape photographers use old folding cameras, taking eight 2¼ x 3¼″ pictures on 120 film: the viewfinders may not amount to much, but the amount of information on the negative is impressive. These are particularly favoured by those who use negative film and do their own printing.

Finally, on the equipment front, a tripod is a useful accessory. Once again, it promotes the contemplative aspect of the process, and it also gives a feeling of occasion. Whilst some photographers would decry this, many agree that the landscape is something you have to measure up to; a mediocre photographer cannot reduce it to his own scale as he could (say) a portrait or a nude. Either he succeeds, or he fails utterly.

After this, it is a matter of the kind of landscape which you want to take.

To begin with, the detail is a good place to start; a single cottage, surrounded by hills, perhaps. Even a patch of flowers, or a ruined shepherd's hut, can be a successful picture. It allows you

*The only way to get the swans where they were needed, **facing page top,** was to wait; the only way to photograph the church at dawn was to get up early.*

Attention to detail, and a willingness to work for a picture, are evident in all the pictures on this page.

to concentrate on form, on the overall shape of the picture (remember earlier remarks on composition), and encourages you to watch out for dissonant areas of colour. A good trick here is to examine the out-of-focus image, which subjugates form to colour. Furthermore, with a detail it is harder to fall into the classic trap which awaits the novice landscape photographer: no main subject.

After you have mastered the close-up detail, you can begin to take more and more in. For close-ups, a standard lens is frequently ideal. After that, landscape photographers begin to split into two groups: those who advocate wide-angle lenses (to capture the sweep of the landscape all around) and those who believe that they can better control their image by using a longer-focus lens to select what strikes their eye.

LANDSCAPES

A 5 x 4″ camera was essential to capture all the wealth of detail in the snow scene on the right; carrying camera and *tripod on a winter's morning was not easy, but the results justify it.*

Neither view is in itself 'correct'; the most that can be said is that the choice of lens depends about equally on the terrain and the photographer. In the mountains, the long-focus approach is frequently all but essential. Otherwise, a picture taken across a valley may be utterly unimpressive – though, of course, if the mountains are big enough, or the photographer chooses his viewpoint carefully enough, even a wide angle would be perfectly suitable. For views of rolling countryside, or pictures with a strong foreground and an extensive background, then a wide angle may well be more appropriate.

It is when you begin to tackle the larger subjects that you begin to appreciate the importance of knowing your countryside, as well as just loving it. For many years, for example, I have been fascinated by the white china-clay mines and waste dumps in Cornwall, my native land. I always promised myself that I would photograph them; but when I came to try it, I found it vastly more difficult than I had expected. There were too many greys, and browns; the white I had in my head hardly existed. As I explored, though, I came to realise that my memory was not really at fault: there are white roads, and white rivers, and a fresh dump is glistening white, but I had been going to old and disused dumps. I also began to appreciate the other colours: the deep milky blue of the water in a pit, reflecting a summer's sky; the sage-green of the hardy plants colonising the old dumps; the battered, rusty kettles; the lorries in enveloping clouds of blue-white dust.

There have been other places, too. The wild rough scenery of Big Sur is another thing I want to photograph – but I hardly know where to begin. The ominous darkness of Dozmary Pool, where the giant Tregagle roars, and where no sensible Cornishman would go at night; the creeks of northern California, so like the lochs of Scotland; the incredible Renaissance jumble of Valetta, the 'city built by gentlemen for gentlemen' after the Great Siege, or the Moorish dignity of Mdina, the old capital of Malta which it replaced. It takes time.

As with many other aspects of photography, the landscape makes two demands which are not immediately apparent. The first is that you should be interested in – even in love with – your subject for its own sake: the casual photographer will very rarely equal the man of passion. And the second is time, a lot of time. When I first read the works of Ansel Adams I was struck dumb by the pictures, but almost dismissed the text: I wrote in my journal, "You too can take pictures like Ansel Adams if you are prepared to spend three weeks on each exposure." I now realise that I underestimated: three months or even three years might not be unusual (though you can always do something else in the meantime), and the investment is worth it. The fact that we can capture the picture in a fraction of a second, and even that metering the Ansel Adams way takes a minute or two, blinds us to the question of <u>when</u> that fraction of a second should be. It is rather like some of the more demanding Zen Buddhist practices: perfect inaction, then (at the appropriate time) perfect action. You see why I say landscape photography is a contemplative exercise!

This does not mean, of course, that there is no place for the record shot; but this can only be an *aide-memoire*, and not a creative picture in its own right. It can act as a spur to drive you back again and again until you have the picture you want – but you should not exhibit it as a work of art unless that curious inner voice tells you that it is. Unfortunately, the landscape has been easy meat for the talker and theorist, and the most incredibly tedious pictures have been explained away as art. The simple guide is always the same: 'I may not know much about landscape photography – but I know what I like!'

THE COLOUR OF THE CITY

Just as the traditional landscape deals with the colours of nature, so too does the city have its own colours. Because the city is, by definition, man-made, the colours reflect the tastes and fashions prevalent either when the city was built, or at the present.

First of all, there is the cityscape – a general view, in the same way as a landscape is a general view of the countryside. There are of course all the variations in light which are to be found in the country, but in most towns and cities the atmospheric haze which builds up during the day – the pollution, if you like – has also to be taken into account. To show some new office development pristine and sparkling, you would need to get up very early on a summer's morning; but equally, you might choose to use the evening's haze. You could use it, for example, to emphasise the cosiness of a village. I will never forget coming down into Okehampton, on Dartmoor, one winter's night. It was bitterly cold, and I was riding a motorcycle. The town lay in its valley, shrouded in coal-smoke. After the clear air of the moors, it was like breathing tar – but it was also a powerful symbol of the warmth available there, of the sense of being in an outpost in a fundamentally hostile environment.

There are many other ways in which you can match a picture to its lighting and atmosphere. For instance, a grey utilitarian town of the industrial revolution looks very different on a summer's day and on a grey misty winter's day. In the one, the

goings, then the afternoon rush-hour – but more relaxed now, without the deadline of the time-clock. This is the time to stop for a drink, or a bit of window-shopping. Finally, the evening, with night-life of various sorts, teenagers cruising in their cars, cinema queues, strip joints, bars . . . and all this slowly petering out, until the town is quiet again in the small hours of the morning, waiting for the circle to start again.

At night, of course, there are the lights of the city – and the effects vary enormously from twilight through to full darkness, with street lights, traffic lights, store illumination, office lights, advertising signs. These are more fully dealt with later.

Rather than using a wide-angle lens for general cityscapes, which might seem the obvious approach, a long-focus lens and a distant high-up viewpoint is often more effective. The perspective is compressed by the long-focus lens, which often emphasises the character of the city: in Stratford-upon-Avon it could mass together the Elizabethan buildings, or equally it could show the towers of downtown Los Angeles against their background of smog. Inevitably, a long-focus lens emphasises haze, so pictures will be moody rather than needle-sharp. The drawback of wide-angles is that it is very difficult to get a really interesting foreground: all too often, a potentially interesting cityscape is dominated by a large expanse of road or park – though in some cases (as always) this too can be effective.

red bricks can be warm and vibrant, projecting an atmosphere of welcome and comfort and the promise of hot tea in back-to-back houses, the hospitality of honest hard-working folk. In the other, the feeling is quite different: of the endless grind, the daily trudge to work, the ever-present threat of the dole queue. Other angles and other lights portray different aspects again: the centre of industry, lively and self-confident; the decaying industrial heartland, discarded as financial wizardry spins more profits than honest toil; the showpiece of modern town-planning; vandalism by architects.

There are also the people to consider in a cityscape. Like the light, they vary through the day. Early in the morning there will be few people; the odd cleaner or early deliveryman. A peak comes at the morning rush-hour, with people and cars packed close together, hurrying, eyes fixed straight ahead, impatient. Then, the normal working day; everyday comings and goings. At lunchtime, a chance to relax; this is when the pretty young secretaries are out buying clothes, the purchasing clerks are eating their sandwiches on the park benches, and harrassed singles are trying to do their shopping. Back to the comings and

*Often, telling pictures of well-known sights can be made at night. Colours are more interesting, and the lights add an air of fantasy to a scene which might be quite dull in the daytime. Rainy streets can be turned to great advantage, too: the distorted reflections make a far more attractive foreground than an empty pavement. Try, also, to take the pictures which are special to **you**, the scenes where difficulty of access or sheer quirky coincidence mean that not many will see them. The Snoopy balloon always raises a smile, and the interior of the stock market has a bizarre quality to it.*

Aerial pictures may be beyond *the reach of most of us, though it is often possible to get surprisingly good pictures by holding the camera close to the window in an airliner as it is coming in to land, and cutting out reflections with a scarf or jacket. Do not hold the camera against the glass, though, as the vibration will cause blurring. Cut blue haze with an 81A filter.*

Instead of going for the broad sweep, you may decide to concentrate on details. These may be as large as a building a quarter of a mile high, or as small as a doorknocker.

In order to photograph buildings in the traditional manner – with strictly parallel sides, so as to avoid the 'falling over backwards' look which results from tilting the camera upwards, you need either a perspective control lens or a technical camera (or a higher viewpoint opposite the building!) – and given the price of most perspective control lenses, a second-hand technical camera could be a better bet. The alternatives are to use ultra-wide-angle lenses, and waste half the frame (not very practical with colour slide film) or to use the same wide-angles and tilt the camera <u>very obviously</u>, so that the 'falling over' perspective is quite clearly intentional. You are likely to end up with a lot of sky in such shots, so a polarising filter and a blue sky make for interesting colour.

The day on which you photograph a building can have an enormous effect on the final result. On a bright, sunny day the same building can be made to look cool and airy, or hot, sweaty, and unpleasant, or dank and shadowed. By choosing a misty day it can be made forbidding or familiar; on a rainy day, it might look threatening, or welcoming, or thoroughly wet and uncomfortable. Unless the person who is looking at the photograph knows the building, who is to argue? To accentuate the effect, filters can be invaluable – either subtle, such as the CC05B which gives a wintry tinge or an 81A to warm things up, or downright bold, like a vivid purple or cyan.

There are many details other than buildings, though. For example, you may choose to make bright, bold colour your sole criterion – in which case you are already more than half-way towards abstracts. Bright roadsigns, plastic delivery trays used by bakers, the vivid red-net bags so often used to contain cabbages

THE COLOUR OF THE CITY

*Very tall buildings, such as New York's World Trade Center, allow 'aerial' shots without an aeroplane. Often, though, much more interesting and creative shots can be made by selecting details or small cameos. The graphic simplicity of the bridge, **below,** defies all the 'rules' of composition, but its impact is considerable. A 5 x 4" camera captured the fine detail, but carefully used Kodachrome could give almost as impressive an effect. The fish-eye perspective **facing page bottom left,** has emphasised the closed-in, protected, feeling of the ice-rink, whilst meticulous attention to exposure and colour balance was needed to convey the opulence and elegance of the buffet scene **facing page top.***

203

and other green-leafed vegetables at city markets, advertising signs, cars, even rubbish, all can afford brilliant pictures. Underexpose for extra intensity, and to help in spotting the colours, throw your eyes slightly out of focus as described earlier.

Another idea previously suggested, which is particularly relevant here is one of decay. Peeling paint, or partially torn-off posters, or even spray-painted graffiti, can all give sudden and unexpected juxtapositions of colour and shape.

Instead of abstraction, there are also the many tiny details which make a city unique. The roadsigns are an obvious example, though as time progresses these are becoming more and more standardised. Who could forget the British posting-boxes, so bright that they have given their name to a colour, 'pillar box red'. And what Englishman could get over the shock of finding that the Irish paint them green? In London, of course, the big red bus is colourful and distinctive – but here we are getting on to the area of travel photography, which is covered in the next chapter.

Buildings and objects are not the only colourful subjects in the city, either. There are always the people – especially the young people, who usually wear the brightest clothes. The 'punk' fashions must surely be the ultimate in personal colour, with fluorescent green or orange spiky-cut hair, though it must be admitted that the clothes are sometimes rather drab. Surprisingly few people mind being photographed, but if you are of a timid disposition you may find that a 105mm lens, or even a 135mm, is easier to use. Alternatively, use a real wide-angle, such as a 24mm, and get in among them: if you are really close, people tend to assume that you are too close to be photographing them, and consequently ignore you.

All in all, photographing a city is a question of getting a feeling for the place; of deciding what you want to say with your camera, and saying it. If the city strikes you as huge and terrifying, then try to communicate that. If it seems a haven of civilisation (which, by definition, it is – 'cives,' from which 'civilisation' comes, is Latin for 'a city'), then portray that. The only way to get good pictures is to have something in mind already, even if it is only something so abstract as 'some typical Venetian colours'. Look and think; and then photograph.

Travel, especially if it is to somewhere sufficiently remote, can be an excellent way to unleash creativity; but there is always the danger that everything seems so new, so exciting, that we are content merely to record what is around us. Whilst this is a perfectly valid approach, it does not necessarily partake much of creativity.

More than almost any other branch of photography, it behoves the travel photographer to choose his equipment carefully. Buying extra equipment at the destination may be impossible or at best expensive, and there are few things more infuriating than realising whilst on location that what you really need is something which you already have – at home.

at the hotel or wherever you are staying, but then you are effectively back to the minimalist school.

A fair compromise is probably one body, your three (or even two) favourite lenses, and a backup – either a spare body or a complete compact or similar camera (I use a 1936 Leica). It is best not to be too battery dependent, and if you do rely on batteries to make sure that you replace them (and preferably carry spares as well) before the trip.

Of course, if you are considering publication, a larger format camera will be useful; consider a rollfilm SLR or TLR. If the camera is likely to be used in very hazardous conditions, simplicity is important too: a Rollei or similar TLR is about as

One of the greatest difficulties in travel photography lies in avoiding clichéd views of well-known scenes. A good way to do this is to incorporate something which is not normally shown: the buildings adjacent to the Leaning Tower of Pisa, the ice of a New York winter. The temptation is always to photograph the famous sight and leave it at that, but the incorporation of the ice, of the archway as a frame for the Taj Mahal, and of the gondolas as a foreground to the well-known Venetian architecture, all make for a picture which is very much more attractive than the bare record. The only way to get such pictures is to spend a good bit of time scouting around and planning before actually pressing the shutter release; the Mughal interior **facing page bottom right** suggests the cool haven which the carved pavilions provide from the glare of the sun, even if the tonal range of the scene is such that shadows are blocked and highlights washed-out.

The choice of equipment varies very much according to the kind of things you want to photograph, the intended use of the photographs, the weight you want to carry around, and (of course) the depth of your wallet.

At the one extreme is the minimalist approach; a single camera and a single lens, with perhaps a simple backup. Whilst there is a certain amount to be said for an automatic SLR, there is a great deal more to be said for one with auto and manual options, and a good meter such as a Weston Master or a Luna-Pro. The single lens is open to considerable personal interpretation. I have tried a 55/1.2 (superb for general applications but often too long) and a 24/2.8 (occasionally too wide and sometimes too slow); if I had one, I think I would compromise with a 35/1.4. Others prefer zooms of varying types, but I find that these are so slow as to be useless for many types of pictures – especially if, like me, you favour 25 ASA Kodachrome.

At the other extreme is the everything-but-the-kitchen-sink school, with three bodies, half a dozen lenses, motor drives, etc. This gives you plenty of creative control, but it is an awful lot of stuff to carry about with you. Of course, you can leave most of it

reliable as you can get, though I prefer my (equally simple) Linhof Super Technica 6 x 9cm. Of course, this sort of thing can get pretty heavy and expensive.

It is impossible to be very specific about equipment, though, and it usually takes a couple of trips in order to decide what is best for you. The advice above is pretty general, and based on my own experience; for example, for a recent trip to California's Disneyland I took only an automatic SLR with standard lens, because all that was needed was a snapshot-type approach to illustrate a book on snapshot photography. On the other hand, a trip to India to illustrate a book on Vajrayana Buddhism involved three Nikons, eight lenses, and a Linhof outfit with three lenses and three backs as well as a Hasselblad. And, of course, the trusty 1936 Leica!

Choosing the equipment is not the only thing to do before you go. You should also research the place as much as possible – borrow or buy books on it, see films, go to exhibitions, anything. You can illustrate two types of things. The first is the accepted view of a place – the soft misty green landscape of Ireland, for example, or the bright sun and primary colours of Southern California – and the second is your personal view; in California, you might photograph the astonishing sunsets through the palm trees, the aircraft stacked up over the airport, or the gaudy seediness of the latino down-town area. There is nothing wrong with the 'accepted view' approach, provided it does not become clichéd and obvious, and indeed I find that it is a necessary counterfoil to the more personal type of work. It is also essential, from a commercial point of view, to have 'establishing shots' which show familiar landmarks such as the Golden Gate Bridge in San Francisco or the Parthenon in Athens. The creativity required for such shots may even be greater than that required for ostensibly more original shots; thinking up a new way to photograph the Taj Mahal is a real challenge to creativity.

The research does not stop when you arrive. Buy picture postcards; they show you the local landmarks (useful for establishing shots) and in some cases serve as Ghastly Warnings about how not to photograph somewhere – though more often they are the work of local photographers who have probably tried many angles and had a more-or-less valid reason for choosing the one they did.

A counsel of perfection advises you not to take pictures as soon as you arrive, but to walk about getting the feel of the place. In Bermuda, for example, one of the most striking things is that the greenery really is as lush as it is shown on the picture postcards – perhaps more so. In Los Angeles, the peeling paint and faded colours in some parts of town (especially the *barrios*, where the photographer with an expensive camera ventures at his peril) are quite Mediterranean. This initial walkabout is designed to stoke up your creative fires; the argument is that if you are deprived of your camera, you benefit both by becoming hungry to use it and by being denied the opportunity to take the 'obvious' pictures.

I do not support this view. The walkabout is an excellent idea, but it carries with it a certain freshness of vision. If you are not carrying your camera, you will see things that you want to photograph – and you will later return, with your camera, to try to take them.

The chances are that they will be gone, or at least that your originality of vision will be gone; and worse, because you are trying to recreate the past, you are not open to the present. Certainly, there will be pictures which you will want to take again, and there may well be pictures which you will later discard as rather obvious, but there are also likely to be some really original and spontaneous pictures.

One of the best things about *travel is the way it refreshes our vision. The top picture is essentially narrative: it tells a story about a way of life. The middle one is almost an abstract, and the one above is* *slightly surreal and threatening. The frozen figures were never meant to be seen from the back, and the contrast between their looming scale and the tiny tourists is rather disquieting.*

Determining exposure can be *extremely difficult when one is faced with the light colours common in hot countries; when this is combined with the bright clear light of the Mediterranean, there is sometimes a temptation to disbelieve your exposure meter. The best solution is to take an incident light reading and then to underexpose by anything from half a stop to a stop and a half; that way, you will get detail in the whites and magnificent colour saturation elsewhere. If you are using an in-camera meter, aim it at the lightest surface which you want to contain any detail, and give three whole stops **more** exposure. Alternatively, take a reading off the palm of your hand, and give half a stop less. These rules-of-thumb are, of course, only a guide: you will need to make adjustments for your particular technique, your film and equipment.*

Successful travel photography is a pretty schizophrenic process. On the one hand, you are trying to show the familiar; things of which people can say, "Ah, yes, I remember that; it was absolutely typical of the place." On the other you are trying to show things which will make them say, "Hey, I never realised that." Furthermore, as nothing short of actually being there can portray the whole *gestalt* of the experience, you are constantly trying to evoke much with little. Perhaps the nearest analogy is with poetry: in the few lines of 'An Irish Airman foresees his death' Yeats manages to summon up the exultation and terror of flying; the silence of the air and the noise of the aeroplane; a deep feeling for the country, and a sense of separation from it; and the essentially similar nature of fatalism and free will. Similarly, Shirakawa's photographs of the Alps, or the Himalayas, or the Grand Canyon, all conjure up a sense of vastness and wonder; of bizarre beauty on a titanic scale; of colours so vivid and yet so unexpected that they remind us of Lovecraft's 'the colour out of space', a wholly new colour never before seen by man.

The important thing is obviously to select from the endless barrage of impressions which you are receiving all the time.

*Opinions are divided about whether to use figures to show scale. My own view is that they should only be included where they are a necessary compositional element, or an integral part of the scene. Thus, the church scene **above** has no need of a figure, but in the temple **right** the eye searches in vain for a fulcrum; a figure in the courtyard would help.*

Although the experience itself is continuous and amorphous, there are certain approaches which you can consciously adopt.

The first is the choice of the general picture versus the detail. The traditional landscape, for example, is a general and narrative picture; it shows how quite a large area looked at a particular instant in time, and tells you what was going on during that instant in time. This does not mean that it is devoid of composition; some of the most beautiful landscapes of all time, such as those taken by Ansel Adams and Minor White, are essentially narrative in nature. A different approach, though, isolates a smaller part of that landscape; instead of being very recognisably 'A view from . . . looking over . .', it becomes, perhaps, 'a typical corner of . . .' (I am not suggesting you use

such corny old titles – but they do illustrate what I mean). Elliot Porter's supremely beautiful pictures are often of this type. A yet closer view isolates perhaps a single plant, a part of a building, a sign, or a vehicle or a figure. Coming in closer still we begin to enter the worlds of close-up and macrophotography, dealt with elsewhere. Once again, no one approach is inherently <u>better</u> than any other; it merely depends on which you find the most interesting.

The second is what one might term the 'political' aspect, which deals with how you approach a subject. This is covered in greater detail later, but it is relevant to travel photography, too. Is Los Angeles the long-legged teenagers on the beach? The bronzed surfers? The teeming consumers in the shopping malls?

TRAVEL

The crowded freeways? The *barrios?* The mansions in Beverly Hills? The smog? The beautiful rolling hills? The endless suburbs? The tourist traps? The sex shops on the Strip? The star-studded sidewalk on Hollywood? The pumps dotted all over the landscape, pulling the oil out of the ground? The skyscrapers in the financial area downtown? The railroads through the streets? The question is not only one of selection of subject: Beverly Hills can either be a symbol of affluence and success, or of conspicuous consumption and feckless waste – or (and this is the way I see it) a middle-class suburb built by *arrivistes* with too much money for their own good.

The utterly stunning fairy-tale *beauty of the snow scene* ***facing page top*** *demanded great patience and preparation. The potential picture had been observed some long time before the right combination of sunny dawn and recent snowfall presented itself. It meant getting up frighteningly early on several mornings in succession, and carrying a heavy 5 x 4" camera* *and tripod. The others are also large-format pictures, which entailed a great deal of waiting. Truly successful travel photography is impossible to combine with casual holidaymaking: you have to be prepared to work long hours, walk long distances, and wait until everything is just right. The simplest single tip is always to rise at or before dawn!*

A third approach might be the 'universality' of a picture. There are pictures which could be taken in Death Valley or in Dublin – except that the quality of the light is different. A typical example is sun-and-sand pictures; you might be able to take pictures in Aberdeen which were indistinguishable from those taken in Ipanema, but the weather is likely to be better in Ipanema and there will be a greater chance of finding scantily-clad and beautiful girls. If you like a particular style of photography, but your home town affords little scope for it, you may be able to practise it elsewhere. Pity the photographer of seascapes who lives in Kansas, or the Dutch lover of mountains!

A fourth spectrum to consider is <u>when</u> you take your pictures. The slanting light of dawn is very different from the overhead light of noon, but both can be used to good effect. Although noon is often said to be the worst possible time for photography, there are certain pictures which are enhanced by it. Imagine, for example, that you want to portray the dazzling burning heat of a high summer in Mexico. The almost vertical light, the inky black shadows, possibly the shimmering distortion of heat haze, are all going to be illustrated far better at noon than in the reddish light of dawn.

Weather conditions, too, are important. Dartmoor, in Devon, is a part of the world I like very much; but there are some pictures which cry out to be taken in sunlight, others in mist, yet others in rain or under a blanket of snow. Photographers who admire Ansel Adams are known to wait months for the light to be just right, returning to the same spot year after year until they get what they want. I believe that this is due to an over-strict interpretation of the concept of 'previsualisation'; but I do not deny that (sometimes) it produces the most excellent pictures.

Above and facing page: *Ancient monuments and pre-historic sites can serve as sources of inspiration to those lucky enough to visit them.*

The small figures of the people in the picture shown **top left,** *emphasise the massive scale of the Buddha statue.*

You may wish to consider how important people are to your photography; photographers as disparate as Ansel Adams and David Hockney seem to do very well without them, but Cartier-Bresson and Eugene Smith concentrate on them. Margaret Bourke-White seemed able to produce superb pictures with or without people, and the pictures of Walter Nurnberg seem to use people as archetypes and touchstones rather than as individuals.

Again, there is the question of <u>how much</u> colour you use in your photography. In the hands of a master such as Shirakawa, there may seem to be little difference between even black-and-white photography and colour (though his colour tends to be monochromatic anyway), but Hockney uses picture-postcard colours to excellent effect, as does Harry Callahan. One of my own favourite pictures – a moonrise over a hill in Wales – is composed of a featureless black hill, a featureless deep-blue sky, and a white blob of moon.

All this intellectualising may seem foreign to the direct experience which I have extolled above, but it is in many ways a preconditioning of receptiveness. The biggest barrier to creativity is a tendency to stick to what you know. By questioning your own attitudes you can make those sudden little leaps which are characterised as 'Hey, I could do it that way instead'; and even if the <u>conscious</u> thought does not cross your mind when you take the picture, it is a pretty safe bet that it will be in there unconsciously, and rooting for you.

COLOUR AT NIGHT

Our Victorian forbears distinguished between instantaneous exposures (or 'snapshots') and timed exposures, which might be short enough to be measured by the time-honoured 'one hippopotamus two hippopotamus' method or long enough to determine with a pocket watch; those with a penchant for photographing the interiors of churches frequently ran into half-hour exposures, and on a dim day the enterprising solar artist might well repair to the nearest inn for a leisurely lunch <u>during</u> the exposure.

Even the slowest modern colour films are around a hundred times as fast as a Victorian 'rapid' dry plate, so during the day we no longer even consider 'timed' exposures, at least out of doors. At night, though, we are forced back upon the old distinction.

Contrary to popular belief, hand-held colour photography at night is perfectly possible; and given that this is likely to interest more people than 'timed' exposures, we can consider this first.

HAND-HELD PHOTOGRAPHY AT NIGHT

There are three weapons in the night photographer's armoury. The first is fast lenses. An extreme speed lens is ideal; for the real fanatic, the f/1 Noctilux for the rangefinder Leica or the f/0.95 Canon Dream for the rangefinder Canon 7 and 7s are available at a price. Next come the f/1.2 lenses from a number of leading manufacturers.

Whilst these are very nice to have, they are still considerably more expensive than the f/1.4s and the gain in speed is only half a stop. Furthermore, unless they are from very reputable makers, their optical quality may not be too exciting.

The f/1.4 is probably a good compromise, but it is by no means essential; an f/2 lens can cover a surprising amount of work, and even an f/2.8 is far from useless. Certainly, you would be ill advised to use anything much slower than f/2, but if you look at some of the work done in the 1930s with lenses as slow as f/3.5, it becomes clear that high speed lenses are by no means essential.

Twilight and dawn often *provide magical and at times unusual lighting effects that can be interpreted in various ways.*

Underexposure intensifies the evanescent colours and captures the feeling of half-light.

The next weapon is fast film. Here, the modern photographer is incredibly lucky in comparison with his pre-war counterpart. The absolute limit for (black-and-white) pre-war films was about 400 ASA, and now this is available as a <u>standard</u> speed (i.e. without pushing) in both colour print and colour slide. By using faster films such as 3M's 650 ASA or a little 'pushing' in processing (or both) speeds of 800-1000 ASA and more are possible without disastrous loss of quality.

There are, however, two things to watch out for when using these films. The first is that there is a very definite limit to how far they can be uprated; anything more than 100% or *(in extremis)* 150% will lead to colour shifts, thin shadows, colour casts, and all manner of untoward effects. The second is the very mixed colour typically found in night lighting – mixtures of mercury vapour, sodium vapour, fluorescent, and tungsten lighting are by no means unusual, and to expect 'white light' colour rendition is unrealistic.

Fortunately, a very wide range of colour effects is acceptable in a night shot; even more fortunately, the fastest films exhibit the best tolerance for mixed lighting, and for the majority of night shots either the daylight-balanced 400 ASA film or the tungsten-balanced 650 ASA film will give excellent results. To be sure, these films are more expensive than their slower brethren – but the difference is scarcely disastrous (certainly a lot less than

*The squiggly trails of head and tail-lights of the traffic in a night shot may be something of a cliché, yet the effect can often be pleasing as shown in the aerial photograph **above**. In the pictures on the **facing page**, they add a mystical quality to the sleeping town.*

***Many of the most effective** night-time shots in cities and villages are taken at dusk, when there is still enough light to give an impression of the surroundings but the lamps are lit. This technique is used **above and right**. A more sophisticated version of the same approach involves making a double exposure a few minutes (or even hours) apart, one for the general scene and one for the lights. Very great care is needed to make sure that the camera is not moved between the two exposures – a solid tripod is essential.*

buying a faster lens) and the processing costs the same regardless of speed. Admittedly some labs charge a little extra for uprating, but this is far from universally the case and anyway, uprating is often unnecessary.

The last arrow in the quiver is a steady hand. Although the received standard wisdom is that you should never hand-hold a picture at less than 1/60 sec. (or 1/30, depending on which authority you believe), you can often get away with slower speeds than this, especially if you can brace yourself or the camera against something during the exposure. It varies widely from person to person, but you may find that by resting the camera on a fence-post or automobile you can achieve a 90% success rate at 1/15, a 50% success rate at 1/8, and some degree of success at even lower speeds.

Remember, though, that even with a slight degree of blur, you may prefer to have the picture rather than pass up the opportunity completely. When I was a student, I used to carry my old Leica, fitted with an f/3.5 lens and loaded with 50 ASA film

COLOUR AT NIGHT

(it was the cheapest available). I have a number of rather wobbly shots taken without support at speeds as long as one full second. They are not artistic masterpieces, but I am still glad that I have them.

As for metering, there is good news and there is bad news. The bad news is that metering in poor light is extremely difficult: the meter may run out of sensitivity, and refuse even to flicker, and in any case the contrast and lighting of a night scene may well differ considerably from the 'typical' scene for which the meter was designed. Spot metering is one answer; zone system metering with a very sensitive meter such as the Luna-Pro is another; a healthy dollop of experience in how to interpret meter readings at night does no harm; but the easiest is to use an exposure table of the type published at the end of this chapter, modifying it in the light of experience as you grow more practised. This fortunately leads us to the good news, which is that metering at night is not very critical anyway.

This is because of the very high contrast which is typical of night lighting, and to a lesser extent because of the different colours of light which are likely to be encountered. With a

On the immediate right we have 'nuite Américaine,' or day-for-night; severe underexposure gives the effect of night. The reduction of the subject to silhouette, and the inclusion of a double exposed sun, gives this picture an eerie science-fictional quality. The picture top is a twilight shot of a thunderstorm, and shows the lightning strikes during a long (45-second) exposure; such shots are usually most effective at night. On the opposite page, the moon has been made an important element in the picture. The best way to do this is to use a really long-focus lens – at least 200mm, and preferably 500mm or even longer – or the moon will appear as a minute blob. Exposures must also be brief; at that sort of magnification, the moon fairly races across the frame. A common way to get such pictures is by combining two separate pictures, one a 'stock shot' of the moon and the other of the rest of the subject, with plenty of clear sky.

conventionally lit daylight scene, we have a pretty clear idea of what we expect to see, but at night we tend to be rather more free of our preconceptions. We are more inclined to accept that the photograph is a photograph, rather than an accurate representation of reality. If the faces are correctly exposed, the clothes may be too dark and the background will certainly be so; but we can look at the faces and accept the picture as correctly exposed. At the other extreme, if the background is lit up like day, the figures may be burnt-out blobs or they may be impressionistic blurs because they have moved during the exposure. If the exposure is long enough, they may even vanish

altogether, which is why there are no figures in very early landscape pictures.

Here, though, we are talking about what our great grandfathers would have called 'timed' exposures, and our techniques are rather different.

PHOTOGRAPHY WITH A TRIPOD

Before going on to anything else, it is important to make one point: if colour films are exposed for appreciably longer (or shorter) periods than their designer intended, they cease to respond in their usual manner. They will lose sensitivity, so that

an exposure which the meter would tell us should be thirty seconds might require fifty seconds, and they will change in colour balance so that filters are required to give us a 'normal' looking image. For example, some films tend to go blue if they are exposed for longer than about 1/10 second. The longer the exposure, the more blue they look and the stronger the brownish filter that is required to compensate. Of course, the brown filter introduces a further extension in exposure . . . in practice, this does not give rise to the infinite series of adjustments it might imply, but it can be quite a headache.

These reciprocity defects, as they are called, are not usually significant until you are considering exposures of a second or more. They vary widely from film to film – some films are designed for quite long exposures, and will respond well at five or ten seconds, and the colour shifts and losses of sensitivity are also very different from film to film.

The information you need may be packed with the film, but more likely you will have to write or call the manufacturer; they are all quite willing to help.

With this major reservation, together with the remarks already made concerning the colour of light at night, there is no reason why you should not embark upon night photography with

COLOUR AT NIGHT

Even shots like these can be *hand-held if you can find something to rest the camera against – a window-sill, or a wall, or a bollard. A crisp, contrasty lens is essential, or everything will disappear*

*behind a veil of light which masks detail and destroys atmosphere. The pictures **above and facing page top** were taken at twilight; the lower one is rather later on a winter's evening.*

a tripod. A good general guide to tripod selection is to use one as heavy as you can bear to carry and as expensive as you can bear to pay. Light flimsy tripods are all but useless, as they allow a camera to wobble not only in the breeze but also as a result of its own mirror vibration: an old professional trick is to increase the effective mass of the tripod by hanging a full gadget bag from it. If a tripod is too insubstantial to allow this, then it is too insubstantial to be of any use anyway.

There are, however, alternatives to full-sized tripods. One is the table-top tripod, preferably a substantial one: most professionals favour the Leitz model, which is surprisingly inexpensive and doubles as a chest pod, together with either the Leitz ball-and-socket head (frighteningly expensive) or a good proprietary model such as that from Kaiser. Another useful professional standby is the beanbag, which can be as simple as an old sock or small bag filled with sand or even beans: used as a cushion between the camera and any support, it allows exposures of a second or so to be tackled with confidence. With these, a 'hands-on' camera release technique may be permissible,

but for the utmost stability you should always use a cable release. If you forget the cable release (and everyone does, sooner or later), try using the camera's built-in self-timer for a vibration-free release.

FLASH OUT OF DOORS AT NIGHT

When using flash out of doors, remember that there will be far less light reflected back from the surroundings than would be the case indoors, so that the flashgun will appear to be giving less light. Furthermore, automation is not much use out of doors; most of the time the gun will be working at full power anyway, and in any case there is the same sort of problem as described with meters, in that the gun is designed to respond to an 'average' scene – into which category a night shot does not fall.

For simple on-camera flash, set the gun to 'manual' and use a guide number 25-50% lower (experiment) than the manufacturer's published number. This should give acceptable results up to the limit of the power of the gun. For instance, one of my guns is rated 100 (feet) at 100 ASA. Out of doors at night I use a guide number of 60 with 100 ASA film, so with an f/2 lens I can use it up to 30′ – though obviously anything nearer the gun than 30′ at that aperture would be overexposed.

A more interesting technique is to use a combination of open-flash and multiple-flash. With the camera on B, each time you double the number of flashes you double the amount of light falling on the film. If you work out, therefore, that you would need to use f/1.4 to get the picture with a single flash, but you are restricted to an f/2.8 lens, you will need 4 flashes (2 x 2). If you wanted to use f/8, in order to get greater depth of field, you would need to use no fewer than 32 flashes (2 x 2 x 2 x 2 x 2).

COLOUR AND ACTION

The most obvious thing about action photography is that it freezes a section of time; the dancer, the skier, the racing driver are all fixed in a single pose. The camera can fix things as we see them – or as we think we see them, which is effectively the same thing – or it can show us things we cannot normally see: the snow kicked up by the skier hanging in mid air, or a twirl of colour as the dancer pirouettes.

There is, however, more to it than this. For example, action may be emphasised by the use of bright or dissonant colours: to return to the skier, the picture seems much more action-packed if it shows white snow, blue sky, and brilliant red ski-clothing. The drably-clad skier against a backdrop of pines looks a lot less exciting, even though he may be travelling as fast as his brightly-clad counterpart, or faster. Also, the choice of lens, camera angle, and composition can make a vast difference – though we will return to this later.

Finally, you really have to be familiar with your equipment. The ability to make rapid adjustments to speed, aperture, and focus is essential, and practice at reloading fast, perhaps on the run, is often very useful. There is no real need for a motor drive unless you want to trigger the camera remotely; in fact, the indiscriminate use of a motor drive not only uses up film at an alarming rate, but also diminishes your chances of getting the picture you want. Anticipation, and serious thought about when is the best time to press the shutter release, can give much better results than simply keeping your finger down on the motor drive button. With a 5fps drive your chances are not too bad; with a 10fps drive they are excellent – but you will be reloading the camera once for every 3-7 seconds shooting.

Aside from the technical considerations, there is also the matter of knowing what you are photographing. This is even more essential in natural history photography, where the old

Every one of these pictures has some blur in it somewhere; the creative aspect of this lies in balancing blur and sharpness to give the impression you want. Experiment and experience, and your own preference, are the only teachers.

With regard to equipment, the usual rule applies: use what you have. There are, however, two or three technical points which can make life a good deal easier.

First, interchangeable lenses are a boon. It is in the nature of action photography that you cannot always be as close as you would like; the standard 50mm lens fitted to most 35mm cameras is often too short, and the 35-40mm wide-angles fitted to many compacts are extremely limiting.

Instead, a short telephoto in the 85-105mm range is very useful, or (for those sports where you really do have to keep your distance) a lens of 180mm or even more. The 135mm focal length is often an unhappy compromise, and really owes its existence to the fact that it is the longest focal length which could accurately be coupled to the rangefinder cameras of yore.

Secondly, fast lenses and fast film are often called for. Unless you are photographing an event where there really is an enormous amount of light about (such as a skiing competition), you may find that the fast shutter speeds required mean that you need correspondingly fast lenses; and if you want to stop down as well, for maximum depth of field, then fast films will be essential.

COLOUR AND ACTION

Experience and anticipation are a very important part of any sort of action photography: the better you understand what you are photographing, the more you are able both to spot a good picture and to see it coming. Few people would go so far as to become bullfighters, but in less demanding activities it is always a good idea to get some personal experience if you can. With this sort of fast-moving and often unpredictable action, you are caught in a trap. You need long lenses, to pull the action close; small apertures, to cover errors in focusing; and fast speeds, to reduce camera shake. Your only saviour is fast film – and then you have grain problems.

injunction is, 'Biologist first, photographer second' but you will always get better pictures if you have some knowledge of the subject you are photographing and some previous experience, so that you know what focal length lenses to use and where the best angles are. For example, at the first four-wheel-drive meet I went to, I took quite long lenses; I did not realise just how close you can get to the action. Now, the longest I take is 105mm, and I find that I use lenses as wide as 35mm quite regularly. It is best of all if you practice what you photograph, be it ballet or all-in wrestling; but even if you do not, then at least spend some time learning about it.

FREEZING AND BLURRING

It is quite tempting to divide action pictures into two types, the 'frozen' and the blurred. The former uses the highest shutter speeds possible to make sure that nothing in the picture is blurred; in the extreme example, drops of water hang in mid-air

as if weightless, and divers are transfixed in time, their bodies just breaking water as unyielding as glass. This used to be considered the standard; it was normal in pre-war photography books (and even for quite some time afterwards) to quote long and complex tables of shutter speeds required to stop various kinds of action at various distances. Apart from such implicitly unnerving ideas as standing within ten feet of an express train moving at sixty miles an hour, there were multiplication and division factors to be considered according to whether the movement was at right angles to the line of sight, oblique to it, or (another alarming thought) coming straight towards you.

The blurred approach, on the other hand, can go to the extreme of showing a few impressionistic whirls and labelling them 'Andalusian dancers'; at an exposure of a second they might be Andalusian, Gipsy, or Republican. Periodically this becomes an overwhelming fashion, but used with discretion it can be very effective indeed.

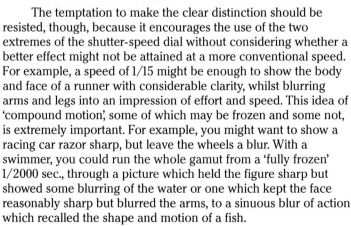

The temptation to make the clear distinction should be resisted, though, because it encourages the use of the two extremes of the shutter-speed dial without considering whether a better effect might not be attained at a more conventional speed. For example, a speed of 1/15 might be enough to show the body and face of a runner with considerable clarity, whilst blurring arms and legs into an impression of effort and speed. This idea of 'compound motion', some of which may be frozen and some not, is extremely important. For example, you might want to show a racing car razor sharp, but leave the wheels a blur. With a swimmer, you could run the whole gamut from a 'fully frozen' 1/2000 sec., through a picture which held the figure sharp but showed some blurring of the water or one which kept the face reasonably sharp but blurred the arms, to a sinuous blur of action which recalled the shape and motion of a fish.

You can also mix a number of sharp images to give the impression of blur and movement, or mix a sharp image (or images) with a blurred one. The former is normally achieved with stroboscopic (multiple) flash, but with some cameras it is possible to use the motor drive to give multiple exposures on a single frame; even if the camera does not specifically provide this feature, pressing (and holding) the rewind button may have the same effect. Alternatively, a straightforward multiple exposure may be possible.

The usual way to get a blurred image plus a sharp one is to use a long exposure and fire a flash during that exposure. If you want to use synchronised flash, you will need to plan the exposure so that the sharp part is at the beginning; it is generally more convenient to use 'open flash' and fire the gun manually. This has the added advantage that you can make more than one flash exposure. For obvious reasons, exposure determination is difficult and a fair amount of experiment and bracketing will be necessary. Another possibility is again a straightforward multiple exposure.

In fact, when you start considering the possibilities of this sort of photography, the options are almost endless. For example, if you use a tripod you can hold the image still at one (or more) points, and pan or tilt to create blur; you can use the various 'motion' attachments marketed by filter manufacturers, which are essentially curved prisms, to 'smear' part of the image; or you can zoom during exposure.

Although the zoom has become almost a cliché, there are still many occasions when it can be used. It requires quite a lot of practice if you are to avoid jiggling the camera or shifting focus, but if you combine it with a flash exposure even this is not a problem. Usually, the most convincing results are obtained by using synchronised flash and zooming from the longest focal length to the shortest; that way, you get the subject sharp, but

COLOUR AND ACTION

227

Mentally, we always tend to associate colour and action; any picture which panders to this preconception stands a good chance of success. It is usually very important to fill the frame with the action: most action sports require a great deal of featureless track, water, etc., which if allowed to fill the picture can be very boring.

COLOUR AND ACTION

surrounded by 'action streaks' as though it is exploding out towards you. Incidentally, it is not necessary to use a zoom lens to achieve this effect; the change in angle of view of any lens as it is focused will give a similar effect. All that you have to do is 'pull focus' during the exposure – the angle of view narrows as you focus closer.

A technique which makes use of blur and motion is <u>panning</u>. If you follow a moving subject, keeping it in the centre of the viewfinder, then you can use a much slower shutter speed than if the camera were fixed. In extreme cases, this allows you to render sharp a subject which you could not otherwise photograph: a racing car might require a 1/3000 sec. exposure to 'freeze' it without panning, and only 1/500 if you panned. Even with slow-moving subjects, though, panning can be very useful. First, it allows the use of shutter speeds which accentuate the kind of compound motion already referred to; secondly, it allows you to use smaller apertures (either because they are all that you have or for increased depth of field); and thirdly, it blurs the background in a way which suggests great speed. This last effect can be particularly effective, whether used to convey an accurate impression (of, say, a racing car) or something more subjective. A runner, for example, can be made to look as if he is literally 'travelling like the wind'.

ACTION AND COMPOSITION

Although the old-fashioned 'rules of composition' are now rightly regarded as useful generalisations rather than rigid rules, there is no doubt that some compositions are more dynamic than others. To take a very simple example, let us return to our skier. If he is just entering the picture, there is a feeling (no matter how irrational) that he has the rest of the frame to ski across; whereas if he is at the other side of the picture there is a feeling of tension, as if he is about to burst through the border.

There are a number of tricks like this, though purists object to some of them. One is the choice of lens; a long lens will 'stack up' the action in a way familiar from coverage of motor races, whilst a wide angle will stretch or accentuate perspective – for example, a wide-angle lens mounted in an aeroplane, and so positioned as to show a part of the aeroplane, will dramatically emphasise the isolation of a skydiver. Another is tilting the camera; we are conscious that mountains have steep slopes, so if the camera is tilted slightly to emphasise the slope we accept this as natural. It is possible to overdo this; there is one otherwise excellent publicity picture of a four-wheel-drive vehicle fording a stream – but if the hill were as steep as the picture shows, the stream would be more like a waterfall than the brook it appears to be in the picture! It is hard to criticise them too much, though, because anyone who has ever tried to show the steepness of a hill (in San Francisco, for example) will realise just how tame it can appear in the final image. It is interesting to speculate how much of this is due to our acclimatisation to exaggerated photography.

Even the time-worn concepts of 'balance' and the 'S curve' can be applied. According to classical theory, a composition had to be 'balanced' with a primary subject and a secondary; if we omit the balancing secondary, there is a certain tension in the picture. Similarly, the old 'S curve' leading into the picture can be used to convey the idea of rapid movement along that curve.

ACTION AND COLOUR

The feeling of action in a picture can, as already mentioned, be influenced by colour. Reds and yellows are considered to be 'advancing' colours – and certainly, small areas of these in otherwise subdued pictures fairly leap out at you. Other colours,

Exposures for lights and other night subjects with some 'Kodak' Colour Films

Film	Subject		
	Lights at night (no shadow detail)	Subjects lit by lights at night (some shadow detail)	Moonlit landscapes
KODACHROME 25 (Daylight)	1/15 sec at f/2.8	1/15 sec at f/2	45 sec at f/2
KODACHROME 64 (Daylight) EKTACHROME 64 Professional 6117 (Daylight) EKTACHROME 64 and 64 Professional (Daylight)	1/15 sec at f/4	1/30 sec at f/2	35 sec at f/2.8
EKTACHROME Professional 6118 (Tungsten) EKTACHROME 50 Professional (Tungsten)	1/15 sec at f/2.8	1/15 sec at f/2.8	20 sec at f/2
EKTACHROME 200 and 200 Professional (Daylight)	1/15 sec at f/5.6	1/30 sec at f/4	10 sec at f/2.8
EKTACHROME 160 and 160 Professional (Tungsten)	1/15 sec at f/5.6	1/30 sec at f/3.5	15 sec at f/2.8
EKTACHROME 400 (Daylight) KODACOLOR 400	1/15 sec at f/8	1/30 sec at f/4.5	12 sec at f/4
VERICOLOR II Professional, Type S and Professional 4107, Type S	1/15 sec at f/4.5	1/30 sec at f/2.8	Not recommended, but try 20 sec at f/2.8
VERICOLOR II Professional, Type L and Professional 4108, Type L VERICOLOR II Commercial, Type S and Commercial 4119, Type S KODACOLOR II	1/15 sec at f/4	1/15 sec at f/2.8	12 sec at f/2

Above: Panning techniques *may require a little practice, but once mastered they can be used to considerable creative effect in the sports or action shot.* **Top**

and facing page: *Polarising filters penetrate haze, reduce reflections and lead to strong, saturated colour.*

such as blue and green, are 'retreating' colours, and lack the psychological impact of the advancing ones. Ideally, the active part of the picture should be in an advancing colour; this is one of the reasons why red ski clothing is standard for photography.

Two other key points are simplicity and contrast. When something really grabs our attention, we are aware of it almost to the exclusion of all else. A successful action picture duplicates this in two ways. First, it uses a few bright simple colours – or at least, it manages to contrast the principal subject with its background. It is, for example, extremely difficult to make an

effective picture of a number of soldiers in camouflage, no matter how dramatic their exploits. The vast majority of successful war pictures are either close-ups of one man, or at most a few, or they use dramatically the colours of war – the red of fire and blood, or the monochrome brown of the trenches.

Of course, it is not necessary to rely exclusively on colour. The famous raising of the flag on Mount Suribachi is a classic example of a composition which works as well in black-and-white as in colour (or indeed when cast in bronze); but such a combination of dramatic events, a penetrating eye, and sheer luck does not often come anyone's way.

In conclusion, it may seem that I have emphasised the calculating aspect of action photography too much; but for every picture which is attained by sheer luck in the heat of the event, there are ten which are achieved by mastery of the craft – and a thousand which are abject failures.

NATURAL HISTORY PHOTOGRAPHY

There are those who wince whenever creativity and natural history photography are mentioned in the same breath: their view is that a natural history photograph exists solely to record its subject as accurately as possible, and that there is therefore no room for creativity.

This argument can be attacked on three grounds. First, to obtain an accurate picture may require a great deal of creativity, albeit not necessarily of the artistic kind: surely Steven Dalton's masterful pictures of insects in flight involved a great deal of creativity in simply working out how to take them. He had to devise special shutters, flashguns, and methods of triggering them both, and then had to persuade his subjects to fly or hop in the right directions.

Secondly, there is no particular reason why a picture should not be both biologically accurate and aesthetically pleasing. It may be unusual, or even accidental, but when it does happen, the result can be doubly pleasing.

Finally, there is no reason why a photograph 'should' be an accurate biological record. Whilst no-one would condone an insensitive photographer who upset the animal and damaged its habitat, why should anyone condemn a photographer for taking an attractive picture even if it does not clearly show the diagnostic features for identifying the species?

Because the field of natural history photography is so vast, it embraces many different kinds of photographer and many different kinds of equipment. There are certain ground rules, though, which are true for all types of natural history photography: these are covered first, after which we take a brief look at different specialised fields.

The first thing is equipment. Whatever your equipment – and it will vary considerably according to your chosen field – you must be totally familiar with it, and able to operate any control at

a moment's notice. Many successful wildlife photographers use automatic cameras to free them from many of the mechanical concerns of photography; the concentration required is (or should be) so great that you have no attention left to spare for the mechanics of operating the camera.

Secondly, you need to be dedicated. Whilst there is a place for anyone with a good eye for a picture to take the occasional

Animals have expressions too. How closely these equate to our interpretation of them is a matter for debate, but there is no doubt that they can look reflective, intelligent, and happy as well as the more usual amusing or alarming. As in many other branches of photography, the secret is often patience – that, and shooting for the percentages.

lucky shot, the person who knows all about his subject obviously has a very much better chance. If you know the habits of the species in general, and (preferably) of your own individual specimen, life will be very much easier. For example, a cat almost invariably stretches on waking up naturally; so if you want a cat stretching (whether a domestic moggie or a lioness), just wait around until a sleeping one wakes up. Furthermore, a cat normally sleeps after eating; so, for the stretching shot, feed the cat – and wait!

This points up the third necessity: patience. Although animals are far more perverse and infuriating than plants, it is

NATURAL HISTORY PHOTOGRAPHY

A good way to gain expertise is to specialise in one animal – such as the big cats, here. After a while, you begin to learn their habits: when they sleep, how they eat and play, the relationship between adults and cubs. Although most of this information is specific, the habit and means of observing can be carried across to other species.

surprising just how difficult it can be to find a perfect specimen of a plant . . . in the right lighting . . . in the right surroundings . . . with a flower open and the dew fresh on it . . . not waving in the breeze . . . The impatient photographer will be content simply to get an image: the good photographer will wait for the <u>right</u> image, though he may expose a lot of film whilst waiting.

Finally, you need to be alert. The difference between a mediocre picture (or no picture at all) and a great picture may be how fast you can spot the subject, get the camera to your eye, and take the picture. Physical fitness helps; ideally, you should pursue a sport such as fencing, which exercises both body and mind.

BIRDS AND LARGE ANIMALS

Most people start in natural history photography in this way, often as an extension of an existing interest. The big problem is that almost all wildlife is wary, and some of it is dangerous too. For the dangerous variety, you should <u>never</u> expose yourself to even the slightest danger without having someone else around to

act as lookout. It is all too easy to become so obsessed with getting a picture that you fail to notice the tiger's mate that is stalking you: it may sound melodramatic, but it does happen, especially with scorpions and snakes.

As for combatting the wariness, there are three possible solutions. One is to cultivate the Red Indian skills of tracking and moving noiselessly; it is not as difficult to do this as you might think. Consider camouflage, too: streaks of greasepaint or cocoa powder on the face, drab, ragged clothing – real Commando stuff. Secondly, you can use hides. Some of these are quite elaborate, and the photographer can live in them for days if necessary, but others are no more than stones, branches, and a bit of green tarpaulin. After establishing the hide, you may need to wait for quite some time for the animals to regain confidence, but quite a useful trick is to have someone else come to the hide with you; he then leaves, with you inside, and since very few animals seem to be able to count, they may well assume that the danger has gone away. The third trick is to use long lenses.

Whilst it is quite possible to get very good pictures using lenses of up to 200mm or so, it is difficult: far more usual are 400, 500, 600, 800, and 1000mm lenses on 35mm. This, incidentally, is one of the several reasons why 35mm is popular with natural history photographers: the longest lenses available for larger formats are often shorter in absolute terms, and certainly far shorter in relative terms. A 500mm lens on a Hasselblad (the longest easily available) is roughly equivalent to 300mm on

When photographing any *animal big enough to be dangerous, always remember that no matter how lazy and cuddly it may look, it can probably move with lightning speed and it may well be able to kill you. This does not only apply to the more obvious animals: a domestic sow, with piglets, can kill in their defence. In European and American wildlife parks, always keep windows closed: in the wild, listen to the advice of your guide, never work alone; always have someone to guard your back. Try to keep calm, and avoid excessive exercise; too fast a heartbeat means camera shake.*

35mm: a 1000mm lens on 35mm could roughly be matched for magnification by a 1600mm on a Hasselblad.

The problems with these very long lenses, though, is that they are large, heavy, expensive, of limited maximum aperture, and require very substantial tripods if camera shake is to be avoided. They also need very clean air: any haze will show up as a degradation of image quality and colour. Many excellent long-focus lenses are quite unfairly accused of poor definition because of this. The rule, then, is to use the shortest focal length you can get away with, as close as possible.

Of course, there are animals sufficiently sure of themselves that you can use lenses of 135mm or even less: with the pigeons in Trafalgar Square, for instance, a 24mm lens is fine. The rules about not startling the animal still apply, and plenty of patience is still needed; a good way to sharpen your stalking skills is to try to photograph a domestic cat. Remember two things, though. With a few domestic exceptions, the only animals which do not fear man are those which can easily take him to pieces: rhinos are a good example. The other thing is that almost any animal

NATURAL HISTORY PHOTOGRAPHY

can and will move surprisingly quickly, so alertness is essential. If the animal is harmless, you will only lose the picture, but if it is dangerous, you can lose a lot more.

To return to equipment, there is no doubt that 35mm is overwhelmingly the most popular. It is relatively cheap, a vast array of lenses is available, the camera is not too heavy to carry for long distances, and you get 36 pictures from a roll. This not only cuts down the amount of film you have to carry about: it also reduces the number of times you have to reload (and the best action always seems to take place during reloading), and it means that you can shoot more pictures. In wildlife photography you are almost always shooting for the percentages, and plenty of relatively cheap film means that you can increase your chances enormously.

ZOOS

It may seem a little odd to consider zoo photography separately, but there are many differences between photographing an animal in captivity and photographing it in the wild. First, you can usually get much closer with far less trouble (and danger). Any good medium telephoto is suitable, with something like a top-flight 70-210mm zoom as the very best option. The flexibility and speed of operation outweighs the slight loss of image quality, which will in any case be invisible on the kinds of subjects you are tackling.

Secondly, the animals are relatively tame; a good deal less patience is required in the average zoo than in the average jungle or other natural habitat.

Thirdly, the environment itself introduces problems. Bars are there for a reason: poking the camera through them is not a good idea, though you may sometimes be able to persuade a keeper to cover you whilst you do so. Obviously, it is better to go along at less busy times if you want to talk to the keepers, who are also likely to be very knowledgeable about the animals in their care. Watch out for obtrusive backgrounds, too; a neutral concrete wall (provided the join between floor and wall is not an obvious straight line) is not too bad, but often there are man-

***Never dismiss the amusing,** the brightly coloured, or the simply unusual as fit only for snapshots; if you don't get any fun out of your photography, why do you do it? Zoom lenses are ideal for such pictures – apart from their inherent flexibility, they can also be used to accurately crop the image in the viewfinder.*

made structures at the back of the cage. A very useful trick is differential focus, with the lens used as wide open as possible; a 135/2.8 is ideal. If the bars are close enough, you may be able to 'lose' those, and if you can throw the background out of focus as well you may be able to achieve remarkably natural-looking pictures. Try to suit the weather to the animal, though: lions look very depressed on a rainy day, but sun can cheer them up considerably.

The last big difference about the zoo is that it is a lot more available than some exotic location in Africa or India, and so affords an excellent opportunity to try your hand at animal photography. The price of admission is usually a good deal less than the price of a single film, so it is an option well worth exploring.

CLOSE-UP AND MACROPHOTOGRAPHY

This is the other type of photography which most people automatically think of when natural history photography is mentioned. It embodies all the difficulties of conventional wildlife photography, with the additional problem that you have to get very close indeed to your subject, you are working with virtually no depth of field, and normally you will be running out of light as well.

Here more than anywhere you have to know the habits of your subject, and here more than anywhere you have to have the right equipment. The former can only be acquired by study of your chosen animal (insect or whatever), but the latter allows a few general rules.

35mm is the usual format, for the reasons already stated and especially because you are shooting for the percentages: with a really difficult subject, one frame out of thirty six might not be a bad success rate. It is also far easier to get close-up gear for 35mm cameras, than for other formats. This falls into two general groups: methods of increasing extension, and special lenses.

In general, flowers are best shown either in close-up, like the daisy **above,** or in small groups. What very seldom works is the long shot, where each flower is reduced to a pin-prick of colour among the green. Incidentally, many photographers carry a small atomiser or spray-gun to get the dewy effect in close-ups.

The normal lens on a 35mm camera can be focused down to about 45cm. There are three reasons for this. The first is that lens mounts to focus closer are considerably bulkier and more expensive than ordinary ones. The second is that the performance of many lenses (especially fast ones) deteriorates dramatically at very close distances. The third is that the marked f/stops no longer hold good, and the lens must be opened up if underexposure is to be avoided.

Extension tubes and bellows get around the first problem, but leave the other two. In practice, many lenses of around f/2 are quite acceptable even when used close up, especially if they

NATURAL HISTORY PHOTOGRAPHY

Flower photography – and
indented any form of close-up – is
a field where the relative merits
of 35mm and rollfilm are about
equal. One offers better image
quality; the other, greater depth
of field, easier handling, and
shorter exposures.

In general, 35mm is best for
broad areas of colour and
graphic shapes, as in the two
pictures **right and top right.**
Rollfilm scores where very fine
detail is paramount, as on the
facing page, top left. Many
serious natural history
photographers own both 35mm
and rollfilm systems; 35mm is
indisputably best to start with.

as 'f/8½'. At 150mm, the factor would be 1.5, so if you set f/8 you would get f/12 – effectively f/11 (the difference is about −10%, less than the variation between film batches).

Going on to special lenses, the cheapest is simply a positive close-up lens, which screws onto the camera lens in the same way as a filter and effectively shortens its focal length, so that the standard extension is enough for a closest focusing distance of (say) 20cm instead of 45cm. With a simple Tessar-type lens, and working at a modest aperture (f/8 or less), these can be very good; the best of them are cemented and corrected doublets in their own right, but no manufacturers commonly encountered (except Leitz) still follow this path. With the wrong lens, or at wide apertures, results can be disastrous: the best way to find out is to check a close-up lens on your camera.

Much more expensive are lenses specially designed to focus very close. The best known and most widely used of these is the Micro Nikkor for the Nikon, which used to be f/3.5 and is now f/2.8. The relatively low speed allows the designer to correct the lens very highly, and in addition he optimises the corrections for a rather nearer subject than a normal lens: at around 1/10 life size

*Specially computed macro lenses are often slower than their general-purpose counterparts, but offer superb contrast and resolution in addition to their close-focusing ability. The spider web **facing page top** is one of the most difficult subjects to expose correctly; ideally, the web itself should catch the light, with a dark background. Bracketing is usually essential, as metering the web itself is next to impossible.*

are reversed (so that the back of the lens faces towards the subject). Faster lenses, or lenses of poorer quality, may vary from the acceptable to the useless.

The increase in exposure can be handled by most TTL meters, but in their absence quite awkward calculations are required. The most convenient is probably $F' = F\left(\frac{N}{N-1}\right)$, where N is the subject distance expressed as a multiple of the focal length of the lens (measure from the middle of the lens). For example, at one foot (300mm), using a 50mm (2″) lens, $\left(\frac{N}{N-1}\right)$ is 6/5. Multiply F (the metered exposure using a non-TTL meter) by 6/5 to get F, the effective aperture when F is set. For example, if you set f/8 you get f/9.6, commonly expressed in photographic terms

(subject distance about 30cm) is best, but performance is still superb at infinity or at 10x life size – though a bellows or extension tube is needed to get this close. Like most similar lenses, the Micro Nikkor focuses continuously down to ½ life size, then uses an extension ring for 1:1 reproduction.

Such 'macro' lenses are available in a number of focal lengths, from around 40mm to 90mm, 105mm, and even 200mm; the longer focal lengths give more 'stand off', which is useful when photographing (for example) insects, but are bulkier, slower, and more expensive than the shorter ones. Incidentally, the Micro Nikkor is so good that many people who own one use it in place of a faster standard lens.

The so-called 'macro zooms' are not always such a good bet: in fact, with few exceptions, their performance close-up is horrible. The best of them all is arguably the 90-180mm Flat Field Series 1 Vivitar, a massive, expensive, slow (f/4.5) lens which was discontinued some time ago, but is in great demand among the *cognoscenti*. The advantage of the zooms, though, is that the diaphragm is normally mechanically compensated to ensure a constant aperture even in the macro mode. This is rather more convenient than the fixed-length lenses, which require either TTL metering or the same sort of calculations as described previously – though for obvious reasons, the longer lenses can achieve a given reproduction ratio with less diaphragm adjustment.

Although forethought is an *important element in creativity, many shots require a snap decision and response, as the opportunity to capture the sight* *can vanish as suddenly as it appeared. Animals in the wild are a case in point, where just a simple record may be the major consideration.*

With any close-up system, though, a major problem is depth-of-field. Depth of field is constant for any given reproduction ratio, no matter how it is achieved, and in extreme close-ups it is <u>shallow</u>. Add to this the need to open up to get a reasonable amount of light on the film, and you have a major problem. The only effective answer is to have lots of light to start with, and the discussions of the best way to light macro subjects can fill whole chapters. The easiest (but most expensive) way is with a ringlight, a circular flash tube around the lens, but others involve the use of large soft reflectors or even a 'Pepper's Ghost' system with a sheet of plane parallel glass at 45° in front of the lens and a flash fired from the side.

Regardless of all the drawbacks of macro photography, though, it is always worth trying to get a picture. At the very worst, you will fail; at the best, you may be handsomely rewarded. Even such theoretically disastrous combinations as a macro zoom and a teleconverter used together have been known to bring home the bacon!

SPECIALISED NATURAL HISTORY PHOTOGRAPHY

There are many fields so specialised that only an active practitioner can know much about them: examples include underwater photography, photography in caves (potholes), the photography of insects in flight, and so forth. As it is impossible in a single book, let alone a single chapter, to explain all the ramifications of the different kinds of specialisation, all I can suggest is that you look at the pictures in this book and elsewhere; if they inspire you to try something of your own, get hold of a specialised book on the subject and use that as a starting point.

REPORTAGE

Reportage, also known as photojournalism, is traditionally concerned with 'telling it like it is'. The classic image of the newspaper photographer is of a hard-bitten type carrying a Speed Graphic; his trendier replacement, the photojournalist, is visualised as being hung about with battered Leicas or Nikons, jetting to far-flung parts of the world and photographing wars and insurrections.

Whilst there is considerably more than a grain of truth in both these stereotypes, there is a lot more to it than that. Photojournalism also embraces the photographers of the Farm Security Administration recording the dire plight of sharecroppers in the 1930s; Jill Freedman's essays, 'Circus Days' and 'Firehouse'; Lartigue's 'Diary of a Century'; Cartier-Bresson's innumerable works; Bert Hardy's sensitive investigations; Gene Smith's hard-hitting 'Minamata'; even (arguably) Bailey's 'Goodbye Baby and Amen' or Diane Arbus's freak shows. Yet each of these is very different in approach, intent, and technique: Lartigue was an inspired snapshotter, the FSA was a Government-sponsored project involving many photographers over a long period of time, and 'Minamata' was the result of one man's obsession.

The attentive reader will have noticed that the works referred to above are primarily (in some cases exclusively) in black-and-white. This is because that has historically tended to be the appropriate medium for reportage, for two reasons. The first is that most periodicals use far more black-and-white than colour; this is especially true in the case of newspapers, although a surprising number of magazines are still a very long way from being all (or even mostly) in colour. Because the pictures were (and often still are) reproduced in black-and-white, it made sense to shoot them in black-and-white.

The second reason is that black-and-white is more tolerant of exposure errors, quicker and less critical to process, and faster. Although photographers like McCullin take careful meter readings under fire and expose their pictures perfectly, most are not made of such stern stuff and correct exposure is the exception rather than the norm. On some papers, this even applies to such dangerous circumstances as mayoral receptions and church tea-parties; the technical skill and knowledge of some newsmen is unbelievably low. Speed of processing is an obvious advantage, as is in-the-field processing and transmission of pictures by wire machine. Sheer film speed is useful, too: although 3M's tungsten-light film is rated at 640 and can be pushed a stop or so without serious quality loss, black-and-white films are still acceptable at 3200 ASA or more: if highlight detail is all you need, effective ratings of 10,000 ASA and more are possible, especially with such gems as 2475 and 2485 Kodak recording films.

Nevertheless, there is still a place – and an honourable place – for colour in reportage. It is not widely known that there are extant some colour pictures from the FSA programme in the 1930s, and now, of course, there is a great deal of colour reportage in the colour supplements of newspapers and in such magazines as Paris Match, Stern, Geo, etc.

The problem with colour reportage is that it is still a relatively new medium. Whilst this may be a source of delight to the innovator, it does make life a little difficult both commercially and from the point of view of reader acceptance. In addition to the technical difficulties outlined above, picture editors are not sure what they are looking for in colour reportage (and may have limited colour budgets anyway) and the person who looks at the photograph may find that it jars with his preconceptions of how a news picture 'should' look.

Because most of us get our knowledge of reportage

Dance studios are an excellent place to practice your reportage techniques. You have to be able to focus rapidly and accurately; to compose almost automatically; to compensate for rapidly changing lighting as the dancers move across the stage; and (perhaps most important of all) to select the best pictures afterwards. These thirteen pictures come from a single 36-exposure roll; the errors have already been weeded out. Put yourself in the place of a picture editor – which **three** pictures would you select?

Colour is being used more and more for 'hard' news, but it is much more usual to find it in 'soft' stories in magazines – pictures which can be set up in advance, rather than snatched in the heat of the moment. Many of these pictures can be extremely beautiful, and they are normally taken with fairly simple 35mm equipment, such as any amateur might have.

photography from newspapers, we are quite happy to see a grainy picture of limited tonal range under the label 'reportage'; the grain corresponds to the half-tone screen used for newspaper reproduction, and the limited tonal range to the quality of newspaper printing. On the other hand, we derive our understanding of colour photography from advertising (where technical quality is usually impeccable) and from our own pictures, wherein the quality is usually surprisingly good. Grain and a general flatness of colour is quite acceptable in a news picture, because we mentally equate it with black-and-white; but colour casts are much less acceptable. It is in the nature of colour film to give colour casts when mistreated during processing, overheated in the camera, or used in lighting for which it was not designed – and as all of these circumstances can arise very easily in certain types of reportage, colour is little used in (for example) war photography.

Even if we could get impeccable colour (and McCullin seems to manage it pretty well), it would still jar upon some sensibilities because it 'prettifies' some subjects to an intolerable

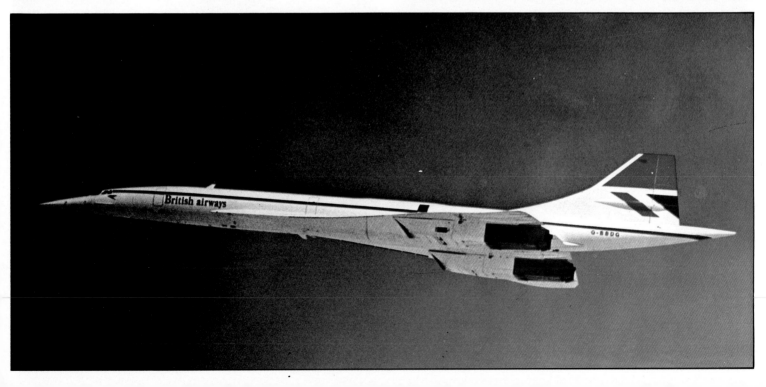

REPORTAGE

Another good way to practice *your reportage skills is on racing cars; at the big professional events, there is little room for the amateur in the best places, but at vintage and 'club' meets you can often get in among the action. Ensure preferential treatment next time with complimentary prints.*

extent. This is once again a consequence of our preconceptions; we are accustomed to cooing over a successful snapshot, 'Didn't it come out well?' We expect pleasant subjects in a colour picture – and when we do not get them, we may not be well pleased. Whilst this means that a really good picture can derive extra impact from its reversal of our expectations, it also means that anything less may be diminished or even demeaned by the use of colour: in simple terms, a war can look too much like a vacation.

Of course, this may be used to good effect when the subject is inherently an agreeable or enjoyable one. A fine example of this is any great State occasion, with a royal wedding or investiture a prime example. All the pomp and glory looks well in colour, because (after all) it was designed to. It was meant to be an occasion for public rejoicing, a holiday, a break from routine – and this fits in well with our preconceptions about colour pictures.

In practice, this effect extends also to several occasions which are not ostensibly purely for the fun of it. A military parade is an excellent example, because once again the intention of the organisers is to stir and enthuse the populace; they want you to forget that the purpose of an army – any army – is to kill people. By extension, State funerals are highly suitable subjects for colour photography; the fact of death is subjugated to the achievements of the dead person in life.

Having thus established that some subjects are more suitable than others for reportage in colour, there are two things to consider. The first is the choice of equipment, and the second is the style or technique.

Equipment is (as ever) a matter of personal choice, but there are two groups of equipment which are widely used. The first is the simple, strong, fast-handling 35mm camera with standard or wide-angle lens. The traditional choice was always the Leica, though the reflex Nikon has supplanted it to a great extent. With a fast standard or 35mm lens, this type of gear is favoured by the photographer who likes to get in among the action. The alternative is the SLR equipped with a moderately long lens – 135-200mm, with the 180/2.8 a long-time favourite – used at a distance to pick out colourful details. Some photographers favour even longer lenses, but the trouble with these is that they are heavy and have limited maximum apertures, though the latter has now been remedied with the 300/2.8 lenses from Nikon and Canon; the drawbacks are now weight and price, instead.

The standard/wide approach is considerably more difficult to handle in colour than in black-and-white, principally because of the extra variable introduced in the form of colour. The black-and-white user can compose his picture so that the principal interest is highlighted, and the rest played down; if need be, an

– sports, games, parades, etc., where it does not really matter all that much if the picture is not particularly good and where in any case the pressure is nothing like as great as it might be whilst covering a war. The other thing which can be covered in colour is 'semi-soft' news, the kind of thing that drags on and on and in which the pictures are not particularly dated: in Vietnam or Afghanistan, for example, it did not much matter whether a picture was a day old or a month old – as long as it was a good enough picture.

Within this framework, there is the question of the attitude adopted by the photographer – what I earlier called the 'political' aspect. In the nature of reportage, what is being photographed is likely to arouse strong emotions. To take the example of Vietnam, the photographer could choose to show the undoubted heroism of many of those fighting there; the equally undoubted cowardice of others; the repulsive conditions in which the fighting was

unnecessarily bright patch near the edge can be darkened during printing to make sure that it does not draw the eye away from the main subject. With colour, instead of tone, this is very much more difficult: there is no intermediate printing process (though darkening can be effected in the final printing process, if the image is to be printed), and whilst an area of red may reproduce on black-and-white as an unobtrusive <u>tone</u>, as a <u>colour</u> it can be all too obvious.

Given that in colour reportage both this and the technical difficulties already mentioned must be mastered, it is scarcely surprising that so little reportage is in colour or that so few photographers are famed for their colour reportage. In practice, therefore, it tends to be fairly 'soft' news that is covered in colour

actually done; what happens to a man (American or Viet Cong) when he steps on an anti-personnel mine; the bars and whore-houses of Hanoi; or any of a hundred other things. Having photographed them, the use to which the pictures are put is another major consideration. Taking the bars and whorehouses, for example, he could portray them as a well-deserved rest for men on (or beyond) the limits of endurance or as a vile sink of iniquity sapping the spirits of innocent young men. Little though I love politics and the mouthings of extremists, I am forced to agree with the oft-repeated sentiment of some Marxist photographers, at least with respect to reportage: every act of taking a photograph is a political act. After that . . . it's your politics.

WE DO THE REST

At the very beginning of this book, I quoted the old Kodak slogan: "You press the button and we do the rest."

So far, we have looked mostly at the button-pushing side; indeed, as stated at the beginning, there is little reason (except, perhaps, in colour printing) not to let someone else do the rest. On the other hand, it is unrealistic to pretend that the photographer's involvement with the picture ends at the moment of pressing the button.

There is simply no space here to discuss at length the creative techniques possible in the darkroom; the afterwork you can perform on the print; the possibilities of hand-colouring, retouching, or mixing photography and artwork; or the best way to present a picture. The creative photographer must, however, be aware of all of this and more besides. The rest of this chapter explores, in no particular order, a number of other possibilities which you may care to follow up.

INFRA-RED AND ULTRA-VIOLET

In colour photography, there are two kinds of infra-red equipment. The first uses conventional cameras and special 'false colour' film. This is a normal integral tripack, but one layer is sensitised to green, one to red, and one to infra-red. All are sensitive to blue, so a blue-absorbing (= yellow) filter is always necessary. Alternatively, filters of other colours may be used: Kodak recommend light green, orange, red, and amber, but you may also care to experiment with 'effects' filters, just to see what happens. The false-colour IR films are very sensitive to heat, and should be refrigerated before use (as well as between exposure and development if much time elapses). Exposure is critical; bracketing is essential. Finally, not all cloth focal-plane shutter blinds are totally IR opaque, so keep the lens cap on between exposures unless you have a metal focal-plane (or leaf) shutter.

The other kind of IR photography records much longer waves, beyond about 14000Å, and requires special 'thermographic' cameras equipped with IR sensors; these are more electronic than conventionally photographic, and are responsible for 'heat trace photographs' showing phantom vehicles in car parks, phantom bodies in beds, etc. They are also staggeringly expensive, and are normally the preserve of government agencies and the like.

There are also two kinds of ultra-violet (UV) photography. The first uses UV 'light' directly, with a filter which is visually opaque. Only the UV wavelengths very close to the visible spectrum can pass through ordinary glass; for shorter

wavelengths, special quartz lenses are used. Much more interesting for the creative photographer is ultra-violet fluorescence photography.

This makes use of the fact that many materials fluoresce, or glow, when UV light shines upon them. The glow is quite faint, so it is usual to take such photographs in a darkened room with the only 'light source' being a UV fluorescent tube (obtainable from many electronics hobby stockists). The light recorded on the film comes from the fluorescent sample itself – which can be something as unusual as a starched shirt, a piece of plastic, a pile of laboratory chemicals, or many common minerals!

When using UV light you should ALWAYS wear goggles and take care to avoid undue exposure to the UV, which can otherwise produce painful conjunctivitis and artificial (but convincing) sunburn. You will not be aware of the adverse effects until an hour or two after excessive exposure, so it is all too easy to forget.

One of the great advantages of *modern slide films is that once you have taken the picture, the processing laboratory really does do the rest. This frees the photographer to concentrate on two things; taking the picture, and selling it. An insight into the commercial world often leaves amateurs feeling that perhaps they would do better not to sell their pictures. A typical art-director's reaction, on looking over the mountain pictures on this page, would be 'where can I put the text?' The flawless azure sky and the wildflowers on the grassy slopes are nothing to him: he just sees it in terms of so many ems in twelve point on fourteen, left justified, and wonders whether he can get all his text in. He will cheerfully chop about a carefully composed picture, and then wonder why the photographer looks pained: 'He's getting paid, isn't he?' This does not mean, though, that anything less than the best is good enough: the picture is* **selected** *on its merit, no matter how it may be violated later. Furthermore, as explained in the text, the larger-format picture has an additional and quite unfair advantage: when you are going through five hundred pictures, it is easier to see. Nevertheless, professional photographers can and do take beautiful pictures, just for their own amusement; much as they prize some of their commercial shots, their favourites were taken for love, not money. Every photograph must be taken as if it were the only one.*

WE DO THE REST

FILM PROCESSING

Standard processing (including speed adjustment) is best left to processing labs. There is, however, a variety of non-standard processing which can be interesting. This is processing positive (reversal) film as a negative. The alternative, processing negative as positive, is not always effective, as most colour negative films have a heavy orange cast to make printing easier. With some films this will decolourise during (reversal) processing, but you cannot rely on this.

The effects are weird and fascinating, especially if you choose your subjects carefully, and the only drawback is that some negative processing solutions will be contaminated if positive film is processed in them – so warn the lab first.

OTHER DARKROOM TECHNIQUES

In conventional colour printing (whether neg/pos or pos/pos) you can of course vary colour by varying filtration; you can also try out 'effects' filters, including 'action makers', starbursts, multi-image, etc.

In a less conventional field you can try tone separation; this involves making three separation negatives (by contact is easiest) from a black-and-white negative (in which case you have one for the highlights, one for the mid-tones, and one for the shadows) or from a colour slide (using whatever effects filters take your fancy). You then print through each of these in turn, using magenta for one, cyan for the next, and yellow for the third.

Very strange and wonderful effects are obtainable with this technique; those who get really hooked start evolving all sorts of variations of their own.

SLIDE COPYING

There is more to this apparently simple operation than meets the eye. The most important thing is that your light source must be consistent both in intensity and colour temperature; most people use electronic flash, though some use photo-floods. To avoid hot-spots, either bounce the light off a plain white card or use thick opal glass or Perspex (Lucite – methyl methacrylate) diffusers.

A good slow standard lens plus extension rings (or better still a bellows) will allow you to get close enough. Faster lenses than f/1.8, or wide-angles for reflexes, or worse still zooms, will give horrible results. Many professionals use an enlarger lens on the bellows for best results.

A problem in straight copying is contrast control; second generation pictures tend to be of higher contrast than originals. If you want the higher contrast (which you may do in creative work), fine. Otherwise, there are three solutions. One is to use special duplicating stock, only available in bulk. The second is to buy an Illumitran or similar with contrast control unit. The third is far cheaper and only slightly behind the Illumitran in convenience; leave some white background around the slide, so that some of the light from the copying table spills and flattens contrast – remember to leave off the lens hood. You can also try using a dirty UV filter.

When you introduce filters, the fun really starts. You can correct off colours, or add colour casts; you can use effects filters (including soft focus, action maker, etc.); and with a little care you can try partial filtering effects – the square 'system' filters are useful for this, and gel filters are even better.

***Whenever you shoot for** publication, always bear in mind how the pictures are to be used – how many, how big, and what sort of layout. The five* *pictures on these two pages would be a fine illustration for an article if used together; but which one sums the story up?*

WE DO THE REST

Even the most hackneyed *subjects can be photographed creatively. Two lighting effects which are always useful are* *shooting into the sun and underexposing, which gives the golden/silhouette effect above, and waiting until nightfall.*

You can also try lightening underexposed slides (darkening overexposed ones is usually less successful), and cropping. Slight cropping can often improve composition, and in exteme cases you can 'pull up' a tiny fraction of a picture so that the dye structure of the film shows up, as described earlier.

You can also 'dupe up' from 35mm to larger formats or 'dupe down' from larger formats to smaller; make 'sandwiches' or double exposures; and make colour negatives (or black-and-white negatives) from colour slides. Incidentally, the effects obtainable with a sandwich and a double exposure are <u>not</u> the same. In a sandwich, the dark part of one slide will obscure anything on the other but the light part will allow detail to show through. In a double exposure, the dark part of one slide will allow the other slide to be recorded, but the light parts will burn out any detail in the other.

Another method of slide copying is to copy the projected image. This is not suitable for high-quality duplicates, indistinguishable from the originals, but it does allow you to experiment with all kinds of projection surfaces. Patterns projected onto nudes are now almost hackneyed, but there is still plenty of scope for experiment; imagine projecting a scorpion or a centipede onto a nude.

The cathedral interior, above, is a prime example of technique in the service of creativity. The rising and swing front of a technical camera were used to preserve the soaring verticals; the high viewpoint and wide-angle lens (90mm on 5 x 4″) convey the airy spaciousness; and the blue light filtering through the stained-glass windows gives the right feeling of coolness and quiet. When you see a picture which really impresses you, always try to work out how it was taken. Do not neglect the everyday, though. Technically excellent pictures, even if they have appeared a hundred times before, are always in demand. Even quite ordinary 'stock shots,' taken with care, can be both attractive and saleable. The pictures on the left, from rollfilm trans-parencies, are a good example.

WE DO THE REST

Some places are so beautiful that it seems virtually impossible not to take a good picture; but when you look closely at the pictures on these two pages, you begin to see just how much artlessness is the result of art. The picture of Mount Fuji is a particularly fine example. The colours are what first catch the eye, with the blue of the sky, the white and purple of the mountain, and the red-gold of the paddy. Then you see the little figures, and last of all you realise that the white streak across the middle is the famous 'bullet train.' Everything – even down to the cloud beside the mountain – is just right. The photographer just mounted his camera on a tripod . . . and waited. The colours in the lakeside scene, and in the picture of Schloss Neuschwanstein, are the colours of autumn. It was not by chance that the photographer was there on that morning. The same goes for the other two pictures: the sun striking the church balances the dark mass of the mountain; the late summer haze on the steep cobbled streets reinforces the weariness of the cyclists. Nothing is left to chance.

AFTERWORK ON PRINTS

Straightforward spotting of prints should be routine; black spots are not usually too bad, but white ones can easily be filled in with retouching dyes. A few people can even do this on transparencies (large format, of course), but this requires skill bordering on the supernatural.

Retouching is another matter. Whilst the sable-hair brush and the knife come immediately to mind, professional retouchers make heavy use of the airbrush – a sort of miniature spraygun, resembling a fountain pen, which can be used to apply dye or pigment to the picture.

Airbrushing is widely used to enhance colours. The beautiful green eyes seen on the covers of many glossy magazines, for example, owe more to De Vilbiss (the airbrush manufacturers) than to nature or photography. White pigments allow too-bright colours to be 'knocked back,' or alternatively they can be 'shadowed' with black. It is also possible to block out unwanted areas: many of the pictures of immaculate machinery to be seen in manufacturers' catalogues started out as ordinary oily greasy machines against a working factory background, but the airbrush has removed the background and repainted the machine so that it appears pristine and as if photographed in a 'cove' with white floor, walls, and ceiling.

Although the airbrush is much employed in what might be called 'straight' retouching, there are also many creative uses which can be found for it. The first is adding colour to black-and-white pictures; the black-and-white face with red lips is maybe a cliché, but similar tricks can be employed to great effect. Secondly, the airbrush leaves no brush-strokes, and may be made to give a very 'photographic' effect. Many of the so-called 'photo-realist' painters employ the airbrush extensively, and among photographers Peter Barry is famous for his melding of photo-graphy and airbrush work to create strange and often surreal

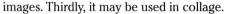

images. Thirdly, it may be used in collage.

Collage literally means 'glueing', and the essence of collage and montage is that the photograph is physically cut up and then glued back together. Parts can be omitted or repeated, and you can incorporate other photographs (or artwork or anything else) as you feel inclined.

When you want the handiwork to be obvious, you can exhibit the work itself; otherwise, you can copy it onto a new piece of film to present a 'seamless' new picture. If you are going to do this, it is best to work on a larger scale than the intended final result: for example, if you want a 10 x 8″ final print, make a work print at least 11 x 14″ and preferably even bigger, so that your handiwork is scaled down in the final picture.

There is also a sort of 'punk' school which tears, burns,

mangles, stains, and otherwise physically attacks prints or even slides. Whilst this can be very effective, one cannot help feeling that it is often done for effect – effect which, when the picture is displayed, turns out to be lacking.

CREATIVE PRESENTATION

Too many photographers lavish great time and effort on making a really superb image, and then file it away and forget about it. If a picture is worth spending time on – either in the taking or in the darkroom – it should also be worth displaying.

For a picture which is in itself a strong image, a plain frame is best; anything too ornate will only attract attention away from the picture. Personal tastes will vary, but a good choice is the modern brushed aluminium for a 'gallery' look, or plain light wood for more homely pictures such as landscapes or portraits.

On the other hand, it is perfectly possible to use a frame as a part of the picture: a heavy ornate gilt frame might suit a portrait, especially one in a deliberately old-fashioned style, and a heavy oak frame might go well with a rich blue sky.

Is there any way to improve your creativity? Yes. For a start, look at every picture you can. Analyse what you like about it, and what is wrong with it. But there is a more active way than that. Set yourself a theme. Before you start to photograph it, think about it: explore all its connotations in your mind. Go through your own picture files, imagining you are a picture editor – that should get you going. Then – and only then – get out and start taking pictures. The theme here is water. There is a lot more that can be said. Why not try to say it?

If you want to sell your pictures, you must also present them well. Transparencies, as already explained, are the only possible medium, and the usual method of presentation is the black card cut-out frame. The transparency (in or out of a projection frame in the case of 35mm) is taped inside the frame, and the whole thing is protected with an acetate envelope, clear on one side and frosted (to act as a diffuser) on the back. The normal size for 35mm and all rollfilm formats is a mask about 9 x 12 cm; this makes them a convenient size for handling and leaves space for any information needed to be typed on a plain white label and stuck to the mount. A typical caption might include place, date, and a brief description of what is going on, such as "Buddhist monastery, Rewalsar (Northern India) 1982." Few people are remotely interested in exposure details, films etc., but don't forget your name, address, and telephone number!

POSTSCRIPT

This book is ended: we have come to the end of the road as far as words and pictures are concerned. I have tried to do three things.

First, I have tried to explain as many tricks of the trade as possible, so that you will not be at a loss when it comes to bending the photographic process to suit your personal vision.

Secondly, I have tried to spark as many ideas as possible. You may not like some of the pictures in this book; you may disagree with some of the text; but the mere fact that you have reacted shows that your critical faculties are in some kind of working order.

Thirdly, I have tried to include a wide selection of work from some of the finest photographers around today. Do not be ashamed to copy them; copying is a traditional way of learning. On the other hand, do not copy them forever. Once you have mastered a technique – try to take it in a new direction. You will have to be pretty original, because many of the photographers featured in this book are very inventive, very versatile, and very creative; and for that very reason, none of them would pretend that he had done all there was to be done in a particular field.

You are not alone, though. This book is over, but every day there is a stream of new images to look at: on advertising hoardings, in magazines, in other books. Learn to look critically at everything you see. In pictures, try to work out what pleases you (or displeases you) about a particular image: is it the colour, the subject matter, the shape, the memories it evokes? Do not be too impressed by the arguments of others: of more than one critic it may fairly be said 'he writes a very fine picture', and in his excellent book The Painted Word Tom Wolfe exposes the absurdity of an art establishment which hides ever-diminishing creativity behind ever-expanding clouds of (nigh-meaningless) words.

Try to apply what you learn from the pictures to what you see around you in real life. You are impressed by a landscape: how could you best express that landscape, compressing a hundred square miles of land into a piece of coloured plastic 24 x 36mm? Would it look best in the evening, with lowering clouds; fresh and bright, in the dawn; sunbaked at noon; grey with rain? The picture you want may not be the easy one: you may have to come back day after day, perhaps year after year if you visit the place seldom, until you can match your vision. By all means take a reference picture, but do not confuse it with the picture in your mind: keep that pristine until you can get it down on film.

Finally, remember that creativity isn't easy; anyone who tells you it is must be lying. It can be frustrating; it can be heartbreaking; it can make you wonder why on earth you don't take up some easier hobby, like lion taming or brain surgery; but when it all goes right, you know why you do it.

Filters and Special Effects

Contents

Most of us probably learned the initials R.O.Y.G.B.I.V. whilst at school, (perhaps as 'Richard Of York Gave Battle In Vain'). Maybe we can still remember that they also stand for the constituent colours of white light – or, more likely, the colours of a rainbow. Either way, both have photographic applications. The former relates to filtration, whilst the latter perhaps gave the inspiration for diffraction gratings (rainbow filters) or prismatic (colour fringe) lens attachments.

R.O.Y.G.B.I.V. stands for red, orange, yellow, green, blue, indigo and violet, which is the visible spectrum. To this can be added infrared and ultraviolet, when 'visible' is in a photographic context. Some educationalists and scientists now exclude the indigo category, for reasons best known to themselves, whilst other scientists object most strongly to white light being separated into six or seven segments. They point out, quite rightly, that there is no such colour as red, only shades of red, etc. For example, both vermilion and carmine can be considered as being reds, yet the latter is an impure red, not found in the spectrum. The difference between theory and practice is that, in photographic terms, pure red, blue and green filters do exist, which for our purposes neatly divides the spectrum into three parts. These have been the basis of additive tricolour

photography since before the turn of the century. When it comes to subtractive colour photography, which is the vast majority nowadays, then the spectrum is once more divided into three sections. Two of these colours are 'cocktails', namely cyan (blue plus green) and magenta (red plus blue), whilst the third colour, yellow, comes neither shaken nor stirred.

Again, it must be stressed that this arbitrary division only relates to photographic rather than general science. The reason for this is that red, green and blue can be absorbed by cyan, magenta and yellow filters respectively, which is where the term complementary colours comes in. The importance of this will be described in the next chapter.

Photographic emulsions do not respond to colour in the same way as does the human eye. As can be seen from the graph below, the eye is most sensitive to the yellow/green area of the spectrum, whilst black and white panchromatic emulsion is particularly sensitive to blue light. Filters can be used to alter this response, the classic example being the use of a yellow filter to bring out clouds in what otherwise would be a plain grey sky. Facing page: A graphic illustration of the breakdown of white light into its constituent colours.

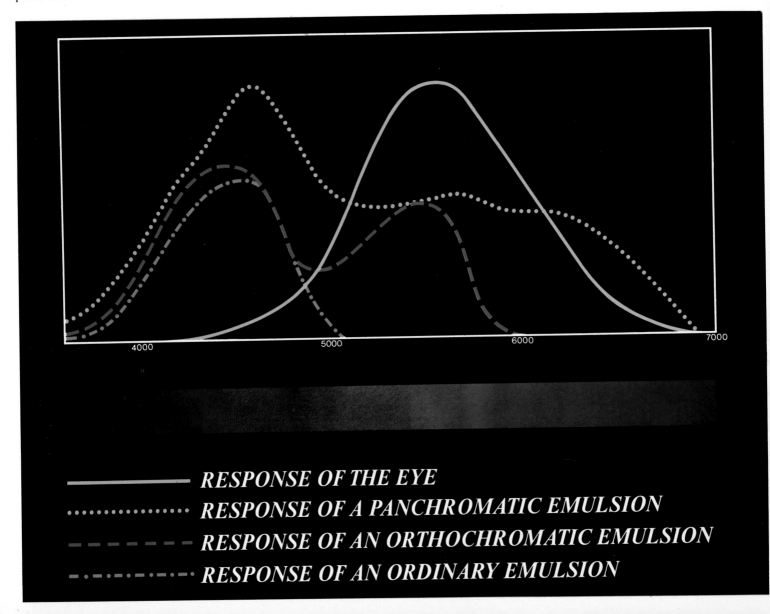

4000   5000   6000   7000

——————— *RESPONSE OF THE EYE*

·············· *RESPONSE OF A PANCHROMATIC EMULSION*

– – – – – *RESPONSE OF AN ORTHOCHROMATIC EMULSION*

– · – · – · *RESPONSE OF AN ORDINARY EMULSION*

RESPONSE OF THE EYE TO COLOUR

For some still unknown biological reason, the eye is more sensitive in the yellow to green area of the spectrum than in other regions. This phenomenon explains the use of fluorescent and sodium lighting, yellow car headlight bulbs and night driving glasses, yellow-green darkroom safelights and the fact that yellow Automobile Association road signs are more legible than the blue of the Royal Automobile Club! As lighting levels become lower, the colour sensitivity of the eye becomes monochromatic in the sense that images received by the retina become apparently more black and white.

As the brain is part of our optical system, it compensates to the degree that we can see a colour as we wish to see it and not as it actually is. A photographic emulsion does not have this advantage. With experience we learn to compensate for this compensation. Practised photographers, who can see the yellow-green cast of a 'white' fluorescent tube, always use a daylight-balanced transparency viewing box and examine colour swatches under the light source to be used for the photograph. Even with this precaution, the human eye/brain can be fooled. Modern technology has produced inks and dyes which contain amounts of fluorescins. These have the effect of making certain materials and products impossible to photograph to any degree of colour fidelity. Try telling a scientifically illiterate client that just because he can see it does not mean one can necessarily photograph it – yet this may well be so nowadays. In the same vein is the designer who wants a colour object photographed on the same colour background and is then disappointed with the result. Whilst a certain amount of compromise can be achieved in lighting, there is no argument that a pair of eyes see stereo-scopically whereas the camera lens is strictly mono. You may have seen a photographer squinting one-eyed at a subject. Now you know that the poor chap isn't afflicted, just being professional – or using experience!

Evaluation of colour can be a subjective matter – or simply personal taste – yet against this, any of us can be colour blind to an extent to which we are not aware. One of my uncles, quite late in life, purchased an expensive brown Harris tweed suit at an absolute bargain price. Arriving home, he was at a loss to understand why his family were horrified at his new peacock blue attire. Likewise, I have worked with a photographer who continually complained to Kodak, Agfa, Nikon, our colour lab and anybody else who would listen, that his results always had a green cast. Perhaps the acid test is to look at the tuning of friends' and family's colour TV sets. But then, just like yours of course, my colour vision is perfect!

RESPONSE of BLACK AND WHITE PHOTOGRAPHIC EMULSIONS to COLOUR

The colour sensitivity of modern emulsions falls into four main categories. These are shown in the table below.:

EMULSION	SENSITIVITY	SAFELIGHT
Super Panchromatic	+ Red Blue Green Yellow	Not advisable
Panchromatic	Red Blue Green Yellow	Blue-green (with care)
Orthochromatic	Blue Green Yellow	Red
Ordinary	Blue	Orange/yellow

35mm users may well ask why all these categories are mentioned, since ortho and ordinary emulsions are not available in cassettes. The short answer is that they are available in bulk

*Colour blindness is the inability to distinguish between colours or, at its more severe, to see them at all. This affliction, of which the sufferer may frequently be unaware, can be tested for by using various charts. Shown **above** is the British American Optical Company colour blindness test.*

lengths, and, since it is easy to load cassettes and develop the results under a safelight, it may be a subject worthy of experimentation for real enthusiasts or those business executives, scientists, doctors, academics and historians, who use audio-visual means of data presentation and recording. For the latter, the availability of high contrast (or line) emulsions is a plus factor.

'Super Panchromatic' was a pre-war designation for the fastest films around at that time. Designed primarily for low light level photography under tungsten sources, the net result was an over-sensitivity to the red end of the spectrum. This category of emulsion still exists today, though don't expect verification of this statement from the manufacturers of 400 ASA black and white films! The practical result of Super-Pan films was a lightening in tone of lipstick reds – generally worn only by the fairer sex, but also not unknown in the theatrical profession. To counteract anaemic rendition of lips – or the necessity to wear black lipstick – various manufacturers developed the pale blue 'half-watt' filter. This gave the effect of darkening red toned make-up to a satisfactory degree, but did have the disadvantage of reducing emulsion speed by around half a stop. Though (as far as I can ascertain) half-watt filters no longer exist in manufacturers' catalogues, the current equivalent for experimenters would be a Kodak Wratten CC20 or 30 Blue gelatin filter.

RESPONSE OF BLACK AND WHITE FILMS TO COLOUR

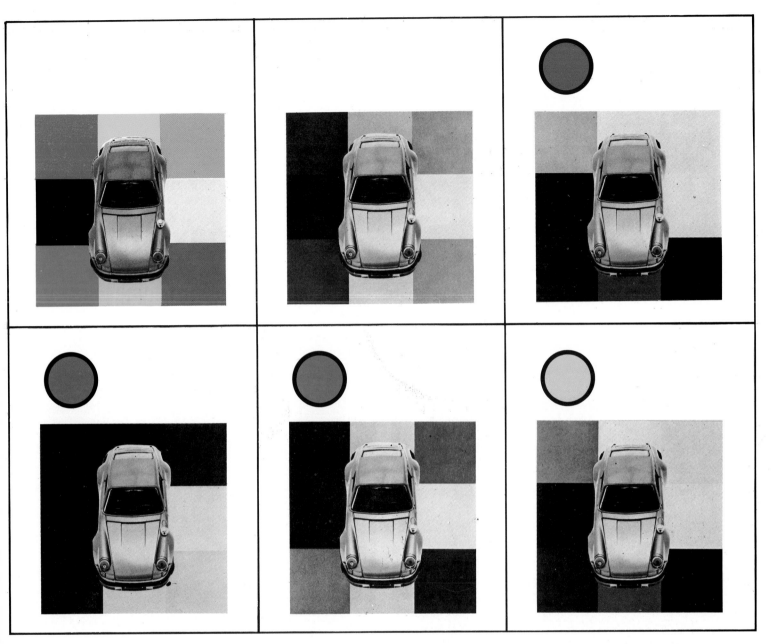

Panchromatic films have the best balanced response to light of all colours, though, in common with all photographic materials, there is an excess of sensitivity to blue light. This is best explained by the photographic phenomenon of a blue sky with white clouds being rendered as a very pale grey non-event, or, in other words, a yellow 'cloud' filter is still necessary, even though it will effectively halve the film speed.

Modern orthochromatic emulsions have a spectral sensitivity extending into orange, although using an orange filter will require a much higher factor than for a panchromatic film. Ortho emulsions in sheet film form can have the same superb tonal gradation as the best panchromatic films, which can be important in copy negative work. When contrast variation is necessary, this can be more easily achieved by visual development under a safelight. Ortho films, like Ilford's obsolete Selochrome, were widely used by medical photographers for fine detail rendition, with increased contrast of various skin conditions. If your nearest and dearest have freckles, avoid experimenting with orthochromatic portraits. The unflattering result will look like somebody's Syndrome.

*Coloured filters, when used in black and white photography, will lighten similar colours in the subject and darken their complementaries. The series of pictures **above** demonstrate this principle, each being the filtered rendering of the original colour picture **top left**. The picture **centre top** shows the tone separation of the unfiltered panchromatic emulsion.*

Ordinary emulsions (blue sensitive only), as found in bromide papers, black and white 'positive' films and some recording films, were historically the first. They are sometimes referred to by the misnomer of 'non-colour sensitive' emulsions – isn't blue a colour? Like some ortho films, they can have a superb tonal range. O.K., they are only suitable for recording black and white original images. However, should you ever wish to copy, say, airbrushed art work, line and wash, pencil drawings and X-rays, there is no better emulsion to use. Development by inspection is even easier than with ortho films – the safelight is brighter! The disadvantage, as stated, is the monochromatic colour sensitivity. Most old books on photography will show the 'black' daffodil to illustrate this point.

COLOUR TEMPERATURE

Colour temperature is a measurement of the incandescence of that heated black box, so beloved by physics teachers. It is expressed in degrees Kelvin, these in themselves being degrees Centigrade +273. Having got this over, it concerns photographers in that it is also a measurement of the degree of redness or blueness of a light source. Lighted candles, at one end of the scale, give a somewhat warm rendition, even on artificial light balanced colour film. Whilst at the other extreme is the sky – which looks pretty blue on a good day. This somewhat crude analogy can also be expressed in tabular form:–

Domestic lamps	ca. 2650 to 2850°Kelvin
Tungsten Halogen	3200°K
Photofloods	3400°K
Blue flashbulbs	ca. 5000°K
Mean noon sunlight	5400°K
Blue sky	12–18000°K

Tungsten type colour films are now balanced to 3200°K, whilst daylight films are for a 5400°K light source. For some

or too blue, use a correction filter taped over the flash head. The reason for this is an excess of ultraviolet, which the eye cannot see but the film can. Obviously with black and white film this is of no importance.

The only other bit of theory relating to colour temperature, which photographers may meet, is mired values. These indicate, numerically, a shift in colour temperature which is constant regardless of starting point. Mired values are either positive or negative. Amber or yellowish filters, which lower colour temperature, have a positive value, whilst bluish filters, which raise colour temperature, have a negative value.

As an example, 5400°K colour temperature has a mired value of 185. At 3200°K the mired value is 312. A Wratten 85B conversion filter is +131 mireds. A Wratten 80A conversion filter is −131 mireds. These are near enough to the 127 mired difference between daylight and tungsten balanced colour films. It follows therefore that a film used in a light source for which it was not designated can, with the appropriate filter, give adequate results. Some German and Japanese filter makers also use mired values for their red to blue correction filter ranges.

*A colour temperature meter, such as the Sixticolor **above** tells us, once we know the temperature for which our film is balanced, how 'blue' or 'red'* *is the prevailing light. Filters, indicated by the meter dial, can then be used to apply correction so as to bring the film into balance with the light.*

international standards reason this was measured at Washington USA in June at noon.

It is also worth mentioning that the colour temperature of tungsten lamps becomes lower with age and with voltage drop. Whether this ever in fact shows up on a colour picture is a matter for conjecture. For the really fussy, there are colour temperature meters on the market. These can be very useful when colour fidelity is important. They do have the disadvantage that they are unable to measure the discontinuous spectrum of fluorescent and other discharge lamps, which is a pity.

Electronic flashes are theoretically balanced to daylight colour films. In practice, even studio units can vary wildly between 5000 and 6500°K. If your results are consistently too red

FILTER EXPOSURE FACTORS

Now that we have discussed the main parameters affecting the usage of filters, it is possible to relate these to an explanation of how filter factors work.

These can best be described as the increase in exposure necessary in relation to filter colour and density, emulsion sensitivity, and the light source to be used.

Unfortunately, even with this information, there is still some theory to come. Those of you who have had enough can skip the next part and come back later.

A filter factor can be shown as being 2X, 3X, 4X, 5X and so on, sometimes in ½X or ⅓X increments. As long as it is a 2X, 4X,

through f1.25, 1.8, 2.5, 3.5, 4.5, 6.3, 9, 12.5, 18, 25, 36, and so on. In practice, these two systems slot neatly between each other, in half stop increments, thus it is possible to express a 3X filter factor at a metered f16 as needing an aperture of f9 – or midway between f8 and f11.

There is, however, a modern tendency to express this as 'f8 and a half', which is equally valid. Most modern small format lenses are calibrated in one stop increments, with a half stop indication (or click stop) – if you are lucky. Large format lenses, nowadays, indicate one third stop divisions – with or without clicks! This is in line with professional E6 emulsions, which can

Exposure measurement should *always be made* <u>*before*</u> *adding a graduated or spot filter* **above** *to the front of the lens. Taking a* *reading with such filters in position will result in overexposure of the unfiltered part of the shot.*

8X filter, exposure determination is simple. Beyond this it is necessary to understand the relationship between lens apertures, shutter speeds and ASA ratings, in order to juggle with say a 5½X or 2⅔X filter factor.

A question I am often asked is 'Why do I have to know about filter factors, when my camera's TTL meter will compensate automatically?' The answer, I am afraid, is that it will not do so in all cases. It may well cope adequately with blue, green and yellow filters, sometimes with magenta, seldom with orange, and not at all with red. This is due to the colour sensitivity – or lack of it – of the measuring cell employed. Reputable camera makers, like Nikon, will admit that exposure compensation is necessary for certain filter colours, and tell you how much extra to allow.

Most modern lenses use the International scale of apertures in the following progression, f1, 1.4, 2, 2.8, 4, 5.6, 8, 11, 16, 22, 32, 45 and so on. This was arrived at in 1910 after nearly thirty years of International Congress of Photography squabbles. However, it was not until after 1945, after the Internationals had won the war, that the rival Continental system was dropped. This progressed

theoretically have up to a one sixth of a stop tolerance, but in practice a third. Shutter priority exposure metering systems invariably work to around a half stop tolerance. Better makers like Canon and Leitz can improve on this.

Shutter speeds double up or halve temporally between marked values. A very few high precision camera makers allow for intermediate settings within stated limits. Some electronically controlled shutters, when part of an aperture preferred metering system, give stepless speeds. These cope beautifully with those filters which include halves or thirds in their factor – providing that the metering colour sensitivity is compatible with the filter employed.

When it comes to time exposures a filter factor becomes easier to allow for. Assuming that the basic exposure reading can be adjusted to show a shutter speed of one second – at one of the possible shutter/diaphragm combinations, the following table shows how simple exposure compensation for filter factors can be:–

Basic exposure	+	Filter factor	=	Adjusted exposure	or	Equivalent exposure increase in stops
1 second		1X		1 sec		0
1 second		1½X		1½ secs		+½
1 second		2X		2 secs		+1
1 second		3X		3 secs		+1½
1 second		4X		4 secs		+2
1 second		5X		5 secs		+2¼
1 second		6X		6 secs		+2½
1 second		7X		7 secs		+2¾
1 second		8X		8 secs		+3

ASA increments are in thirds, which gives yet a further way of compensating for filter factor increases in exposure. There is, however, a very great danger in that failure to reset the ASA dial of camera, or meter, can result in ruining the rest of the film by over-exposure when the filter is removed. The same applies to those cameras which have an exposure compensation dial. These are usually calibrated in half stops within a range of −2 to +2. 'Against the light' buttons, fitted to some automatic exposure cameras, are of plus one stop (2X), or sometimes plus two stops (4X), value. Again, a TTL system will not compensate correctly for some filter colours. If in doubt then bracket your exposures towards over-exposure.

The following table shows what happens when an ASA scale is used for filter factor compensation. An ASA 400 film has been used as the norm.

ASA setting	400	320	250	200	160	125	100	80	64	50
Filter factor	1X	1⅓X	1⅔X	2X	2⅔X	3⅓X	4X	5⅓X	6⅔X	8X
Equivalent exposure increase in stops	0	+⅓	+⅔	+1	+1⅓	+1⅔	+2	+2⅓	+2⅔	+3

Colour photography is where we finally meet all those filters with one third and two third fractional increases of factor – in profusion! As previously mentioned, there is less latitude, i.e. exposure tolerance, in colour than there is in a black and white emulsion. Furthermore, a pale filter over the lens has a far greater effect on colour balance than the same filter would have on monochromatic tones. Hence the one third fine tuning.

The last part of this section is by way of an explanation. Related only to black and white photography is the question of the light source and emulsion colour sensitivity affecting the filter factor.

Daylight at 5400°K contains more blue and ultra violet, yet at sunrise or sunset can be as red as 2000°K. Artificial light at 3400°K and below, contains more red and yellow than daylight. The green content of both sources is about the same.

All black and white emulsions are, if anything, over sensitive to blue light – this is where they get their daylight ASA rating. Consequently when used in artificial light which contains less blue, there is a drop in emulsion speed. This doesn't really matter with 35mm and 120 rollfilm, where a thinner negative has

advantages. It does matter with sheet film and Polaroid materials, where perhaps as much as a one stop loss of emulsion speed becomes critical. Because of this situation, it follows that filter factors can be of different values between the two light sources. The table below is an average of several manufacturers' data.

DAYLIGHT FILTER FACTORS	FILTER				
	Red	Orange	Yellow	Green	Blue
Medium speed panchromatic	8X	4X	3X	3½X	3X
Medium speed orthochromatic	–	NR	5X	4X	3X
ARTIFICIAL LIGHT FILTER FACTORS					
Medium speed panchromatic	5X	2½X	1½X	3X	5X
Medium speed orthochromatic	–	NR	2½X	3½X	5X

Whilst we probably all realise that using colour filters means increasing exposure, this is not so for grads or spots. Colour effects filters on colour *transparency film depend for their success on the colour they impart to the image, so err on the side of underexposure for maximum effect.*

Throughout the latter part of this chapter there may appear to be some mathematical inconsistencies, and I admit to a certain amount of rounding up and down. This is in line with practice, rather than the theory of academics arguing methods of calculation and decimal points. Whilst it is possible to measure the difference between exposures made at f1.4 and f1.5, between 1/100 sec and 1/125 sec, and between ASA 400 and ASA 450, most of us use our eyes for assessment rather than densitometers.

All lens manufacturers go to great lengths to produce the best optical performance which their marketing structure will stand. Yet having purchased a standard of optical excellence which their forbears would have committed murder for, both professional and amateur photographers alike will then deliberately go about destroying that image quality with a layer of organic glass (i.e. plastic) in a suitable attachment. All in the interests of creativity. Never let it be thought that I am against sticking things in front of a lens; throughout my professional career these very devices have often made the difference between success and failure – and in consequence between eating and starving. Nevertheless, I can assure those who have not tried it that it is possible to see a marked difference in definition between transparencies taken with and without a plastic filter – even with the naked eye. Of course, the larger the format the more likely one is to get away with it!

peril. The movie business, because of the limitation of using a single shutter speed, i.e. 24 frames per second – or 1/60 sec., has traditionally been far more expert in the use of filters than even the most advanced stills photographer.

For the last forty odd years, ciné cameramen have used special filters to give exactly the on-screen effect that they – or more likely, the director, requires. To this day, certain camera operators have 'secret' filter combinations made up. One such could be, say, a combination of Wratten 85 + neutral density + graduated neutral density + crosstar. Of course, with the Hoyarex, Cokin and other systems one can build up the same combination, but shooting through perhaps as much as 10 to 12mm of plastic gives an effect perhaps most kindly described as interesting. By comparison, glass/gelatin/glass sandwich movie filters are about half this thickness, and although they may cause slight focus shift, they will have less effect on definition and

Twenty odd years ago Leica enthusiasts argued and discussed, in print, the question of filters debilitating image quality – and this with Leitz! To be fair, Leitz probably produce the finest filters around – even with Zeiss still in the market, yet the progenitors of the Leica eventually admitted that although their superb filters were plane parallel to within a few microns (i.e. very flat indeed), in optimum photographic terms there was still some slight image degradation.

This debate began long before the advent of multi-coating; a technique which has helped to alleviate those problems which occur by adding what is in effect an extra lens element and air space! To sum up, it can be said that a good quality multi-coated glass filter will have little apparent effect upon image quality, provided that a good sized lens hood is also used. Plastic filters, partly by their nature, and more so because of the ingenuity of Jean Coquin, whilst existing in a sophisticated range at budget prices, can be discounted by optical purists only at their creative

image contrast. We are of course talking about big image magnifications rather than the snapshotter's postcard-sized colour print.

Gelatin filters, extant since the early days of photography, are fragile – even though lacquer coated, and whilst becoming as expensive as organic filters, are still much cheaper than glass. So where is the advantage? 'Gels' have little effect upon the definition of a lens, being nominally only 0.1mm thick, even when two or three are used together. They exist in a huge range which is totally unmatched by any other filter system. They cannot be multicoated and need a deep lenshood for this reason. Plate camera users invariably attach gels to the back element of a lens – ergo inside the camera, or sometimes even between the lens elements. This is not as horrific as it sounds, having been standard plate maker practice since the year dot.

With careful handling, gelatin filters can last for many years and furthermore take up little space in the gadget bag. I have

Kodak Wratten gels which are around twenty years old and still in usable condition. Keep gelatin filters in all their original packing and ensure that they remain flat and dry. The colour of synthetic organic dyes used may change in time, though my oldest gels show no marked colour difference when compared to a freshly purchased filter of the same designation.

Acetate filters of similar appearance to gelatin, are now marketed in a big enough colour correction range to rival Kodak's Wratten series. Whilst they are supposedly as optically clear as gelatin filters, my feeling is that, in comparison, they are slightly cloudy. This suspicion does not show up in practice, and after all, acetate has been used as a rollfilm base material for many years. Certainly, most colour printing filters are made of acetate for its greater resistance to heat.

C.P. filters, however, are not optically suitable for use over a lens. Cokin make an acetate 'Creative filter' set, and state that –

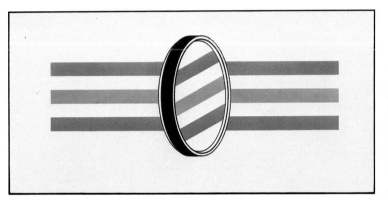

Filters, like lenses, come in varying qualities, and whilst it is argued that all filters degrade the image, poor examples can produce noticeably inferior results. Cheap glass filters are not always optically flat, leading to fall off in quality, whilst polarisers and neutral density filters may give poor colour rendering. For creative purposes, a second-rate filter may be ideal, in that it can reduce a lens' inherent 'bite.' The diagram above illustrates the effect a poor filter has on the light it transmits.

'optical definition is not the same as normal optical filters.' Cemented filters are the oldest type around. They appeared in various shades of yellow as soon as orthochromatic emulsions became available. Used primarily to give an enhanced sky rendering on black and white negatives, they were also known as ortho screens.

A cemented filter consists of a gelatin filter sandwiched between two pieces of thin, optically flat glass, and glued together with Canada balsam. If this sounds somewhat crude, remember that camera lens elements are stuck together in the same way.

These filters are widely used by the cinema industry and to a lesser extent by large format professional photographers. It is not generally known that many proprietary polarising and rainbow (diffraction grating) filters are still made in this way. If you are unlucky enough to drop one and cause it to start separating, you will see the rather nasty, characteristically blotchy appearance of the now useless filter.

Special combination filters and very large sizes can still be supplied to special order. In fact if you are prepared to pay for it, then anything can be made.

Last, and commonest of all, are the dyed-in-the-mass glass filters. It is perhaps surprising that, in spite of all the ancient stained glass windows around the world, this is a comparatively modern process. For some reason (other than the Leica and Contax), coloured glass filters first appeared in Germany in the late nineteen twenties, being generally available in colours other than yellow by 1935, when exotic coloured glasses like graduated green or yellow, infrared and ultraviolet were catalogued.

Postwar reparations allowed other countries to take advantage of German technology at no cost. In Britain, Chance glass from Pilkington Bros. gave rise to a spate of badly made filter holders and their contents, in a range – other than various yellows, which had been the pre-war pattern. Even the burgeoning French photographic industry could see the logic of this market. America had been producing some dyed-in-the-mass glass filters during the war, though really wedded to the 'home-grown' Wratten cemented filters. It was, of course, the Japanese who finally produced glass filters of a standard equal to pre-war Germany's best, albeit many years later.

The quality of glass filters still varies enormously. Not only in terms of the glass used, the degree of parallelism between faces, but also ultimately in the thickness of the final product. It is much easier to make a thick filter, for fewer get broken in manufacture. The best glass filters are thin, which means less diffraction, though there is then the problem of fragility. This can be overcome by the use of tension springs to hold the filter glass against the front rim of its mount. Rolleiflex filters, for instance, will rattle when shaken hard, but seldom seem to break when accidentally dropped. At one time, Leitz and Zeiss were so proud of their thin filters that both engraved the company logo minutely on the glass!

WHY USE FILTERS?

When we photographers first encounter filters, there is a tendency to be confused by what we learned in art class, where mixing colours produced the immediate shade we required – well sometimes! A colour cast in colour photography works in the same way, though the film will see the effect more strongly than the eye. Where the confusion between painting and photography occurs is when dealing with complementary colours, an understanding of which is necessary for black and white photography, neg-pos colour printing, the correction of colour casts in transparencies and pos-pos colour printing processes.

The chart below illustrates the make-up (or breakdown) of white light for both additive and subtractive colour photography processes.

The triangle below shows the *relationship between colours, with complementaries shown opposite one another. A filter absorbs and hence darkens its complementary colour whilst lightening its own colour.* ***Facing page bottom:*** *Square plastic* *filter systems of the Cokin type are an affordable and flexible method of increasing creativity. Filters and effects can be combined to make even the mundane appear dramatic, as in the filtered fish-eye shot* ***facing page top.***

ADDITIVE		
	Absorbs	Reflects/transmits
RED (= Yellow + Magenta)	CYAN (= Blue + Green)	RED
BLUE (= Cyan + Magenta)	YELLOW (= Red + Green)	BLUE
GREEN (= Cyan + Yellow)	MAGENTA (= Red + Blue)	GREEN

SUBTRACTIVE		
	Absorbs	Reflects/transmits
CYAN (= Blue + Green)	RED	CYAN (= Blue + Green)
MAGENTA (= Red + Blue)	GREEN	MAGENTA (= Red + Blue)
YELLOW (= Red + Green)	BLUE	YELLOW (= Red + Green)

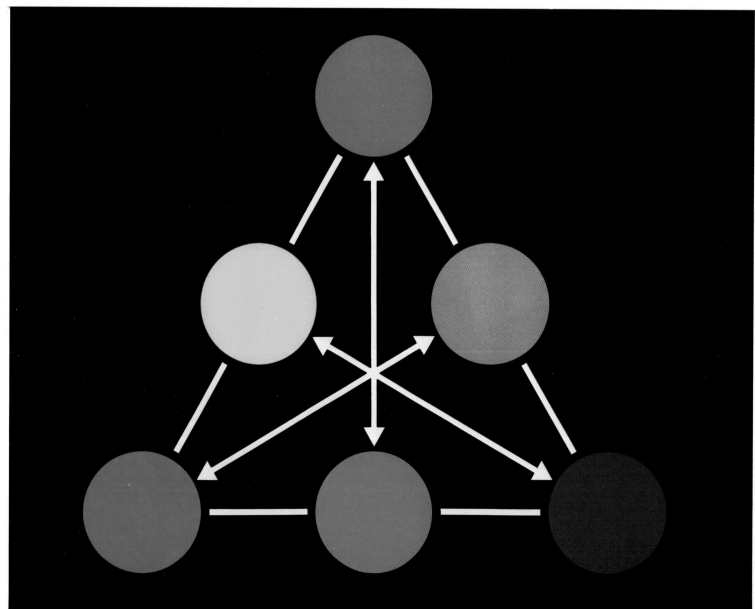

FILTERS FOR BLACK AND WHITE PHOTOGRAPHY

Any good black and white film can record a range of tones in excess of a ratio of 100:1. The figure is still impressive, even when reduced by about half in the final print. These lovely theoretical figures are arrived at by measuring black, grey and white densities from a negative of a black, grey and white original.

Unfortunately, most subjects are composed of colours. It is quite possible to find two colours which, whilst readily separable to the eye, will, when photographed, be rendered in the same shade of grey. To correct this situation we must use a filter. If the subject colours happen to be complementary, then something has to go, in which case we would filter for the colour which needs to be predominantly rendered. It is as well to observe the cardinal rule in filtration, which is: 'A like colour will lighten tone, whilst a complementary will darken.' This in turn can be used to correct, emphasise or exaggerate tones at will. Just to complicate matters further, there is the question of degree. Just how absolute theory differs from practice is shown in the following table:

Subject colour	Filter to lighten tone Maximum – minimum (transmits)	Filter to darken tone Maximum – minimum (absorbs)
Red	Red-orange-yellow	Green-blue
Orange	Red-orange-yellow	Green-blue
Yellow	Orange-yellow	Blue-green
Green	Green-yellow	Red-orange
Blue	Violet/blue	Red-orange-yellow-green
Violet	Violet-blue	Red-orange-yellow-green

Apart from the use of 'mixed' filters such as magenta and cyan (covered elsewhere), there is also the yellow-green compromise still offered by many filter makers. This has the effect of darkening the sky whilst lightening foliage. Salmon coloured filters were in vogue in the late 1930s, when dramatic skies were all the rage. These gave the effect of moderately darkening a sky and deciduous foliage tones, whilst conifers became virtual silhouettes. The nearest modern equivalents are Wratten CC30 magenta, or a proprietary FLD colour correction filter.

Filters for b/w photography can be placed into four main categories. These are: correction, contrast, detail and haze penetration, all of which can overlap in function to any degree the photographer chooses. Black and white film has a colour sensitivity which differs from the eye in that most emulsions over-react to ultraviolet and blue. We are all aware of the phenomenon whereby a beautiful blue sky with white clouds is recorded as a bald non-event. Whilst this is mostly as a result of the nature of photographic emulsion, it can also be because an area of sky is relatively brighter than other parts of the subject and in consequence over-exposed. Contrasty films, developers and over development can cause or add to this effect. Apart from the aforementioned, the usual remedy is to use a filter to absorb the excess 'blue' light. In ultimate terms, this is normally a yellow-green or medium yellow filter of between two and three times exposure factor.

Contrast filters can fit partly into the correction filter category. Where the subject is a light-coloured building against a blue sky for instance, the use of anything between a yellow and red filter will effectively increase the contrast between subject and background, whereas a flat, hazy landscape, photographed through an orange or red filter will gain in contrast due to the elimination of the softening atmospheric conditions. Monochromatic subjects, such as magenta stained tissue section on a microscope slide, will need a complementary filter – in this case deep green – in

order to produce sufficient contrast, and this really is the name of the game. The final result may be a false rendering of the subject, but clarity is the desired effect.

In a different category are the detail filters, where a filter of like colour to the subject is used. Probably the best known is an orange 'furniture' filter, which will bring out the maximum grain detail in stained woodwork. For rosewood or dark mahogany, even a red filter can be used. Careful printing is necessary, as otherwise an object of dark toned wood could appear to have been made of pine or teak!

Haze penetration filters range from the colourless ultra-violet, through yellow and orange to red for maximum effect. It requires considerable experience, or a knowledge of meteorology, to know with some degree of exactitude which to use. As a rough guide, a UV is generally only used at the high altitudes encountered in mountain or aerial photography, where anything stronger will result in a sky which is darkened too much. Nearer sea level, one uses yellow, orange or red filters, depending upon the amount of haze penetration desired and the degree to which a 'normal' to black sky is acceptable. On dull days a red filter can be used, which, whilst darkening foliage will also increase the overall contrast of the scene. Haze filters will not penetrate mist or fog, so if in doubt try the lot!

With the exception of the huge Kodak Wratten gelatin filter list, a quick glance at any top manufacturer's catalogue is likely to provide a range of filters for black and white photography which consists of something like six colours, of which at least two are likely to be supplied in differing strengths. These could well consist of yellow (in three strengths), orange, red (in two strengths), yellow-green, green and pale blue. This is apart from ultraviolet, infrared and those filters primarily intended for colour photography. A summary could well consist of:

Colour	Approximate factor	Use
Light yellow	1½ x	Mild correction of sky tones. Stronger at high altitudes.
Medium „	2 x	Stronger correction of sky tones with mild haze penetration properties.
Dark „	3 x	
Orange	4 x	Over correction of sky tones. Stronger haze penetration.
Light red	6 x	Dramatic sky rendition. Strongest haze penetration. Use for 'moonlight' effects.
Red	8 x	
Yellow-green	3 x	Standard correction filter. Darkens sky and lightens foliage.
Green	4 x	Similar in effect to medium yellow but lightens foliage to a greater degree.
Pale blue	2 x	For correction of skin tones under artificial light.

For the inexperienced, and long before the days of Polaroid, there were monochromatic (or panchromatic) vision filters. Intended for use in front of the eye, or camera viewfinder, these would render any subject in monochromatic tones, or at least a semblance of such. They would effectively give the photographer a guide as to the rendition of coloured objects on b/w film, or to a subject's tonal differences. Traditionally of deep blue glass, they are nowadays either an olive green colour or, as Kodak describe their current Wratten 90 P.V. gelatin filter, 'a dark greyish amber.'

Whether panchromatic vision filters are in fact of any use is a subjective matter, though there is no doubt that they do reduce the eye's adaptability in assessing tonal differences.

Above: Cloud detail can be enhanced to varying degrees by using yellow, orange or red filters.

COLOUR CORRECTION AND LIGHT BALANCING FILTERS

The whole field of colour correction filters for colour film is generally considered to be a Kodak benefit, even though Wratten designations have become the generic nomenclature. To be fair, although Agfa still make a set of camera filters – primarily intended for their non-E6 emulsions, these are only generally known and appreciated on the European mainland.

Kodak colour correction filters fall into three main categories. There are the 80 series blue filters, intended to convert daylight balanced colour film emulsions to artificial light conditions, and their antitheses the 85 series orange/brown, or amber filters. Apart from their intended use, the 80 filters can be used as 'moonlight' filters in daylight, whilst the 85 series can be used to produce – or enhance – a sunset. In either case do not allow for the approximately one stop filter factor, as this amount of under exposure adds to the effect. A TTL metering system will have to be 'cheated' by use of the ASA setting if a reading is taken with the filter attached.

The second category of Kodak filter is the warming 81 (brown) and 82 (blue) series of filters. Primarily intended for colour temperature correction, these are designed to work in smaller increments than the 80 or 85 conversion filters. The 81 family are widely used by fashion and portrait photographers as suntan filters. The exposure factor of ⅓ to ⅔rds of a stop is ignored, thereby producing a slightly dark and warm transparency.

Colour negatives produced with 81 filtration will make the final printing easier – if this is the effect you are after – but in this case allow for the filter factor. The 81EF filter, as the strongest of the range, is generally used only in very overcast daylight conditions where the light is decidedly blue. The lighter 81C and 81B are my preferred filter strengths for general use, rather than the still paler 81 and 81A.

KODAK LIGHT BALANCING FILTERS

These filters are intended for use over the camera lens to raise or lower the colour temperature of the light reaching the film by much smaller increments than conversion filters.

Filter Colour	WRATTEN Filter Number	Exposure Increase in stops*	To obtain 3200K from:	To obtain 3400K from:	Mired Shift Value
Bluish	82C + 82C	$1^1{}_3$	2490K	2610K	– 89
	82C + 82B	$1^1{}_3$	2570K	2700K	– 77
	82C + 82A	1	2650K	2780K	– 62
	82C + 82	1	2720K	2870K	– 55
	82C	⅔	2800K	2950K	– 45
	82B	⅔	2900K	3060K	– 32
	82A	⅓	3000K	3180K	– 18
	82	⅓	3100K	3290K	– 10
	No filter necessary		3200K	3400K	–
Brownish	81	⅓	3300K	3510K	+ 10
	81A	⅓	3400K	3630K	+ 18
	81B	⅓	3500K	3740K	+ 27
	8C	⅓	3600K	3850K	+ 35
	81EF	⅔	3850K	4140K	+ 53

*These values are approximate. For critical work they should be checked by practical tests, especially if more than one filter is used.

Chart reproduced by courtesy of Kodak Ltd.

Blue 82 filters are frequently used in early morning, late afternoon or winter sun conditions to take out the excess warmth of the light, particularly when any degree of subject colour fidelity is necessary. Under these conditions, a certain amount of experience, or experimentation, is necessary in the absence of a colour temperature meter, though be assured that any 82 filter will effect some improvement. Unlike the 81 series, 82's can be used in combination for even greater correction.

As mentioned above, manufacturers other than Kodak use 81 and 82 designations. These will not necessarily match the original, but will usually still work in a pleasing manner.

Kodak's third category of colour correction (CC) filters is for even finer tuning of colour transparency materials. The range consists of six colours namely: cyan, magenta, yellow, red, green and blue, in a range of six densities from CC05 to CC50. Each designated density of each colour is roughly comparable in the degree of colour shift, though not in the exposure factor required.

The primary use of CC filters is in correcting mild colour casts. This tends to be the prerogative of professional studio photographers, where there is time to shoot a test transparency. It is not unknown for a colour laboratory to have a consistent processing colour bias. Here the professional will have a constant CC filter pack to correct this. Likewise he may well have a favourite CC filter which suits his particular electronic flash unit or lighting technique. There are also many subjects which do not reproduce on film in the same colour/s as they appear to the eye. The client may well insist that his product does so, which can call for a very odd CC filter combination. Bounced light can produce colour casts which need to be filtered out. A CC15M or 30M (Magenta) is a good starter for correction of a yellow-green fluorescent lighting colour bias on daylight emulsion. Other needs for CC filters are; reciprocity shift – where a long or ultra-short exposure changes the colour balance of an emulsion; underwater photography, which requires a CCR (Red) filter; and the colour corrections required when making duplicate trans-parencies – especially when duping film is employed.

manual exposure compensation. Checking the camera's exposure readout with and without the filter, will show how closely (or otherwise) the meter cell's colour sensitivity copes with the filter makers recommended factor.

Judging which CC filter to use for correction on a test, or clip, transparency is partially subjective but mostly a matter of experienced colour vision. The first essential is that the transparency is examined on a daylight corrected viewing box, or even by projection. Holding a 'tranny' up to a window or fluorescent ceiling light is not good enough, even if it is the common practice of people who should know better.

Colour corrected fluorescent tubes are made by Phillips (and others) specifically for the graphic arts and photographic trades. They are not much more expensive than conventional tubes. I should add that they are only for viewing, and are not suitable for use as a photographic light source.

Let us assume that a test transparency is too blue, but of

The list of uses for CC filters is almost endless – at least in the studio, where after making a test shot, one always ensures that the final photograph is taken on the same film batch number as the test. Oh yes, I nearly forgot to mention that professional colour emulsions can vary in colour rendition from batch to batch!

With transparency materials, it is important to consider the final colour effect that you wish to achieve. Facing page: An 81 brown warming filter was used in the top shot to enhance skin colour without upsetting the overall colour balance. The

three pictures above, from left to right, show the effect of using daylight film unfiltered, with 85C orange colour correction filter and with 80B blue filter, normally used with such film under tungsten light.

KODAK COLOUR COMPENSATING FILTERS

Cyan	CC05C	CC10C	CC20C	CC30C	CC40C	CC50C
Exposure Increase*	⅓ stop	⅓ stop	⅓ stop	⅔ stop	⅔ stop	1 stop
Magenta	CC05M	CC10M	CC20M	CC30M	CC40M	CC50M
Exposure Increase*	⅓ stop	⅓ stop	⅓ stop	⅔ stop	⅔ stop	⅔ stop
Yellow	CC05Y	CC10Y	CC20Y	CC30Y	CC40Y	CC50Y
Exposure Increase*	–	⅓ stop	⅓ stop	⅓ stop	⅓ stop	⅔ stop
Red	CC05R	CC10R	CC20R	CC30R	CC40R	CC50R
Exposure Increase*	⅓ stop	⅓ stop	⅓ stop	⅔ stop	⅔ stop	1 stop
Green	CC05G	CC10G	CC20G	CC30G	CC40G	CC50G
Exposure Increase*	⅓ stop	⅓ stop	⅓ stop	⅔ stop	⅔ stop	1 stop
Blue	CC05B	CC10B	CC20B	CC30B	CC40B	CC50B
Exposure Increase*	⅓ stop	⅓ stop	⅔ stop	⅔ stop	1 stop	1⅔ stop

*These values are approximate. For critical work they should be checked by practical test, especially if more than one filter is used.

Chart reproduced by courtesy of Kodak Ltd.

As CC filters – up to a 30 density – are not intense in colour, most TTL exposure metering systems will compensate for the filter factor automatically. The 40 and 50 densities in red (particularly) and magenta (sometimes) will usually need

correct density. Place it on the viewing box and try putting a CC20 yellow filter over half of it, the idea being to bring the blue cast back to a neutral grey. Upon examination, the CC20Y overcorrects, producing a yellow rather than grey tone. Next try a CC10Y, which looks just about correct. Some photographers prefer to wave the filter to and fro across one eye, whilst viewing the transparency. Whichever method is preferred, we still end up with a CC10Y correction. The trick then is to use HALF the visual density, i.e. CC05Y, over the lens. The reason for this is the different response of an emulsion in comparison to the eye.

Transparency evaluation by projection works in a similar fashion, except that in this case the test filter is held over the projection lens. It is quite possible to bind a gelatin correction filter together with the transparency, thereby saving a reshoot. Here one would of course use a visual correction density. Transparency retouchers are capable of dyeing a CC density into a transparency, but this is a skill beyond the ability of most photographers and best not attempted except in desperation.

ULTRAVIOLET FILTERS

The wavelength range of the normal photographic spectrum falls between 3250 and 7000 on the Ånström Scale(AU), or can be measured in Nanometres (nm), which are numerically the same, less a zero! The response of the eye falls approximately between 4200 and 6800AU, whilst the ultraviolet region is between 3250 and 4000. It therefore follows that photographic emulsions, with their high sensitivity towards blue and ultraviolet, can produce a result which the eye cannot appreciate until it sees the photograph!

Any sunlit long distance subject, such as mountains or water, is likely to show both a loss of contrast and definition, and in the case of colour films, a blue cast. This is because under these conditions a high proportion of ultraviolet radiation becomes scattered in the atmosphere to produce haze. This should not be confused with mist and fog where there is water vapour and/or dust present as well. Atmospheric haze scatters very little red, little yellow, some green, more blue and a helluva lot of ultraviolet. Conversely, and perhaps confusingly, there is less of a problem with UV at altitudes above 6,000ft (2,000m), for, though the UV content is higher – as sunburn enthusiasts will attest, the atmosphere is thinner, so the scatter is correspondingly lower. This is, however, not true for aerial photography where pictures are taken through the atmosphere towards the ground.

The reduction of ultraviolet can be achieved in several ways. The development of rare earth glasses, some with UV absorbing properties, multicoating techniques and even UV absorbing lens element cements, have all contributed to the modern lens' 'warm' colour rendering, with its reduction in ultraviolet effect. Many current lenses in fact no longer need an ultraviolet absorbing filter for normal use. The practice of using a UV filter at all times is unnecessary. I appreciate that there is the excuse of lens protection, but what are lenscaps for? All too often an expensive lens is degraded by the use of a cheap filter. If you

The ultraviolet filter can be virtually ignored where filter factors are concerned. The extra exposure required is minimal and camera meters will allow for this automatically. There are several different filters marketed under the general term 'ultraviolet.' They reduce to some extent the blue cast caused by ultraviolet rays but *the effect of all but the stronger varieties is negligible except at high altitudes or by the sea. They do serve, however, as efficient lens protectors, but this must be balanced against the fact that, being mounted on the front of the lens, a lenshood is particularly important to counteract flare.*

must pursue this route, then buy the best multicoated filter around.

UV filters fall into several different categories:

Filter colour	Suitable film	Approximate factor	Typical example
Clear	B/w only	1.1 x	Nikon L37, L37C
Clear (stronger)	B/w only	1.2 x	Nikon L39
Very light yellow	B/w only	1.3 x	Kodak 2A
Very light yellow (stronger)	B/w only	1.5 x	Kodak 2B
Pinkish	Colour + b/w	1.2 x	Kodak IA (skylight)
Pinkish (stronger)	Colour + b/w	1.25 x	Nikon LIBC
Very pale amber	Colour + b/w	1.3 x	Kodak 8l, Nikon A2
Very pale red	Colour + b/w	1.5 x	Hasselblad CR1.5, Kodak CC 05 Red
Very pale magenta	Colour only	1.3 x	Kodak CC 05 Magenta

As these filter factors are so low, they can in most cases be safely ignored.

The loss of definition and contrast due to ultraviolet scatter in black and white work can be corrected to any degree the photographer wishes. On the other hand, it can be left alone – or even enhanced – if this gives the desired effect.

Assuming that a reduction is required, then there is a choice of colourless and yellow filters, through to the over-correction of orange and red if maximum haze penetration is the name of the game. Colourless UV filters are primarily used at high altitudes where anything stronger will produce an over-dramatic sky rendition. This is particularly true in winter sunlight, where the sky is an intense blue anyway. 1A skylight and 1B filters are virtually interchangeable with their colourless counterparts. Very pale yellow filters fall somewhere between these and a 2x yellow or yellow-green tone correction filter. Pale amber or red filters perform about the same function as a skylight, whilst a CC05M has virtually no effect.

Colourless UV filters for b/w work can be used with colour films, though the effect is negligible except at high altitudes; much better to use an 1A or 1B. Pale amber, red or magenta filters all absorb about the same degree of ultraviolet and are primarily used to add a degree of colour correction as well. German lenses used to give a bluer rendering than their warmer Japanese counterparts – some still do. This is where the additional warmth of amber, red or magenta may be preferable. Their other use is with telephoto and long focus lenses, where haze is apt to be amplified, or with zoom lenses of low contrast characteristics.

Colour films also have some degree of colour bias between 'warm' and 'cool', which can affect their sensitivity towards ultraviolet and its subsequent rendering. This is just as much a subjective matter as over-blue mountain or seascape pictures. All too often the photographer's memory is short and he will accept the final result as truth. Likewise, there are those who prefer snowscapes with blue shadows as a result of too much UV. "They are more picturesque, even if incorrect," I was once told by an art editor!

Ultraviolet casts can also occur with electronic flash, particularly with powerful studio units, where a standard filter pack could be, say, a Wratten 1A + Wratten CC05 Yellow. As any colour cast can be a combination of lens, film, flash unit and colour lab, this is a matter for experimentation, though as a rule there is no harm in always using a skylight filter when an electronic flash is employed. It is usually possible to tape a gelatin filter over the flash head and forget it.

POLARISING FILTERS

Synthetic polarising material was developed in 1934 by the brilliant Dr Edwin Land of sunglasses and instant picture fame. The first such camera filters were produced by Leitz and Zeiss a few years later. Light is composed of a wave motion vibrating around a central axis. If it is restricted to one plane, we have polarised light, which can be obtained in several ways. One is by reflection from a non-metallic surface such as water, glass or paint – where the effect is greatest when reflection takes place at angles of between 30° and 40°; is less at other angles and disappears altogether at 0° and 90°. Light is also polarised quite strongly in those sectors of the sky at a 90° angle to the sun. At other angles the effect is weaker and vanishes at 0° and 180° to the sun. Another method is the use of a special screen. What this polarising filter does is to suppress light vibrating in one particular plane, whilst freely passing light vibrating in a plane at 90° to it.

In practice, by revolving a pola filter on the lens, it becomes possible to reduce or eliminate a reflection by coinciding the plane of suppression of the filter with the plane of reflection of the subject. In the case of a sky the result is similar in that removal of flare or reflection effectively darkens that subject.

For those who are interested, polarising material consists of a gelatin film holding in suspension a multitude of double-refracting, dichroic, ultra-microscopic and similarly-orientated crystalline needles of luteocobaltic periodosulphate.

Yes, Well!!

The cobaltic bit explains the bluish tinge of the better pola filters. A greenish tinge in a cheap filter will produce a corresponding colour cast.

All polarising filters have to be laminated between optical glass flats, though Kodak do sell the original in gelatin form. Polarising filters destroy a certain amount of resolution, so adding

281

The deep blue of the sky, the clean white of the far building and the brilliant greens of the meadow in the superb shot **left** are all typical of the improvement that a polarising filter can provide in ideal conditions. Compensation for filter density has to be made when making exposure readings, but be careful not to overdo this; slight under-exposure will help to accentuate the richness. A rather better known property of polarising filters is their ability to reduce, or eliminate, reflections in surfaces other than metal. The most obvious example is that of glass, in which reflections can be very distracting. In the pair of pictures **top** the reflections **left** have been considerably reduced **right,** allowing the contents of the shop window to be seen more clearly. In the pictures **above** the reflections in the lid of the box **left** have been completely eliminated **right.**

POLARISING FILTERS

this factor to poor quality glass flats, colour and mount, means that a cheaper filter is capable of pretty nasty results. Likewise, because they are of cemented construction (or should be), there is a possibility of separation should the filter be dropped or subjected to heat and/or damp. The better manufacturers use edge sealing and multicoat the optical flats, which all helps. Nowadays polarising filters are produced in two variants – the traditional linear being augmented by the more recent circular type. The latter works in exactly the same way, but is designed for use with those TTL metering systems which utilise polarising matter as part of the light receptor. The use of a conventional linear polariser in such cases will produce errors in exposure readings. The camera makers handbook should warn of this. Among the independents who produce both types are Hoya and B + W.

Because of the necessary density of polarising material there must also be an exposure increase. This will be between 2.5X and 4X. Strangely, perhaps, the lower factors come from the better manufacturers. Two polarising filters may be used together, but watch out for vignetting, particularly with wide angle lenses. When polarising filters are used in tandem, they can become a variable density ND filter, or be used as a ciné fading device. The loss of resolution can, however, be high.

Pola filters have three distinct uses, with both black and white and colour films: the elimination or reduction of reflections and flare, to darken a sky, and to increase contrast and colour saturation.

Reflections can work both ways for the photographer. On the one hand he may wish to take a reflection out of a shop window – fine – on the other hand he wishes to photograph a blue sea and sky. Perhaps the shot would look better with a darker sky, so out comes the polarising filter. The sky has now been rendered darker but the sea has gone dirty grey. Quite simply he has polarised the blue reflection of the sky out of the sea. Had he been using black and white film, then the effect would have been similar to using a medium yellow filter, i.e. a darker sky and some elimination of haze to increase overall negative contrast. The result would be at its strongest with the sun behind him.

The toughened glass screen of a motor car can show up with a pattern when photographed with a pola filter. Though this tends to occur mostly in a studio situation, I have had it happen when shooting through both coach and aircraft windows.

Fortunately there is no need to expend film when trying a polarising filter, as the eye gives an accurate indication of what the film will see. Non-reflex camera users have had to use this technique since pola filters were invented, first obtaining a setting, and then transferring filter to camera at the same setting.

A rather specialist use for polarising filters is in the photography of oil paintings. No matter how one lights them, there will always be highlights somewhere. Using a conventional, ninety degree, two light copy set-up, with pola filters over each light <u>and</u> on the camera, gets over this problem.

Expensive but nice!

A polarising filter, for rather complex scientific reasons, polarises, as its name implies, light passing through it. One of the ways this particular property of polarising filters affects us as photographers is that it intensifies and cleans colours. This is most noticeable in skies, which take on a much deeper blue, allowing clouds to stand out quite dramatically. On dull days, however, it has no such effect; instead it simply cuts down the light reaching the film and can, in fact, serve as a weak neutral density filter.

NEUTRAL DENSITY FILTERS

The use of neutral density filters started in the film industry many years ago. A fixed shutter speed of 1/30 sec (now 1/60 sec), meant that depth of field – controlled by the lens' iris diaphragm, could not be varied except by reducing light intensity, which in daylight was not possible. Nowadays, with a still camera – loaded with 400 ASA film – and a trip to the beach, the same situation exists. Too much depth of field can be a detraction to an outdoor portrait, or any other subject which needs to be 'lifted' from its surroundings. An analogy is the picture which looked great (at f1.8) in the SLR viewfinder, but when processed (in f8 form) is disappointing!

Neutral density filters can be obtained in strengths from an arbitrary 1¼x to a massive 10,000x factor. Or from ¼ stop to 13½ stops. Even denser N.D's can be used for Solar and other scientific photography. Neutral density filters can be marked in exposure factors like, say, 2x, 4x, or 8x, or may frequently be found with density marked in a geometric progression, such as 0.3, 0.6 or 0.9. This goes back to the days of black and white cinematography, where a one stop increase in exposure corresponded to a 0.3 increase in negative density.

Whilst most N.D. filters can be used with either b/w or colour materials, they do vary in colour from maker to maker.

There is a tendency for the cheapest to give a slightly green cast, or occasionally blue. This doesn't matter for b/w work or for colour prints, where the printer can make the correction. In colour transparencies, a green cast can do nasty things to skin tones. 'Warmer' emulsions, like amateur Ektachrome, Fujichrome, and Agfachrome 100 can cancel out a slight green cast. Obviously the greater the filter density the greater the colour cast. Additionally there is the question of optical clarity. If you habitually use a deep N.D., I would recommend the use of an expensive glass, or appositely a cheap gelatin filter!

Variable density N.D. filters are a combination of polarising and N.D. technology. In their simplest state they use cross polarisation between two pola filters in order to produce a darker image. Rotating one filter in relation to the other can produce varying exposure factors of say 2x to 4x. When a N.D. filter is also included, the factors can rise to a 3x to 8x range. Cinematographers use Vario-N.D. filters to fade a scene in or out. Professional stills photographers use them to adjust the ASA speed of Polaroid materials to match the emulsion intended for the final photograph. In both cases neither loss of definition or colour cast is important.

SLR users will find one big disadvantage in using the deeper neutral density filters, in that the viewfinder image also becomes 2x, 4x, or what have you, darker. This can be overcome by using a frame – or optical – viewfinder in the camera's accessory shoe, and framing the subject this way. A more expensive alternative is another camera body loaded with slower film!

NEUTRAL DENSITY FILTERS
'Wratten' 96 Filters

Neutral-density filters absorb light of all wavelengths throughout the visible spectrum and thus permit the reduction of light intensity by a definite ratio. They have many uses in all branches of photography and scientific optical work. These filters are not intended for use in the ultraviolet or infrared regions of the spectrum. Density values, percentage transmissions and approximate filter factors of Neutral-density filters are given below. Other densities can be built up by combining two or more filters, e.g. ND 5.0 can be obtained by combining ND 1.0 and ND 4.0.

Name	Density	Percentage Transmission	Filter Factor	Exposure Increase (in stops)
ND 0.1	0.1	80	1¼	⅓
ND 0.2	0.2	63	1½	⅔
ND 0.3	0.3	50	2	1
ND 0.4	0.4	40	2½	1⅓
ND 0.5	0.5	32	3	1⅔
ND 0.6	0.6	25	4	2
ND 0.7	0.7	20	5	2⅓
ND 0.8	0.8	16	6	2⅔
ND 0.9	0.9	13	8	3
ND 1.0	1.0	10	10	3⅓
ND 2.0	2.0	1	100	6⅔
ND 3.0	3.0	0.1	1,000	10
ND 4.0	4.0	0.01	10,000	13⅓

Chart reproduced by courtesy of Kodak Ltd.

If the light is very bright, or we have loaded with fast film, and require either a wide aperture, slow shutter speed, or both, then an answer is the neutral density filter. For the pictures on the facing page a wide aperture was required top to show only the child in sharp focus, and a shutter speed of seconds was needed bottom to blur the running water. Neither would have been possible without neutral density filters. Foreground, subject and background sharp above, and separated via wide aperture/ neutral density above left.

INFRARED BLACK AND WHITE

Infrared filters, for black and white photography, vary in density from deep red to the visually opaque, and must be used with a special infrared sensitive film. Infrared emulsions were introduced in the middle nineteen thirties for aerial photography, since one property of using these long wavelengths is the penetration of haze. Other properties include the ability to differentiate between deciduous and coniferous foliage and between them and camouflage! There are medical uses, where for instance it is possible to photograph the subcutaneous layers of human skin in order to show vein, and sometimes artery, configuration. Inevitably, as soon as infrared emulsions became available in 35mm form, the process was also exploited by pictorialists and newspaper photographers. An infrared landscape has a black sky, with grass and deciduous trees being rendered as white. Photo-journalists were quick to discover that pictures could be taken by this so-called 'black light', leaving the subject unaware that a photograph had been taken. There was a spate of pictures taken of cinema audiences, and the like, illuminated by means of a flash bulb covered with an infrared, and therefore visually opaque, lacquer. There were also oblique aerial photographs, taken from over London, which showed the south coast over sixty miles away.

One classic infrared photograph, taken in the Himalayas, 'reached' a distance of one hundred and fifty miles. During the last war, German photographers took pictures across the English Channel, which clearly showed the opposition's radar installations. Since infrared is also heat, there were gimmick photographs taken by the 'light' of an electric iron. In fact everybody had fun!

Since infrared is a long wavelength, camera lenses do not give correct focus at their engraved settings so an adjustment must be made. Most lenses will have a correction mark for infinity, which is an increase in camera/lens extension of 1/300th of the lens' focal length. This same rule applies for the

Dark skies, white grass and foliage as well as tremendous haze penetration are what can be expected from black and white infrared film. Conventional black and white developers can be used in processing, and pronounced grain should be expected. The film should be kept refrigerated, loaded in darkness and if used in a viewfinder camera with cloth shutter, the lenscap should be kept on between exposures. Because of the density of some of the appropriate filters, extended exposures may be necessary. Bracketing is recommended in this somewhat imprecise area of photography.

markings of other camera/subject distances. In practice this means correction of unmarked lenses as follows:

<u>Focal length</u> when infinity setting is required

  35mm use   33ft (or 10 metres) setting
  50mm use   50ft (or 15 metres) setting
  90mm use   90ft (or 27 metres) setting
135mm use 132ft (or 40 metres) setting
200mm use 200ft (or 60 metres) setting

    Since the 'feet' settings roughly correspond numerically to the focal length of the lens, this is an easy one to remember. Thank you Leitz!

    Shorter than 35mm focal lengths need no correction from the normal infinity setting, provided the aperture used is not wider than f11 – f16.

    The ubiquitous SLR must be used on a tripod, since viewing through the necessarily dark red, or opaque, infrared filter is impossible. The alternative is to use an optical viewfinder in the camera's accessory shoe. Coupled rangefinder cameras are easier to use – with one exception. Bellows are not opaque to infrared for anything other than a short time. It is sometimes possible to wrap them in aluminium foil for protection. Keep the lenscap on for protection if your camera has a rubberised cloth focal plane shutter.

    Before loading an infrared film into the camera, read the instructions. These will tell you that the camera must be loaded in total darkness. The felt light trap of a 35mm cassette is not opaque to infrared. Likewise, since infrared is also heat, the film should be kept cool in order to avoid fogging. Its shelf life is short, so if you do not intend to use it soon after purchase keep it in the refrigerator. Six months is about the maximum storage time, though I have used Kodak film which had been refrigerated for a year, with satisfactory results.

    Infrared film is grainy and of low contrast. You should increase development by 20% when using a Kodak D76 or Ilford ID11, MQ Borax type of developer. If using Kodak D19B, or other contrast developer, then times can be normal. Finer grain developers are not recommended.

    The intensity of infrared within daylight or artificial light cannot be accurately measured, so it is always advisable to bracket exposures by at least one stop, and preferably two, over the normal meter reading. Most infrared films are around 40 ASA when used with an 8X deep red filter, less with the ultimate opaque type. Leitz, for instance, quote the exposure factor of their deepest filter as being between 8X and 60X in daylight.

    The whole technique of infrared photography may sound complex, yet it is something that every photographer should try at least once – preferably in the summer when there is more foliage about.

INFRARED COLOUR

The techniques of using infrared colour film – or false colour as it has been described – are not so very different from the black and white version except in filtration. Perhaps surprisingly, the standard filter is a deep yellow, which means that an SLR is usable! The reason for this is in the sensitization of the basically Kodak Ektachrome three layer emulsions. Infrared Ektachrome was developed during the U.S.A.'s space programme. It is now widely used for surveying and forestation work as well as for military purposes.

Using the normal deep yellow filter again separates the camouflage from the trees. Conifers are rendered as a deep red. A further benefit is that tree and crop disease can be recognised by a colour difference from the norm due to a change in infrared reflection from the foliage. Inevitably someone had to try changing the filter colour, or leaving it off altogether. The results can be of a startling science fiction nature. Skies can become green or magenta or yellow, whilst the infrared reflection qualities of everyday subjects have to be tried to be believed. There is no alternative but to use a lot of film, experimenting with filter changes as well as subjects. The whole exercise must be regarded as a gamble, but when it comes off – wow!

Developed primarily for *scientific purposes, infrared colour film can nevertheless be used to great effect in pictorial photography. The key to success with this unpredictable medium is experimentation. For focusing, distances should be set against the R mark on the* *lens. Dramatic colour shifts can be obtained by altering filtration, suggestions for this being given in the leaflet packed with the film. The pictures shown **top and bottom right,** were taken using Y2 and No. 11 Wratten filters.*

FOG FILTERS

Fog filters are the antithesis of UV and haze filters in that they artificially induce a degree of 'mistiness.' Made in two forms, the earliest and still current, fog filters are blue or violet in colour. What these do is enhance the over-sensitivity towards blue and violet light possessed by all black and white emulsions, with a consequent loss of contrast in the negative. With an exposure factor of between 4x and 10x it hardly seems worthwhile.

In comparison, the more modern dichroic fog filter has a lower exposure factor and is usable with both black and white and colour films. Invariably produced in at least three grades – often more, the dichroic fog filter can have a factor of between 2x and 6x. If there is any snag, it is a certain loss of definition, but then the very nature of the filter makes this unimportant. For once, a lack of coating does not matter either, so the cheapest fog filters work as well as the best. My only proviso to this statement is that if you intend to use, say, a sky filter in conjunction with a dichroic, then better quality filters will produce less overall degradation of the image.

With perhaps a choice of five grades of fog filter, as in the GOYO/TORA range, it may be difficult to decide which one to choose for 'starters.' If in doubt, purchase a mid range density. Fog filters can be used in tandem, subject to the usual warning about the possibility of vignetting with wide angle lenses.

You will find that the milder grades of fog filter can sometimes be used to produce a different kind of portrait. Because of their nature, it becomes possible to use much more contrasty lighting than usual: indeed, a single light technique is often adequate. Used out of doors, it is as well not to use a fog filter on a subject which has clearly defined shadows. Even after these are degraded, the result will look more like an accident rather than a deliberate attempt at producing something different. Perhaps surprisingly, I have yet to meet a fog filter which produces a cast on colour film, and (for once) TTL exposure meters will compensate automatically for the filter density. However, there is a strong case to be made for overexposing by half a stop, which adds to the fog effect. For the sake of an extra frame, try it both ways at your first attempt and take it from there. Finally, for the impecuneous, it is possible to use an evenly fogged b/w negative for experimentation before purchasing the real thing.

*Some of the most attractive landscapes can be taken in foggy, or misty, conditions. As usual, however, just as when we don't want fog we get it, so, when we want it it's not there! This is the time to employ the fog filter, which is available in varying strengths, and certainly imparts an impression of mistiness to a subject, as may be seen in the comparative shots **below,** and the beautiful subject **right.** Filters, of course, cannot show recession in the same way as real mist, and you should choose a day when there are no strong shadows, as their presence immediately gives the game away.*

GRADUATED FILTERS

Graduated filters have become a college student, amateur and 'art' photographer's cliché – which is a pity. Not that they and M. Coquin are entirely to blame, as art directors have been requesting fall-off backgrounds for years now, so that a headline can be reversed out of an advertisement, brochure or showcard. 'Grads' were invented by film cameramen many moons ago. At first they were homemade from neutral density filters until technologists found not only ways of graduating without steps, but also how to do it in glass as well as plastic and gelatin. Most graduated filters around today are plastic.

Apart from the usual neutral, blue, green, orange, red and yellow types, there are exotics like pink, emerald, mauve and tobacco. Cokin hold the record with a range of 14 filters, by providing two densities of each shade, whilst B + W make eight colours and two neutral density filters in glass. Cokin is unique in marketing two graduated fog filters which are very useful for those not wishing to go the whole fog!

The Actina/Filtek catalogue not only lists ten graduated filters but offers the same range of colours plus the added ingredient of slight fog. Known as pastel grads, they give more gradation than other filters of this type.

Grads are available in either circular or rectangular form, the latter having the advantage that the 'horizon' of the filter is invariably adjustable in the mount. Both types can be revolved

Graduated filters are an extremely useful addition to any photographer's creative armoury. Available in a variety of colours, they can transform a rather dull shot **right** *into a dramatic one* **below and below right.** *Take care, however, that the 'join' doesn't look too obvious* **below!** *Exposure measurement should be made* <u>without</u> *the filter in position; otherwise the deep colour of the sky* **facing page** *will be lost.*

GRADUATED FILTERS

When using graduated filters, unless you want to produce an obviously unreal, and startling, result, try to match the mood and feeling of the location to the colour of the filter. The various strengths of 'tobacco' graduated filters, used for the pictures on these pages, are usually very effective; they don't jar the eye and are not too far removed from nature's colouring – given a little imagination! The picture **right,** had a filter not been used, would have been almost monochromatic and, it might be argued, far less interesting. All these 'grads' can, of course, be used to colour one side of a shot if that is what is wanted.

through 90°, used upside down or at an angle. Square and oblong filters are usually large enough to be used with most lenses, including wide angles, and have the advantage that they can be used (with adaptors) on several different lens mount sizes.

The first rectangular graduated filter for still photography was made for the Rolleiflex camera over 40 years ago, and as it had an adjustable 'horizon' mount, no exposure increase was necessary. The same is true today providing a TTL reading, made without the filter attached, can be held on manual or memory. Otherwise a half stop decrease to the indicated reading is the usual compensation, in order to avoid over-exposure.

Graduated filters are affected more by focal length than aperture. Compared to the standard lens, a wide angle will produce a sharper 'horizon' whilst a telephoto, or long focus lens, will provide more graduation, providing it is not used at its smallest aperture. To a certain extent this is also true for any normal focal length lenses.

Any graduated filter can be used on black and white film. The tonal effects upon the parts of the subject being 'filtered' are just the same as if a full filter of the same colour was used, except that that portion of the subject will be rendered darker. The

GRADUATED FILTERS

degree of darkening will depend upon the colour and density of the graduated filter.

When used with colour film, the filter colour will add a cast of the same colour to the subject area covered. Here the mix of colours is similar to a paintbox. For instance, a yellow filter over a blue sky will produce a green sky, and a red filter over green foliage will produce brown foliage. This is, of course, a matter of degree, and some very intense grads are quite capable of obliterating the subject colour.

It is possible to use graduated filters in tandem, so that a subject can be tinted in two colours. Likewise, two same colour filters, or a colour with a neutral density can be used to make a more intense filter. Doing this with plastic filters will ensure a loss of definition which may or may not be acceptable.

*The landscape with horses facing page, top is certainly attractive as it stands. The lower picture, however, shows just how dramatically the whole mood can be changed by the use of a graduated grey filter. Now the sky is dark and threatening, and the horses stand out in sharp contrast. Shown on **this page** are some further examples of the change that can be affected by the use of yellow, orange and tobacco graduated filters.*

HALF, DUAL AND TRI COLOUR FILTERS

Half colour, dual colour and tri-colour filters come into the same category of construction in that they all consist of a glass/gelatin/glass sandwich. Half colour filters have a single colour 'gel' across the mount aperture. Most makers give a choice of about four colour options, whilst Hoya have a range of eleven, including two neutral density filters. Some makers allow for rotation of the mount, whilst cheaper alternatives require the filter holder to be partially unscrewed from the lens mount. The effect of a half colour filter is to add a colour tint to either a foreground or background – or for that matter to either side, or even diagonally. An increase in exposure is seldom necessary unless the effect required is to lighten the foreground. This is achieved by allowing for the filter factor of the coloured half.

Dual colour filters perform a similar function, except that each half is (usually) in somewhere near complementary colours. Typical combinations are: Red/Blue, Orange/Green, and Yellow/Mauve. Obviously, since the filter is totally coloured, an increase in exposure is necessary. This can vary from 2X to 6X, depending upon the individual makers colour densities. A third variant of this filter form is the Tricolour. In this instance, the filter

The pictures featured on these pages, whether they are universally liked or not, are certainly arresting, and this is often the purpose of the photographic image. Plenty of *film should be shot when attempting subjects like these, with exposures bracketed and slight changes of filter position; most of them are not identically repeatable.*

HALF, DUAL AND TRI COLOUR FILTERS

glass is divided into three colours in either three plane parallel or 120° segmented form. A rotating mount is normally fitted as standard.

Using any of these filters requires a certain amount of experimentation before they can be mastered. The effect of lens 'taking' aperture is drastic. When viewing with an SLR camera at full aperture, the effect may be either too gradual or just right. But, by the time the lens is shut down to its smallest stop, then the division(s) in the filter glass will be rendered sharp in the final result. As reducing lens aperture gradually produces an equally gradual effect, a depth of field preview control on the camera is useful, to say the least, in evaluating the final result. It may be that when using a fast film in bright light, it is necessary to use the camera's highest shutter speed, or even to employ an additional neutral density filter, in order to allow for a wide enough aperture setting.

This effect also varies with focal length, in that longer lenses are easier to use with these filters than wide angles. With the latter, the horizon of a landscape shot may have to be positioned exactly half way up the frame, in order to achieve a pleasing division of tone.

Whilst half colour filters do not theoretically require any increase in basic exposure, it may be that a TTL metering pattern will not now read correctly. It is as well to note the exposure readout with and without the filter in place, and to note any discrepancy for future reference. Dual colour and tri-colour filters alike may also fool the camera's metering system, since colour sensitivity of TTL meters varies from maker to maker. The camera's handbook should mention any compensation needed for orange and red filters, as these are the usual culprits. Again, a practical preview can well save future disappointment.

As far as professional photography is concerned, the use of strong filters, especially mixes of colour such as can be produced by half colour, dual, or even tri-colour filters, is usually at the request of a client or art director, or an attempt by the photographer to create something 'different.' Many photographers spend a good deal of their time photographing girls or couples by the sea and, after all, one seascape is much like another. Different models, clothes and ideas all help – as do special effects filters. The combination of colours can be startling, restful – or however you choose to interpret the feeling.

HALF, DUAL AND TRI COLOUR FILTERS

Although many of the effects created by half or multi-coloured filters can appear weird and unreal as, indeed, they should – that is often the intention – they can also be used simply to enhance what already exists in the picture. This is true of the beautiful, geometrically-composed shot **facing page** *of Muttart Conservatory in Edmonton, Canada. Another example is shown by the picture* **below,** *with its dramatically deepened sky and sea. The picture* **right** *was taken through a tri-colour filter and, additionally, a multi-image prism.*

POPS, PASTELS AND SEPIAS

This section is about using those filters primarily intended for black and white work on colour film, or vice versa. Modern marketing techniques have produced a situation whereby these applications have seemingly become a separate photographic entity, whereas in reality the categories of pop and pastel filters, for instance, are in fact only extensions to the uses of filters which have been around for a long time. This statement in no way denigrates those manufacturers who produce these items, indeed they are to be commended for providing an awareness of a creative technique, which has, until recently, nominally only been the province of the experimentally minded or those in the audio visual field.

Any pop, pastel or sepia filter will have its near equivalent in the Kodak catalogue of gelatin filters, albeit that Kodak's intended use was for some abstruse scientific application. Most pop filters for instance can be equated with the following:-

WRATTEN DESIGNATION	COLOUR
11	Emerald Green
21/22	Oranges
15/16	Chrome Yellows
25	Intense Red
30/31	Shocking Pinks
34A	Violet
44	Turquoise
46/47	Intense Blues
58	Intense Green

Some of these filters have a pretty high factor but then so do many pop filters. The oft repeated warning about TTL metering systems still applies.

The result of using pop filters can be startling, though whether one likes the end result is purely a matter of taste. The deeper colours, and red in particular, will give a totally monochromatic result often with an apparent lack of resolution and contrast. Any of the 'combination' colours such as magenta, cyan or yellow-green may allow an intense subject colour to show through. There are no hard and fast rules on this, it is simply a matter of having a go. Two of the most effective subjects can be the sun upon water or a silhouette. Since these are largely monochromatic anyway, a bit of colour enhancement can only add interest.

Conventional red, orange, yellow, blue and green filters for black and white photography can perform the same function as a Wratten or pop filter, providing that there is sufficient intensity of colour, or alternatively that under-exposure (of a colour transparency material) can be employed to heighten the colour enhancement.

Pastel filters too can be equated to the densest Wratten colour correction filters, though the Actina ten-filter pastel range adds three colours which Kodak haven't yet produced in a suitable strength. Pastel filters, like pop filters, work well with subjects of high contrast and yet in addition can produce ethereal results when used in flat lighting conditions, to give an end effect

***Once we get into the realms of** bright, or 'pop' colours in filtration there is seldom any doubt that we are going for effect, rather than enhancing reality. Blue swans, green snow, sea and sky are not what we expect to find in nature.*

Nevertheless, providing you do not attempt to take every shot in this way, startling and attractive pictures can result. Once again, all these filters can be combined with starbursts or any other filters you care to try.

which appears to have been taken in coloured mist.
Monochromatic subjects can be considered to work the best, as
strong subject colours will show through a pastel. The choice of a
sympathetic filter colour can still give a feeling of reality – but
enhanced reality. Pastels are also suited to photography of
people, particularly when a romantic feeling is required. The
addition of a soft focus or diffusing filter will heighten the result,
as will a small amount of over-exposure on colour transparency
film. Colour negative workers can always make a lighter print.

Pastel filter factors range from virtually one to about +1½
stops. As they are not of high density, most TTL metering systems
will cope adequately, though this will vary with differing filter and
camera maker combinations.

Sepia filters can be described like 'An 85B by any other
name would work as sweetly'! This is the basis, though an 81EF
could be added to taste. Using a Wratten 85 series alone will
produce a redder sepia tone, adding an 81 will make the result
yellower. There is plenty of room for experimentation and plenty
of proprietary sepia filters for those who want one off the shelf.
Incidentally, as with all other filters, one maker's sepia will not
necessarily match another's, and the results are better in daylight
and with electronic flash than with tungsten, where the results
can be too 'hot'.

I suspect that sepia filtration first occurred in the cinema
world, where black and white footage mixes more easily with
colour when toned sepia. The same is true for audio visual
presentations, or even television – if they can be bothered.

Sepia filters work well in portraiture for special effects.
Brunettes become auburn and redheads become very red, whilst
blonde hair becomes a colour not found in nature, only in a
bottle! Still life sets can work well in sepia, provided that the
subject's colours are warm toned, blues and greens are apt to be
neutralised.

Exposure factor varies between +⅔rds and +1½ stops. A
half stop under-exposure, on colour transparency stock, can
often help by adding richness to the end result. The exception is

It would be easy to make the
statement that certain colours
are better than others for certain
pictures, but whether a colour
works well or not depends
entirely on whether it pleases
you and achieves the result you
want. However, most people

would find the pale yellow/
*green **top**, the pink **right**, the*
*blue **above** and certainly the*
*sepia **facing page** acceptable*
and attractive, but they would
probably be less happy with the
*heavy magenta **above left**.*

It is best to include strong shapes in pictures when using strongly coloured filters. The deep colours have the effect of rendering objects as silhouettes; therefore they should be recognisable from their shapes as buildings, ships or whatever. The alternative is to give more exposure so that detail is visible, but this weakens the strong colour. The sun in shot helps to give variation to the colour by providing a lighter tone around it. In the original transparency **facing page, bottom left** the sun was exactly in the centre of the frame. The lens was stopped right down and this has created the 'halo' visible across the buildings. There is no mistaking any of the subjects on these pages, and 'wine dark seas' – and skies – are yours to command **left and below!**

portraiture, where the skin tones should be nearer to nature as the added warmth of the filter colour is sufficient in itself.

Filters specifically intended for colour photography can be used with black and white films. Probably the most useful is an 85B which gives much the same sky rendering as a deep yellow or pale orange. An FL-Day or FL-B filter does the same thing to a lesser degree. The amber 81C and EF work like a UV filter at high altitudes to reduce haze and give a darker sky rendition, whilst the blue 82 filters will act like a half-watt filter for artificial light portraiture on fast panchromatic film. The 80 series blue filters are too strong for anything but colour correction, i.e. strengthening a yellow subject, or alternatively can be used to emphasise haze and fog in a landscape. Only the densest CC filters are of any use with black and white films, and then only for mild tonal correction. Both CC50 Yellow and CC50 Green may be used as sky filters.

*The rather delicate colours in the pictures **left and facing page top right** are not intrusive and lend an added feeling of 'romance.' Most fish-eye lenses **below** are provided with built-in filters. The curvature of the front element and the field of view makes the use of conventional filters impossible. All the pictures in this section should be considered merely as ideas; experiment, combine filters, find out how far you want to go along the special effects road, but remember that good photography is what counts.*

COLOUR BACK

The unique Cokin colour back filter set is a means of colouring the background whilst retaining normal colour in a foreground subject. This set is primarily intended for fashion or portrait photography, but can be adapted for other uses. The principle is to use complementary colours and synchro-sunlight flash technique. For example, if the cyan filter is placed over the lens, this will colour the whole subject in that colour. However, if the flash is now covered by a complementary orange filter, the subject will appear in normal colour, whilst the area of the background not lit by the flash will remain cyan. The Cokin filter set comprises:

> mauve + yellow
> orange + cyan
> cyan + orange
> yellow + mauve

The flash and filter sizes are different. Like Jean Coquin, I will give my explanation of this technique in a hypothetical situation. An ASA 64 film exposed in sunlight could need an exposure of 1/125 sec at f11. The subject, a full length figure, is ten feet from the camera. To light this figure correctly from the camera position would require a flash guide number of 110 with ASA 64 film, or in other words, 110 divided by ten feet = f11. Assuming that this is possible, we have a complete synchro-sunlight flash balance. This is the starting point for colour back filters. Each of these pairs of filters has a filter factor which must be allowed for. Here comes another complication and that is, that whilst the orange/cyan pair virtually match in factor, the yellow/mauve filters have about a stop discrepancy between them which must be taken into consideration.

The Cokin brochure quotes 'Be patient, and follow a set method, because even if the principle sounds easy, the application can be quite tricky. So only use these filters if you feel capable of patience and method.' I wholeheartedly agree!

Those of you who read on may care to have a few extra tips. Most modern SLR cameras (excluding the latest Nikon) will only synchronise an electronic flash at a maximum shutter speed of 1/125 sec. This directly relates to the factor of the electronic flashgun which in turn relates to flash/subject distance. There is a lot to be said, in this respect, for using either a medium format or older 35mm camera with a between lens shutter. The ubiquitous Compur will synchronise up to a 1/500 sec (indicated) speed. This has the direct benefit of allowing a lower powered flash unit to be used in bright sunlight conditions. It may be that the old Retina, Vito B or Yashicamat will be brought out of retirement for use with colour back filters, as an alternative to buying a more powerful flash unit.

As usual, TTL metering systems must be used in a manual mode, as must (generally) automatic flash units. There are exceptions but it would be pedantic to quantify this for every situation. Ultimately, the photographer must exercise his own judgement.

Colour back filters are not very intense, so they must be regarded as degrading rather than obliterating the background colours, the exception being when the tones are light or white. Once more, the phenomenon of a green sky (blue + yellow filter) and other combinations of subject and filter colour must be taken into account.

In the controlled environment of the studio, conditions are somewhat easier. A background of white or pale grey can be chosen, which makes life easier, as does the option of flash/ subject distance for exposure balance. Shutter/flash synchronisation speed is no longer relevant.

90° MIRROR AND DATE ATTACHMENTS

The principle of photographing a subject so that the 'victim' is unaware of the camera goes back over fifty years. Intrepid explorers of the 1920s, having discovered the new lightweight Leitz 35mm camera, also found that the Leica could be fitted with a right angle viewfinder, in order to take pictures unobserved of the shy, reticent or religiously opposed.

The modern 90° mirror attachment performs the same function, but with greater disguise. Consisting of a cylinder with a circular cut-out and a 90° surface silvered mirror set within, the attachment can be used on any 35mm or 6 x 6cm SLR camera, provided that a lens of at least double the normal focal length is used. Use of a shorter focal length will give rise to image vignetting. Some zoom lenses, due to their construction, may also give rise to cut off. As there is no general rule in this case, it must be a question of try before you buy. A single filter may be used, providing it is not in a deep mount, behind the mirror attachment. Exposure loss through the 90° attachment can be up to one stop. A TTL metering system will compensate for this; otherwise make test exposures at plus half and plus one stop over the meter reading.

All mirror devices have a revolving mount, which allows for vertical or horizontal pictures. As well as sideways use, the attachment can be used for taking pictures upwards, or, for foot fetishists, downwards! It is better to make rotational adjustments before taking photographs, in order to avoid oblique pictures.

*The 'colour back' system is described in the text and has many applications. One is shown **facing page** in which the pale sky has been rendered a deeper blue. The key to the system is patience. Take your time, think about what you are trying to do, and be prepared to experiment.*

*Left and below left is shown the 90° mirror attachment. Longer than normal lenses should be used to avoid vignetting, and the film will show a reversed image of the subject. This item is ideal for use in situations where 'furtive' photography is the only way to get the picture – as in some countries where the inhabitants object to being photographed. The date attachment, **below**, as its name implies, allows the date to appear in the bottom corner of the picture. If a lot of photography is undertaken it is useful to be able to 'date' the first frame of each day's shoot to ease future identification.*

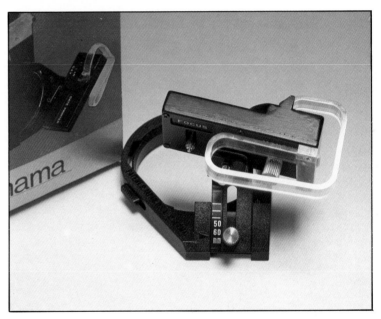

Another unique device from HAMA/Enterprise, enables those with a sense of history, or a scientific bent, to record the date on film, with a relative degree of simplicity. This budget-priced device, at least compared to data backs, can be fitted to 35mm, medium and large format cameras, provided that the lens mount size is between 49 and 58mm.

After fitting the date printer to the lens mount, there is an adjustment for date position, focus of the superimposed image and, of course, day, month and year (up to 1990). An additional control is scaled for focal lengths of between 30 and 60mm for 35mm format, though it is suitable for equivalent focal lengths on other formats.

The date image appears in frame as a blocked out section, in a choice of either top left or bottom right corner, on a rectangular format, or near either edge of any side of a square format. Allow for approximately a 24 x 30mm crop on a 35mm frame if the date is to be excluded for some reason.

The green plastic light collector produces a VDU-like data image on film. When working indoors, it may be necessary to use a separate light source to 'power' the date recorder.

COLOUR, SOFT AND MIST SPOTS

Centre spots can be considered as a filter with a hole or clear area in the centre. This aperture is about a third of the filter width or circumference. Centre spots come in two distinct types: those where the area surrounding the spot is clear neutral density or colour; and those where the surround is a diffuse neutral density or colour. A further variation is for the surrounding area to consist of a fog filter, or sometimes to have a texture similar to a ground glass focusing screen.

Most makers of plastic rectangular centre spot filters have a range which consists of both neutral density and colours. The Filtek catalogue lists 'clear' centre spots of three neutral density and ten colours, whilst Cokin make two mists, two clear neutral density and five clear colours. Hoya produce their mist spots in plastic squares and also a round soft spot, in glass, in a conventional mount.

The function of all these filters is to concentrate attention on the middle of the field, although in the case of rectangular filters the centre of interest can be adjusted within frame. The

Any coloured filter has the effect of darkening the photographic image, and we normally compensate for this by allowing extra exposure. It is very important, however, to remember that, in the case of colour filters with clear central areas, taking light readings with the filter in position will mean overexposure of the clear centre – except in those instances where a narrow-angle, spot-metering facility is provided in the camera. In the case of 'mist spots,' where a clear central area is surrounded by a soft area, then exposure readings are not affected.

COLOUR, SOFT AND MIST SPOTS

Attachments which provide clear central areas surrounded by some form of image degradation or diffusion – which may take the same form as a soft focus filter, a diffuser, a fog filter or even a close-up lens – can also be combined with other attachments. Thus, two clear centre spots can be mounted together to increase the out-of-focus effect of the

outer area, or a mist spot can be combined with a magenta colour spot filter, and so on. With square filter systems it is not necessary to have the clear area in the centre; it can be positioned wherever you wish to achieve the result you want. All attachments are merely starting points for your own creativity.

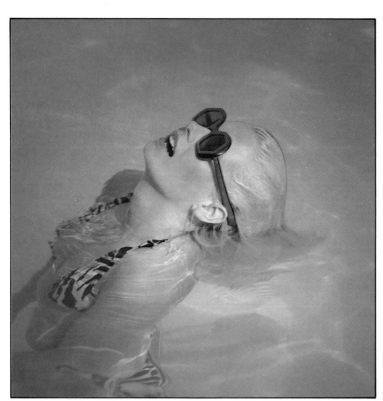

319

neutral density centre spots darken round the subject, the fog and 'ground glass' types add white flare, whilst the colours simply tint the surrounding area.

Centre spots may be used in combination. Those with an actual hole in the middle provide superior definition for obvious reasons.

These filters are suitable for any focal length of lens. A wide angle will produce a smaller sharper 'hole,' whilst a telephoto, or long focus, lens will do the opposite. Normal and longer focal length lenses can produce more blending between subject and surround, particularly if wider lens apertures are employed.

Once more, I am afraid, TTL metering systems will produce over-exposure of the centre area of the picture unless the filter factor of the surround is allowed for to some degree. The exception to this is those rare cameras which have a TTL spot metering facility. Any camera fitted with a depth of field preview control enables the user accurately to gauge the centre spot effect.

Facing page: A blue centre spot has the effect of darkening the blue of the water, whilst a yellow combines with the blue to produce a greenish surround. A mist spot was combined with a soft focus filter for the shot *below. A clear centre spot surrounded by a close up lens was used to make the pictures on **this page,** which accounts for the double images and strong softening.*

321

Denise, facing page, is featured *several times in pictures taken specially for this book. For this one the photographer used a sepia filter combined with a soft focus attachment with clear centre spot. The colouring, pose, clothes and props all match the mood and location admirably. For the picture **top left** a mauve centre spot was used, and for the shot **left** the model was positioned so that the strong sunlight coming through the doorway spilled onto the white blouse at the edge of the clear area of the soft focus centre spot. An orange centre spot, soft focus and underexposure made the subject **below**.*

VARIPOL, VARICOLOR, MAGICPOL

Like so many other categories of filters, there emerges from time to time a generic term to describe a particular type. It may be that one particular manufacturer was first in the field or spent more money on advertising, or whatever: one name will stick with Joe Public, and from then on . . .

The varipol filter consists of one normal polarising filter and one coloured polarising filter. These may be sold in sets comprising a 'master' plus a choice of three colours, or as individual filters. Varipols consist of two types. The single colour variety in red, orange, yellow, green, blue and purple could well be described as dial-a-shade. As with variable density filters (same technical background), it is possible to select a shade of colour amounting to a filter factor range of between approximately 3x and 8x.

Double colour varipols achieve the apparent 'magic' of changing colour as the mount is rotated. This may be achieved by the use of two coloured polarisers. A typical example is the Goyo/Tora range of red to blue, red to green, red to yellow and yellow to blue. B + W make a purple, which miraculously changes the image colour from blue to purple to magenta to orange in that order. If I have any criticism of the varipol filter, it is that, unlike a variable neutral density, there are no graduations which, at least, give an indexed guide to exposure. I have yet to meet a TTL exposure system which can cope with these, and if it is of the type which needs a 'circular' pola filter then manic bracketing or experience is the only way.

New additions to the ranges of filters and attachments are constantly being made available. One of these is a combination of grey and coloured polarising filters and yet another makes use of two coloured polarising filters plus grey. By these means colours can be changed by rotating the mount. All the pictures on these pages were made with just the one filter. An unfiltered shot **above** *is included for reference.*

Varipols do not always act as a normal polarising filter when used in their combined form, but separated, a neutral 'master' will. A coloured back half can be used as a monochromatic polarising filter, providing that the mount allows separation without damage. It is sometimes possible to achieve two colours simultaneously by using a bi-colour varipol. This is of necessity a matter of the subject's planes of polarisation being exactly right. There is no guarantee that all makers' products will work this way, for there are too many variables. All I can stress is that when conditions are right the result is unusual, to say the least. All varipol filters can be tried in front of the eye in order to gauge the effect.

CROSSTARS

Crosstar has become the generic term for those devices which render a light source as a point with anything between two and sixteen 'beams' emanating from it. These can be produced by scribing, etching or moulding indentations into plain glass. Whilst it is possible for the impecunious to attack the old UV filter with a glass cutter, most manufacturers make a better job of it. However, the do-it-yourself approach is quite valid for special applications.

Commercial crosstars invariably produce regularly spaced beams, though Actina do produce an irregular 6 point star and Goyo a vario-cross, in which the angles of a four point star can be varied at will. It is possible to use most crosstars in combination.

Crosstar masks, in effect, alter the shape of the lens' iris diaphragm. We are all familiar with the TV cliché/sloppiness of thirteen hexagonal blobs racing across the frame when a light source is in shot. Using a zoom lens plus a crosstar mask can produce this effect, but with a star instead of a hexagon.

The last category of crosstar is the radial type which breaks up the beams into a series of crosses – or, if out of focus, a series of blobs. The effect can also produce a photograph which appears to have been printed through a coarse newspaper screen. Lots of light sources in shot are necessary in this instance.

Crosstars are essentially plain, preferably optical glass, filters with lines etched into the surface. The simplest have lines at right angles to each other – which provide a four-pointed 'star' when a light source or reflection is included in the picture area. Further lines etched between these angles produce even more points to the star effect, usually up to a maximum of 32, though two filters can be combined to give an even greater number.

CROSSTARS

Night scenes with street lamps and other light sources are an obvious subject for crosstars, as is the sun. Be careful, however, when including the sun in any shot; looking directly at the sun with the naked eye, or through a camera, can cause permanent eye damage. Even when the sun is partially obscured by branches or fronds **top right,** the light is still far stronger than is realised.

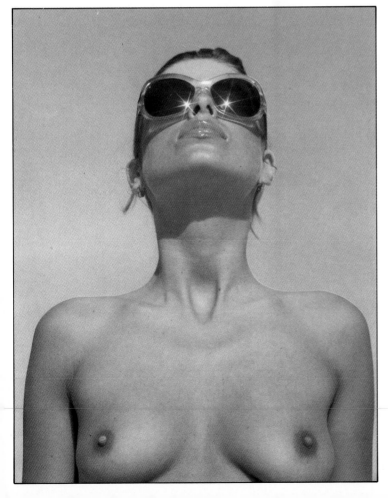

*Reflections in water, whether it be an expanse of water or droplets on flowers or grasses, can be given added sparkle by the use of a crosstar. Underexposure adds to the 'starlike' feeling, and the stronger the reflection the more pronounced will be the star. It is interesting to note that, in the shot of droplets of water on grass **facing page**, the grossly out-of-focus highlights in the background, rather than producing stars, show the actual pattern of the filter. Because of their curved surfaces, both the lenses of the sunglasses the model is wearing **left** show the same reflection of the one light source. With some crosstars it is possible to vary the angle between the rays **above**. Such attachments are usually referred to as 'varicross' filters.*

Mount and filter quality can be important. The cheapest crosstars are uncoated and fitted in a non-revolving mount, which means that they have to be unscrewed from the lens mount to change the angle of the beams. Since a light source must be included in shot, I would recommend the best filter you can afford – and use a good lenshood for the same reason. Rectangular lenshoods should be used with care, as any rotation could cause vignetting.

The lens aperture employed will affect the size and shape of the 'star', as well as the definition and contrast of the overall image. The lens' widest aperture will produce the longest, widest star, as well as the lowest contrast. There will also be a degree of image softening. The wider the maximum aperture of the lens, the more pronounced the effect. As a general rule, it is better to shoot at about two or three stops below maximum aperture, unless you are prepared to shoot a lot of frames to know what the effect will be at each and every aperture. Under exposure is a *sine qua non*, unless the background is dark or the subject is a night scene. Crosstars need no increase in exposure.

DIFFRACTION GRATINGS AND PRISMS

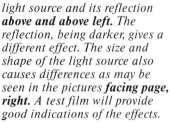

Diffraction gratings (also known as rainbow filters) work in a similar fashion to Crosstars, except that the beams emanating from a point source are rainbow coloured. This effect is achieved in several ways. By microscopically ruled parallel lines either on glass, or printed in gelatin then sandwiched between glasses, or by moulding very tiny prisms onto glass. Diffraction gratings are available which give beams in numbers from the usual 2x, 4x, 8x and 16x to 18x, 36x, 48x and even 72x. With the 'high powered' filters, a point source against a dark background is rendered as surrounded by a concentric rainbow, sometimes with dark radial interspaces. Due to the nature of the diffraction grating, it is also

Diffractors go by many different names: Cosmos, Galaxia, Univers, Andromeda, Nebula etc. etc. They all have specially etched grid patterns which split the light in the manner of prisms but without distorting the image. They require a light source in the frame and benefit from under, rather than over, exposure. It is interesting to include the main

light source and its reflection **above and above left.** *The reflection, being darker, gives a different effect. The size and shape of the light source also causes differences as may be seen in the pictures **facing page, right.** A test film will provide good indications of the effects.*

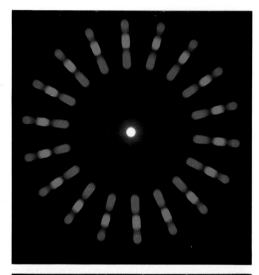

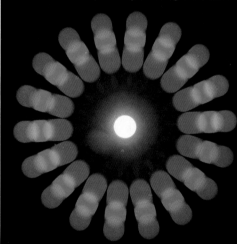

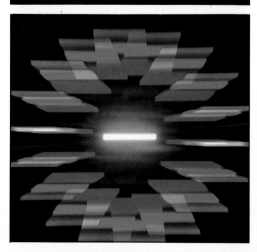

possible to produce diamond and parentheses shapes as well as variations on the wheel. All diffraction gratings have a greater effect upon image contrast and definition than do crosstars. The amount of flare produced can be drastic, though underexposure can 'cure' this. On the other hand, induced flare may add something to the final result. The choice is yours.

A prism used in front of the lens, to achieve image distortion and colour fringing, is an old idea now available in commercial form. The results are invariably somewhat abstract and without definition. They work better on longer, rather than normal, focal lengths if separation of the colours is the prime *raison d'être*. Since the image is refracted through the prism, some degree of photographer contortion will be necessary. As Jean Coquin puts it – "To photograph a subject placed in front of you, you might have to aim at the sky, the ground, or to the left or right." Prisms induce flare. Ergo, a light source in shot can be disastrous.

DIFFRACTION GRATINGS AND PRISMS

There is no doubt that the use *of diffraction gratings, by whatever name they are known, can be overdone. It would be a grave mistake to take every shot using such an attachment. But then, this is true for all special effects; it is invariably best to take one with and one without and see which pleases you best. There is no doubt that a poor shot can seldom be improved by adding an effect. The picture **top left** is ordinary, and adding colour has not altered this; it remains ordinary. Whether the picture **facing page** works well with the colours is for the viewer to decide: certainly the impression of 'walking through a rainbow' is eye catching and interesting.*

VIGNETTERS MASKS AND FRAMES

If there is one family of lens attachments which I loathe, then it is the rash of vignetters, masks or frames currently available. These are invariably sold in sets containing hearts, clubs, diamonds, spades and keyholes, etc. I cannot really see any point in photographing a nude through the latter, but then it's not my particular hang-up! The binocular cliché – formerly used in bad 'B' movies and now the province of TV – is totally incorrect, as anyone who has ever looked through them will attest. Should this not be evident, then a consultation with an optician is a matter of some urgency. Yet for all my hymn of hate, there is a use for some of these devices.

I cannot improve on the Hoyarex catalogue description of their technical mask set, so make no apologies for quoting it here. Their illustrations show how masks can be employed tastefully and to good effect.

"The Technical Mask Set consists of 15 black vinyl masks each measuring 72 x 72 x 0.3mm. There are 10 different pre-shaped masks and 5 plain masks for you to cut out your own designs. Place the masks in the Hoyarex Gelatin Holder (sold separately) and then slot into the Filter Holder in the same way as any other square Hoyarex Filter.

Strong light sources cause spectral highlights to assume the same blurred shape of the mask's perforations giving creative 'montage' effects.

The Technical Masks are particularly effective when used with telephoto lenses between 100-300mm set at the widest aperture. Using small apertures with standard and wide angle lenses has the opposite effect – to the point where the mask's effect will completely disappear. Therefore, for good results always use a wide open aperture by either adjusting the shutter speed or by using a Hoya Neutral Density filter to obtain correct exposure. As the exposure reading will vary according to the mask and lens used, it may be necessary to mount the camera on a tripod. Test shots are the safest way to evaluate the various effects and therefore assure the desired picture.

Additional sets of 15 Black Plain Masks are also available."

The small, cut-out shapes provided by various special effects system manufacturers can be used to produce highlights of their own shape above. The more usual 'peephole' effects are also illustrated and have uses limited only by the photographer's imagination. The keyhole, however, would normally be used to look 'in' rather than 'out.'

MULTIPLE IMAGE PRISMS

There are now at least a dozen variants of the multiple image prism on the market. For once, these were not invented by Jean Coquin, but, I am assured, originated from Spiratone in New York – out of Japan, in the early nineteen sixties. Any device which has been in vogue and used to the extent of becoming boring, will still attract a new generation of photographers sooner rather than later. The multi-image prism, perhaps more than any other attachment, fits into this category, although my feeling is that graduated filters will run a close second before long. In case it sounds as if I am anti-prism, let me assure you that I am not. Indeed the three I own have several times got me out of trouble by enabling an uninspiring subject to be rendered in a different way. As devices for editorial photography I would not be without them, even though it could well be a couple of years or more before I use one again.

Any prism attachment will produce multiple images of the original subject on film, the number of images being directly related to the number of prism facets. These can range from two to seven, with the juxtaposition of the images again relating to the arrangement of the prism faces. This gives the advantage that any prism can be immediately typed just by looking at it – ideal for secondhand bargain hunters!

or three side by side images. Again a revolving mount, turned through 180 degrees, allows the images to be one above the other. Turning the mount less than this figure provides stepped images. An unusual variant of the two face parallel type is the B + W made close-up prism. This is of ca 7.5 dioptres strength – which is powerful for a close-up lens, and should only be used at small lens apertures in order to ensure adequate definition.

A fourth type of prism is the offset parallel type, more often known as a repeater prism attachment. Here the faces start from halfway across, and can be between two and five in number. This gives the effect of a stroboscopic photograph, with a 'leading' subject and between two and five extra over-lapping 'following' images. Using the rotating mount alters the image dispersion as with other parallel prisms.

The ingenious and quality B + W company have now managed to produce colour prisms. These consist of a spectrum with a choice of six faced prism (without clear central area), and a three faced parallel type. Introducing colour allows a much greater degree of subject tone variation than with a clear equivalent. Used on a white, grey or pastel subject it can produce some very startling effects.

Prism attachments can be used on any normal or longer

There are four basic types of prism attachments, the commonest being the kind with a plane central area. This can be circular, with anything from three to six angled surfaces radiating from it, each of which will provide an additional image to the central one. This central area can also be triangular, square, pentagonal, or hexagonal – again with the appropriate number of surrounding sectors. All of these produce a single central image, with a regular pattern of secondary images around it.

The second type of prism has no clear central area. Made only with three or four prismatic faces, a regular pattern of three or four images is produced. A rotating mount allows the triangular or square pattern of images to be moved at will around a central axis in the frame.

The third type of prism has parallel faces which provide two

focal length lens. With wide angle lenses there is always a chance of vignetting due to the depth of a prism mount. This will happen particularly at the smaller lens apertures. It is sometimes possible to use an oversized prism plus a step ring to get over this problem, but only with a wide angle lens of moderate angle of view, and a not too deeply recessed front element.

The choice of subject for prismatic techniques must rest with the photographer, however, as a guide, a light toned subject against a medium to dark background is likely to 'read' better than the reverse situation. For the same reason, a simple subject is likely to be the clearest, whilst anything complex could easily go towards the abstract. Opinions vary as to how far the prime lens should be stopped down. There is no doubt that a smaller aperture produces sharper images of both subject <u>and</u> prism facet

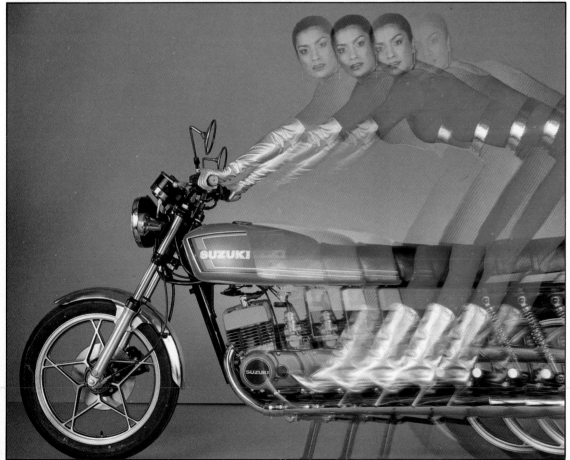

A multiple image attachment in which the planes, or faces, are parallel is sometimes described as a 'repeater' or, maybe, a 'speed filter.' The flowers in the right picture **facing page** do, indeed, look as though they are falling because our eyes tell us that the strongest image – at the bottom – should be the latest image; therefore the flowers must be newly arrived in that position. This shot could have been taken with the strongest image at the top of the picture to give a 'magic beanstalk' effect. The studio shot **left** also conveys this impression of movement, this time across the frame. Whilst it is very obvious that neither the motor cycle nor the model are really moving, the impression is still quite strong. A multiple image prism with no clear centre, and with each segment dyed a different colour, was used to produce the two near-abstracts **above**. Where the faces meet there is an even greater multiplication of the image of the group of figures.

shape, as well as perhaps pulling a background into sharp focus. As with some other lens attachments, I can only suggest a three aperture trial run.

An SLR camera fitted with a depth of field preview facility saves two exposures! For the same reason, and since all prisms are fitted into revolving mounts, an SLR camera will take the guesswork out of image placement. This revolving mount can also be used to double expose in even more images. Alternatively, with the camera on a tripod and a half or one second exposure, it is possible to blur the extra images around the central image, by rotating the prism during the exposure. A prism with a central plane surface should be used, and the subject must be static. I have often been asked if it is possible to use two prisms together in order to produce even more images. The answer is a very qualified 'yes'. You may like or dislike partial images – which can occur.

Mixing dissimilar prisms can be quite interesting. The biggest snags I have found are that the resulting thickness of glass produced a poor quality image, there was vignetting with a standard focal length lens, and the prisms needed to be taped together. The advantage is that you can try the effect on an SLR – without having to use any film!

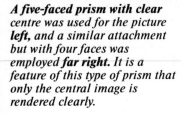

*A five-faced prism with clear centre was used for the picture **left,** and a similar attachment but with four faces was employed **far right.** It is a feature of this type of prism that only the central image is rendered clearly.*

***The pictures on this page, with** the exception of the flower shot, show further examples of the uses to which the parallel-plane prism can be put. As with most of these attachments, it can usually be rotated in its mount (if not it must be unscrewed slightly in the filter thread) to position the secondary images wherever they are wanted. With parallel prisms, the closer the faces the more faces there are, and more images will, therefore, be repeated, thus giving a greater impression of speed or movement.*

DOUBLE EXPOSURE DEVICES

Variously known as double mask, dual image or double exposure mask, these devices exist in two forms: those which mask out half the frame and those which mask out a smaller section or shape. To use these attachments it is virtually essential for the camera to have a double exposure facility, a rewind button, or interchangeable magazines. Anything else involves marking the film leader or backing paper accurately, rewinding and re-exposing, which in the case of model shots gets silly. Yet having said this, I know of a landscape photographer who pre-exposes the full moon in pre-determined positions on numerous rolls of film. These are then taken around the world and suitable subjects double exposed in. It may be astronomically incorrect for a Hemel Hempstead moon to appear over Nevada, but who will know – or even care? Most double exposures necessitate the use of a tripod, particularly if the subject is to appear with itself. The film business, having invented the technique, still perseveres whenever a character has a double or a twin.

With a double exposure facility, or interchangeable magazine camera, the use of a double exposure mask presents no problem. Failing this, the rewind button can be depressed, the shutter wound and the second exposure made. The disadvantage of this method is that the film can move between exposures. Even by taking up the slack in the film cassette and taping over the rewind knob before the second exposure is made, there is still the chance of up to 2mm error. In the cases of either a straight double exposure mask or a shape mask, this becomes a hit or miss operation. The cliché of a girl's head appearing in a bed of

*Cokin double exposure masks were used for both these subjects; the picture **right** with the double mask, which blanks out the central portion of the frame, which can then be re-exposed using the second part* *of the attachment. For the shot **below** the sliding double exposure device was used. Note that the slightest movement of the tripod-mounted camera results in a double image in the centre of the picture.*

flowers will not be affected by a millimetre error, though a degree of planning is necessary in order to have both girl and flowers in close proximity.

All double exposure masks work on a replacement basis. The first exposure is made with either half of the frame blanked off, or a shaped mask is used to perform the same function. The blanked off half of the frame is then re-exposed by sliding the attachment across the frame. In the case of a shaped frame, its negative shape is replaced by its positive or vice versa. In either situation the masks must register with each other.

The aperture and focal length of the lens employed has a distinct bearing upon the image overlap, or lack of it. As a guide, a wide angle should be used at between f4 and f5.6; a normal lens at between f8 and f11, and a telephoto (or long focus) between f11 and f16. As with so many other lens attachments, a wide angle will produce a sharper cut off, whilst a tele will be more diffuse in this respect. A depth of field preview facility and a grid focusing screen help to gauge alignment and final result. Medium and large format users can always check out with a Polaroid.

Exposure readings must be checked and held before the attachment is fitted, as otherwise over exposure from a false reading will result. Finally, a dark or complex background will tend to disguise any masking error. A black background allows the use of deliberate image overlap.

Above is another example using *the double exposure attachment. This can also be used to take images one above the other, as well as side by side. A child up a tree, for example, can look down on itself sitting on the grass. The other two pictures on this page are the result of straightforward double exposure in camera. This requires the provision of some means of disconnecting the film drive between exposures, usually by means of a double exposure button or lever on the camera. Failing this, the rewind button must be held in, the rewind knob held securely, and the lever wind operated. The pictures **facing page** are the result of exposing a film on shots of the moon, rewinding, repositioning the film <u>exactly</u> in the camera, and making the subsequent exposures.*

DOUBLE EXPOSURE DEVICES

To take the multi-coloured waterfall **facing page,** the photographer divided the total exposure by the number of different colours he wanted in the finished shot. This required a neutral density filter to increase the exposure to manageable proportions. It was then a matter of mounting the camera on a tripod and making a series of exposures on the

same frame, each through a different coloured filter. Thus, if the exposure was, say, four seconds at f16, each exposure was made at one second. Waving the camera about with the shutter open, in front of a point light source, was the method used to create the abstract **facing page top left.** Several exposures were made on one frame, each through a different coloured filter. A similar method was used for the shots **above and right,** but this time the camera was securely mounted facing upwards, a torch was attached to the ceiling with string and swung in a circular pattern, and the shutter opened. Again, several exposures were made through coloured filters. A light, or lights, covered with coloured gels and moved around to create a pattern, with the camera shutter open and the studio blacked out, was followed by a flash exposure on the model to produce the shots **facing page bottom.**

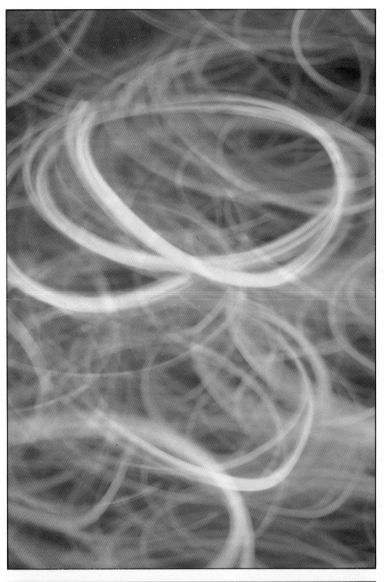

DO IT YOURSELF

No matter how ingenious attachment makers become, there is always some photographer producing a do-it-yourself gadget. Realising this market, there is even a Cokin creative filter set, which can be hacked about at will. Perhaps the following story does not really come into the lens attachment category, yet it illustrates a point. Some years ago I knew a travel photographer who had a triangular pegboard device which fitted his camera from a tripod bush (apex) to forward of the lenshood (base). The holes in the pegboard could be filled with grass, flowers and/or fitted with a square frame. This miniature garden was used to hide the foreground of unfinished hotels. With a beach attachment likewise, and the frame (suitably decorated), provided a nice surround for head shots of pretty girls. As all of

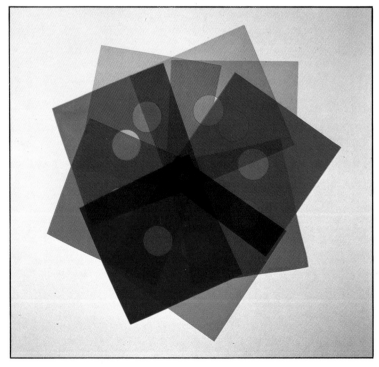

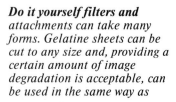

Do it yourself filters and *attachments can take many forms. Gelatine sheets can be cut to any size and, providing a certain amount of image degradation is acceptable, can be used in the same way as* ordinary filters to colour the subject. Transparent tape can be added to increase the softening effect and holes can be cut quite easily, as above, with the aid of an engineers compass scriber.

The effects that can be achieved using the types of filters shown can be very similar to those obtained using proprietary items. They can be cut circular, to fit standard filter holders, but it may be found that changing from one colour to another is a fiddly, time-consuming business. A simpler method is to hold the squares of gel in front of the camera lens – though this requires that the camera is a single lens reflex. Several such squares, with or without an aperture cut in the centre, can be fixed at one corner by the use of a paper fastener, as in the illustration. By this means several filters are always to hand and hardly any space is taken up in the gadget bag. The more scratched the filters become, the more useful they are to soften and degrade the image and to scatter light. As an alternative, if no single lens reflex is available, a 'tube' can be fashioned from the gel, which fits over the lens mount. A little experimentation is required to determine the correct length, but both the pictures **above** were taken using this method.

this could be used hand held, he preferred it to his previous portable foreground technique of carrying a table, cold drinks and sunglasses etc, in his car.

One of my favourite gadgets is the 75mm diameter base of a cut glass tumbler. Salvaged from a washing-up accident, it fitted neatly into an old lens hood. Attached to a standard or wide angle lens it turns mundane subjects into colourful abstracts. There is no point in focusing but the effect does change with the lens aperture used. 'Cut glass' transparencies have been sold for record, book and brochure covers, as well as for backgrounds to an audio-visual presentation. You can try this effect by inverting a complete tumbler over the lens.

The 'Romantic' image is one that lends itself to soft focus, degradation of image, and so on. It may seem ridiculous that we go to the expense of buying lenses that offer superb, biting sharpness, and then go to considerable lengths to destroy that sharpness – but such is

fashion, in photography as in anything else – and you have the advantage of sharpness for subjects that require it. Be careful in your choice of colours. Try not to introduce jarring colours, either in filtration, clothing, props or setting when attempting such pictures. The overall feeling should be one of calm and tranquillity. Smart clothes do not blend well with the idea, and this is why rather old fashioned, soft clothing features so much in settings like these. The minimum depth of field should be used; sharpness in the background is normally to be avoided.

Not yet manufactured is the 'gizmo'. Inspired perhaps by an American who used a tube in order to 'think' images on to a Polaroid film? The gizmo consists of a cardboard (or metal) tube about twice the length and diameter of a standard lenshood. Lined with mirror plastic – or aluminium cooking foil – it enables head shots of pretty girls to be surrounded by interesting abstract shapes and colours. It is better if the model is framed by colours and shapes to start with, though even a street background will do. It is essential to use a wide shooting aperture and it helps if the gizmo is adjustable for length.

Speckle filters consist of various coloured – or all the same colour – gelatin spots, casually arranged around a clear centre

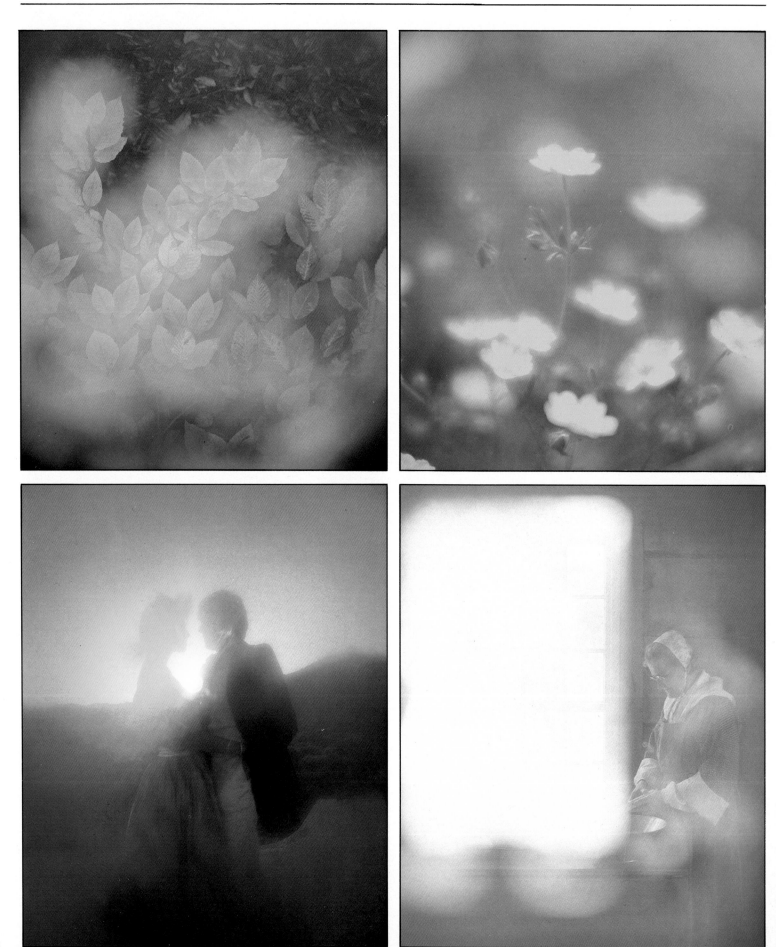

area. These spots can be cut out with scissors (larger) and/or produced with a ring binder paper punch (smaller), and then bound between lantern slide cover glasses, or in a 6 x 6cm slide mount. I have also seen this type of filter produced by using self adhesive clear plastic on a cover glass, a scalpel then being used to cut a clear centre area.

A Kaleidoscope filter is produced by the same means but the gelatin, or acetate, is cut into triangular or oblong shapes. Toy kaleidoscopes can be modified for photographic use although the image quality of the main subject will be poor.

Both speckle and kaleidoscope filters can be taped to the front of a lenshood in the absence of a suitable holder. They should be used at a wide lens aperture, as smaller openings will bring the filter into sharper focus.

In a similar vein is the use of an unwanted colour transparency – again with a hole cut in it. This should be at least 6 x 6cm, or part of a 5 x 4″ as otherwise it will not be big enough to cover a lenshood aperture.

Speckles, kaleidoscopes and old transparencies all work well in conjunction with a gizmo, particularly if the main subject is photographed against a white background. I could also mention home-made distortion filters, and how to produce your own graduated filters, to say nothing of stripeys – but then one has to leave something to the imagination of others, doesn't one?

Filters you make yourself may not be as predictable as the manufactured variety; they may not always produce the result you expect, but they will invariably produce 'different' pictures. If that is what you want, then sweet wrappings, crumpled cellophane, nylons and net curtaining can all be used – the limit is your imagination and ingenuity.

DO IT YOURSELF

The picture on the facing page has something of the look of an impressionist painting. It was produced by standing a sheet of hammered, frosted glass, such as is used for bathroom windows, in front of the subject. Note that the flowers closest to the glass appear relatively undistorted compared with those further away, which become merely coloured shapes. The picture **above left** shows, better than words, how imagination and ingenuity can produce a striking image. A blue gel with cut out centre, held well in front of the lens **left** transformed a rather ordinary shot. The same technique was used for the picture **above,** exposure being calculated for the background so as to preserve the silhouette. Notice how the yellow of the sun has combined with the blue of the gel to create the green flare under the glass. Moving the camera, or the gel, even a few inches would have changed the feeling completely.

CLOSE-UP LENSES

There are two ways to achieve close-ups. The first is to extend the distance between lens and film plane by means of extension tubes or bellows, and the second is to use a close-up lens. The former needs adjusted exposure when a TTL metering system is absent, whilst the latter does not, under any circumstances. Extension tubes or bellows can achieve subject/image ratios of 1:1 with ease. Close-up lenses are not really satisfactory at ratios of more than 1:4.

For many years close-up lenses were known by the generic name of Proxars – a trade name of the Carl Zeiss company who did so much to popularise the idea. The range was then nos. 1, 2 and 3. These figures correspond to a dioptre, which is a focal length of one metre. Strangely perhaps, a two dioptre lens has a focal length of half a metre, a three dioptre of a third of a metre and so on. Unfortunately, what was a nice standard of measurement has not been adhered to by many manufacturers, so that one maker's number four lens could be number four in his range and not necessarily of four dioptres. I can only suggest that you check maker's figures before purchase.

The optical result of adding a close-up lens to a prime lens is effectively to shorten the focal length of that lens, which means that the combination can focus closer within the range of the existing focusing mount movement. Most close-up lenses come with a table which at least shows camera to subject distances of an approximate nature, when a standard focal length lens is set to infinity or its closest focusing distance. Leitz, in their traditionally

mount. After all, you are in effect adding an extra element to your prime lens, with all that this entails, and this is what you pay for. The very best close-up lenses are achromats, which are of two element cemented construction. Using two glasses of different refractive indices allows for greater corrections to be made. This is not of great concern if your subject is a flower or a kitten's head, but if the original is linear and you need edge definition, then an achromat is essential.

Close-up lenses are not suitable for every type of prime lens. Few (if any) 50mm f1.4 and no f1.2 lenses are suitable candidates. After all, this is not what they were designed for. Exactly the same is true for wide angle lenses where there is a good chance that fall-off in illumination and vignetting will occur. The exceptions to this are the non-retrofocus wide angle lenses used on rangefinder focusing cameras, which can be used with close-up lenses. However, there are then framing problems.

Three component sets of close-up lenses can be used in combination which allows even closer camera/subject distances. As long as one realises that this is adding perhaps three extra elements and six air/glass surfaces to the prime lens, and that there will be a decrease in contrast and resolution, then this is fine. A flower subject, for instance, could still be attractively rendered.

Zoom lenses, with a shortest focal length of 70mm and up, can be used with close-up lenses, though most now seem to have a built-in macro facility anyway. Like longer telephotos and long

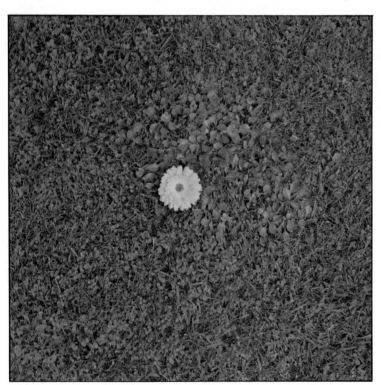

precise manner, also give reproduction ratios, field sizes and depth of field for whichever lenses in their range are suitable. Dioptre strengths range photographically from 0.25 (weakest) to 10 (strongest). There have been 20 dioptre lenses made, in an attempt to reach 1:1 subject/image ratio. These were so strong that the results were awful, the same unfortunately being true of many of the 10 dioptre lenses around.

The quality of close-up lenses varies as much as with any other lens. The best will be made to the same standard as the makers camera lenses, be multicoated and fitted in a precision

For ultimate quality, extension tubes, bellows and/or a well-corrected micro lens are unbeatable for close up work. Bellows and tubes, however, do have the disadvantage that, because of the increased extension between lens and film, valuable film speed is sacrificed. Shallow depth of field, or long exposure times, *have to be accepted. Light, easily carried and used close up lenses, therefore, are very useful items indeed and can provide acceptable quality. Closest focusing distance with a Hasselblad and 80mm lens is shown **above left,** and **above and right** the dramatic difference that can be achieved with close up lenses.*

CLOSE-UP LENSES

Patience, timing and anticipation are important requirements in taking close ups such as those **below, right and bottom.** *Creatures that appear to move relatively slowly*

actually move much faster than is realised, and the lack of depth of field can make them appear as meaningless blurs. Flowers are favoured subjects for close ups. They allow ample time for composition to be considered and are very beautiful in their own right. Soft focus lenses, or diffusers, can be combined with close up lenses **left** *to create soft, ethereal subjects of considerable appeal. The shot of marbles in a glass jar* **right** *was taken using a Bronica SQ and +3 close up lens. All pictures on these pages were taken hand-held.*

CLOSE-UP LENSES

focus lenses, zooms use the fractional dioptre accessory lenses. If there is any disadvantage at all, it is that good, large diameter close-up lenses need good, large diameter bank balances to finance them – but then so do big filters.

Anyone who has taken close-ups will know that the biggest problems are lack of depth of field and working in your own shadow. For these reasons I tend to use close-up lenses mainly with modest apertured lenses in the 90 to 150mm focal length range. Not only do they stop down to f32, but are also a nice compromise in the subject stand-off distance. I also have a preference for long focus rather than telephoto construction for reasons of definition.

*With subjects parallel to the film plane **left**, the shallow depth of field inherent in close up work can be used to maximum advantage. Otherwise* *you should focus on the part of the subject **above and top right** that contains the most detail, interest or importance.*

Macro-zoom attachments have been around since the sixties, and perform much the same function as a 50/55mm prime macro lens. Like early zoom lenses they do not hold focus between settings, though with any close-up work, it is easier to move the camera backwards and forwards for focusing. Fitting a macro-zoom attachment to a macro lens can be a startling experience. At the closest setting the subject will be literally inside the macro-zoom lens mount. There is, as always, a price to be paid for convenience. The macro-zoom accessory is bulky and more expensive than a set of reasonable quality close-up lenses, against which it does not compare too favourably in either definition or contrast, unless used with a prime lens of simple construction, in order to cut down the total number of lens elements between subject and film.

Split field lenses are an ingenious combination of half of a one, two or three dioptre close-up lens and a half empty filter mount. What these can achieve is a close-up of a foreground subject with a view to infinity in the top half of the picture and render both sharp at the same time. To do this, set the camera lens to infinity and then move the camera backwards and forwards until the foreground subject is sharp. Small apertures produce the most satisfactory results. The effect is similar to that which can be produced with an ultra wide angle lens, but without the extreme perspective. Split field lenses can be used turned through ninety degrees so that a foreground object can be to one side of the shot, or turned through a further ninety degrees to allow, say, overhanging flowers to be rendered as sharp as the background.

It is also possible to focus a subject through either 'half' in order to blur the other half of the picture. In this case use a larger, rather than a smaller, lens aperture. Since half of this attachment is 'open', a good lenshood will help to avoid a 'join' showing. A variation of the split field lens is the eccentric spot attachment made by B + W of Germany. This consists of an eccentrically located clear circle within a close-up lens. A rotating mount enables a distant subject to be blended into a close-up shot – within the confines of radial movement and format shape.

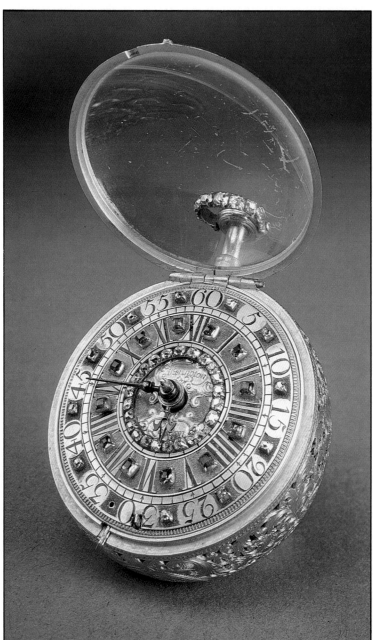

Of all the attachments we can buy to fit on the front of our lenses, the close up attachments provide us with by far the most dramatic change in the way we view our surroundings. Suddenly, our photography takes on another dimension; the ordinary, everyday things we always took for granted can be viewed, and recorded, in an entirely new way. The commonest items take on a new significance; the rusty old bicycle bell becomes an engineering abstract, and the champagne cork reveals its texture when sidelit. A dandelion seed head is transformed into an object of even rarer beauty when positioned directly in front of a light source such as the setting sun or a street lamp. Close up photography is also an exceptionally accurate way of recording a collection of small items such as jewellery, stamps, coins, matchboxes or whatever. Such a photographic record, besides being useful as a reference, is also very valuable in the case of insurance claims made on items lost or stolen.

CLOSE-UP LENSES

Given plenty of light, permitting the use of a small aperture and fast shutter speed, close ups are quite easy. It is when the light is low and we cannot stop the lens down far enough to render sharply the depth of even a shallow subject, such as a moth **below right,** that we need the small, front-mounted flash units **right** specially designed for close up work.

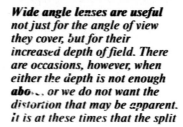

Wide angle lenses are useful not just for the angle of view they cover, but for their increased depth of field. There are occasions, however, when either the depth is not enough **above,** or we do not want the distortion that may be apparent. it is at these times that the split field close up lens comes into its own **facing page.** This item is essentially half a close up lens – in varying strengths – and, used carefully, it can be most effective. Bear in mind that there will invariably be an out of focus band between near and far subjects.

PLEASE
KEEP OFF
THE GRASS

WIDE ANGLE AND TELEPHOTO ATTACHMENTS

Wide angle and telephoto attachments were produced in the first instance to enable owners of fixed lens cameras to keep abreast of those with more expensive equipment, at least in creative terms. Mainly a post-war phenomenon, these devices have been marketed for Instamatics, Polaroids, various rangefinder cameras and even single and twin lens reflex cameras. They are still around today.

Wide angle converters increase the angle of view of a standard lens by between 25% and 35%, or in approximate terms, turn a 50mm standard lens into a 35 to 30mm. Telephoto attachments have been made which increase the standard lens' focal length by 50%, 100% and 400% respectively. These lenses were often sold as a pair. In the case of a non-reflex camera, a double format viewfinder was supplied, or sometimes an adaptor which clipped over the camera's existing viewfinder. TLR's were provided with an extra viewfinding lens. The performance of these attachments can only be described as adequate – the telephotos being much better than the wide angles, where edge

which amounts to about 300mm focal length and f16 maximum aperture. Those made for the Zeiss Contaflex SLR camera were surprisingly good within the optical limitations imposed. All monoculars are clumsy to operate on a camera, but function normally when used with the eye.

Anamorphic, or wide screen attachments, emanate from the world of cinematography. These compress the image in one dimension, and stretch it in the other. A normal ciné frame ratio of about $1\frac{1}{3}$:1, can be stretched to $2\frac{1}{2}$:1, or more, depending upon the make of lens used. An anamorphic projection lens is used to 'restore' the image upon the screen. Some of these attachments can be fitted to a 35mm SLR. The resulting distortion of the image is not dissimilar to that produced by a prism, but without colour fringing and with rather better definition. They work best on subjects like the interior of a forest, or anything else long and thin, but they are not too good for photographing people! Anamorphic attachments are still available new at a reasonable price.

definition of a sort only becomes possible at small apertures, and curved distortion of straight lines is always present. For those who are happy with enprints and a simple camera, these attachments will provide an extra dimension at low cost. The experimentally minded will also have some fun.

Monocular attachments are in effect half of a pair of binoculars with a filter ring fitting. They are usually 6 x 35 rating

*Telephoto and wide angle attachments can be used as cheap alternatives to prime lenses on SLR cameras, or as the only means of altering the view of a fixed lens camera. The pictures **left and far left** show the effect obtained with a wide angle attachment on a standard focal length lens. Different perspective can be achieved with such attachments fitted to wider or longer objectives. Vignetting and fall-off in image quality is a characteristic that should be allowed for, and this can be cropped out at a later stage. **Above:** Fisheye attachments produce exaggerated views and distort nearby objects.*

FISHEYE AND SUPERWIDE ATTACHMENTS

Fisheye and superwide lens attachments share a common function in that their effect upon a prime lens is to increase the angle of view of that lens, and also to render straight lines as curves. This statement must be qualified in that a horizontal or vertical line, falling exactly in the centre of the picture, will be rendered as a straight line. However, each few degrees of camera tilt will promptly render that line progressively more curved. The maximum angle of view of these attachments varies between 110° and 180.° This is increased towards the maxima stated by the use of a short prime focal length lens, or decreased by using a longer than normal focal length.

In the former instance, the classic, circular fisheye image will be produced with the use of say 20 – 28mm focal length lenses on 35mm format. The only variation will be the size of the circular image on the negative or transparency, not the included angle of view. A 180° attachment needs a larger prime focal length in order to fill the frame, and provided that the maximum filter mount diameter of the prime lens used is not above about 58mm, then these attachments can be used on 6 x 6cm, 5″ x 4″ or even 10″ x 8″ formats!

There are two distinct types of fisheye/superwide converters. Those which affect exposure and those which reputedly do not. All the 180° converters which I have examined reduce the effective aperture of the prime lens in proportion to the focal length of that lens. As an example:– the Kenko/Cosmos attachment for 180° pictures requires any prime lens to be used at its maximum aperture. A conversion scale on the lens, shows that a 35mm focal length + attachment will have an effective maximum aperture of f5.6, a 100mm lens becomes f11 and a 200mm lens becomes f22, etc. etc.

As all attachments need to be stopped well down in order to achieve any degree of definition at the edges of the field encompassed, it follows that a large format user could well be working at an aperture of f256.

The newer 110° fisheye/superwide attachments are primarily designed for TTL 35mm cameras, where any induced exposure increase is automatically catered for. When used on larger format cameras, they still work admirably but exposure compensation is necessary, certainly when working from a hand-held meter or with electronic flash. Since most professionals also check out exposures with Polaroid film, they are less likely to make mistakes in this area.

Both types of attachment can be a useful creative tool, witness the fact that the top lens manufacturers produce both as prime objectives. Whether you like the results or not is a subjective matter, yet as a professional, I would hate to be without some sort of fisheye facility. But then I only have to use it once a year in order to justify its continued existence.

When it comes to choice of subject matter, high curvature lenses with their inherent distortion are better employed with inanimate, rather than animate, subjects. At best, the family dog, portrayed as having a huge rubber 'hooter' and miniscule body, will accept the resulting mirth as being a sign of affection. The human family member portrayed likewise, could well not share the same emotion. It takes a lot of self confidence to accept a parodied image.

***Although wide angle and** telephoto attachments generally impair the resolution of the camera's lens, they can nevertheless be used on many occasions when fine detail and straightness of line is not an essential. With such devices* *fitted to a viewfinder camera, it is of course necessary to compose the picture via a matched accessory viewfinder. The pictures, from top, show the effect of using a standard lens, wide angle and tele attachment.*

VARIZOOM

From HAMA in Germany, although made in Japan, the impressive Varizoom attachment shortens or lengthens the focal length of the prime lens by 25%. Designed for use with 35mm format lenses of 100mm focal length and above, it would appear that the prime use of this attachment would be for zoom effect shots. Yet when taking photographs from a fixed position, the focal length variation could well be of paramount importance. I have used the Varizoom on a Hasselblad, for which it was not designed, with the following effect. There is vignetting with the 150mm Sonnar lens at apertures below f5.6, unless either of the 16 on backs are used to give a 6 x 4.5cm or 4 x 4cm superslide format. With the 250mm Sonnar there was no problem.

This table (of rounded off figures) gives you some idea of focal length changes when using a Varizoom:

Focal length of prime lens	Zoom range with attachment
100mm	75 – 125mm
135mm	100 – 170mm
150mm	120 – 180mm
200mm	150 – 250mm
250mm	200 – 300mm
300mm	225 – 325mm
400mm	300 – 500mm
500mm	375 – 625mm

The Varizoom is not suitable for use with the compact mirror (catadioptric) lenses now on the market or with focal lengths of less than 100mm, as vignetting will occur.

The multi-coated Varizoom specification is sophisticated enough to utilise moving elements, therefore the barrel does not extend with focal length changes. However, the attachment is a varifocal rather than a true zoom, in that the focus does not hold between minimum and maximum settings. In practice this is of no great disadvantage, least of all in terms of cost/effectiveness!

One extra bonus is that when used at its 'wider' setting, a closer focusing distance between camera and subject is possible: not a macro facility but still useful. Series 7 filters may be used between the attachment and the prime lens by means of a special ring. Alternatively, there is a standard 58mm front thread. I would recommend a larger than 58mm lenshood, by means of a step-up ring for the shorter prime lens focal lengths.

The makers state that no exposure adjustment is necessary with this attachment.

Subjects like these can be produced with the aid of a zoom attachment, which must be operated through its range during exposure. This sounds easy, but timing is important. The camera must be tripod mounted and, if there is action in the frame it works best if it is towards the camera position **below** *and the centre of the shot is positioned to one side. With static subjects, such as the vase of flowers* **right,** *the situation is easier. Again, the camera must be tripod mounted and the zooming action very smooth, with half the exposure completed before 'zooming.' Changing focus has a similar effect as, of course, does a zoom lens.*

SOFT FOCUS ATTACHMENTS

For almost as long as lens designers have been computing sharper and sharper lenses, photographers have tried to destroy that resolution for various reasons. Indeed, the lens manufacturers, realising this need, gave in gracefully and designed special soft focus lenses – a situation which still exists. Those of us who have a penchant for soft focus, or would like to try it, do not normally go straight out and buy a special lens. It is for this reason that soft focus attachments have been made, thus allowing for experimentation or the occasional need.

Why should any photographer wish to produce soft focus effects when surely those days are left behind? Perhaps, like stereoscopy or romanticism this is a cyclical occurrence. It could be tied in to the world of fashion, nostalgia or the rediscovery of

an era in the cinema. Yet in spite of this there has always been an element of practicality. Portraiture, for reasons of human vanity, has always been the most prolifically practised subject in all forms of graphic art – including photography. Whereas the painter could ignore the passage of time when portraying ladies of an 'un'certain age, the camera could not. I have long conjectured that this was the reason for the discovery of soft-focus lenses, later for negative retouching, and nowadays make-up for T.V. appearances.

I once assisted a very famous portrait photographer, who had been commissioned to photograph the chairman of an

internationally respected company. It was my juvenile misfortune to deliver the finished results. Lord M. just happened to be in his office and told me to wait. "Rubbish," he exploded. "The man's made me look like a bloody baby. Take them back – and don't you dare send me a bill!" Needless to say, Lady M. was delighted with her pictures from a previous sitting. The moral of this story is, by all means use soft focus for landscapes, children, the ladies or whatever else suggests, but never for masculine portraits.

Soft focus lenses and accessories are both fascinating and infuriating to use; no two are exactly alike in effect. There are three co-related factors in soft focus work which must always be taken into consideration if the best results are to be obtained. The first is the degree of enlargement of the final result, the second is

the taking aperture of the lens, and the third is the strength of the diffusing medium.

In the days when a portraitist always produced the same sized final print, it was easy to control the degree of diffusion. Likewise, Hollywood in the twenties and thirties was working to a standard screen magnification. This is also true today for the transparency enthusiast filling his forty or fifty inch screen at every showing. The photographer who prefers prints will find that a soft focus picture which is 'correct' at enprint size will be over the top when he makes a 10 x 8″ enlargement. Conversely a negative which produces a 'correct' 10 x 8″ print will be too

Backlighting, particularly with the light source within the frame, degrades the photographic image to some extent. This is one reason for the development of multi-coating, but not even the very best multi-coating methods can entirely prevent some degree of flare. For the purposes of soft focus rendition this is all to the good; we can use this image degradation, add a pale pastel filter, plus a soft focus attachment if desired, to produce very soft images. With the subject in indirect light **facing page right** it is surprising how little effect a weak soft focus filter has. In these circumstances it is sometimes necessary to use every means we have to achieve the softness we want. For the shot **facing page left** a medium strength soft focus plus a fog filter and a crosstar were used. Without highlights, the crosstar served as a second soft focus filter!

sharp at enprint size. This situation can, however, be easily overcome. Most soft focus attachments work in the same manner in that the degree of image diffusion and flare is greatest at maximum lens aperture, becoming relatively less as the aperture is reduced. A print worker can therefore make two, or more, negatives at different apertures thus allowing for all eventual degrees of enlargement. The alternative is to make three negatives with different strengths of diffuser, all at the same taking aperture. The better makers market three grades of soft focus devices for just this reason.

As soft focus attachments induce some degree of flare at wider apertures, this sometimes needs to be taken into account. In the studio it is possible deliberately to use more contrasty lighting than usual. Expressed as a ratio, when using colour materials, this would be in the order of 1:3 instead of a more usual 1:4 maximum contrast between highlight and shadow areas. On the other hand, you may wish to produce a soft, high key effect. In this case use your normal lighting set-up. A hard backlight, bare bulb (or electronic flash), out of sight and facing camera, behind the model's head, will add to the effect. By the same token, outdoor portraits taken against the light – with preferably a dark background, can be effective for blondes and brunettes alike.

Before moving on to comparisons between the different soft focus attachments, just a word about diffusion in the darkroom. It would be nice to think that it is always possible to 'add' soft focus to any shot at this stage. Unfortunately, the effect is to spread the shadows into the highlights instead of the other way round. This may at first seem a nonsensical statement, but a practical test will show the very obvious difference. The compromise – and it is just that – is to diffuse for part of a print exposure. Usually a quarter or third is sufficient, though it all depends upon the type of diffuser employed, and the end result desired.

One of the earliest accessories for soft focus effects was the Modulo. This has the appearance of a UV filter engraved with a series of concentric rings. The strength depends upon the number of circles engraved. A modern variant also has radial lines engraved from the outside of the smallest circle to the edge of the glass.

Concentric soft focus 'filters' are very sensitive to lens aperture. To go beyond two stops from maximum in a number one, or three stops in a number three, will produce hardly any effect – unless the degree of enlargement is big, although this can vary slightly from manufacturer to manufacturer. This type does, however, have the advantage that contrast loss is low and definition good.

Other attachments of this type are crosstars and diffraction gratings. Whilst not intended to be soft focus devices, they will perform this function when used at wide lens apertures. The degree of diffusion depends upon the number of rulings – or put another way, the number of 'points' they are intended to produce. Image contrast is lower than the Modulo type and decreases as the rulings increase.

*Portraits of women have for many years proved ideal subjects for the use of soft focus. The highlights spread into the dark areas to a greater or lesser extent depending on the strength of the soft focus attachment used. Because of this spreading of light areas, light subjects **facing page** are* *preferable to darker ones **above left.** It is not always necessary to use a soft focus attachment to create a soft focus effect. The shot **left** was taken using a sheet of plain glass, which was lightly sprayed with water, between the subject and the camera.*

SOFT FOCUS ATTACHMENTS

The commonest soft focus attachments around now are of the dimples and pimples types. Since the introduction of so many organic glass (i.e. plastic) filter systems, it has become easier to introduce the kinds of imperfections which will give a soft focus effect upon film. In its mildest form, the dimpled type resembles the glass from an anti-Newton ring slide mount glass. In fact one of these can be used over the camera lens for a mild soft focus effect. Dimpled glass – or plastic, is available in several grades, the finer types only being suitable for 35mm work, whilst the heaviest tend towards the image flattening quality of a fog filter. The pimple type has a raised moulded pattern upon one surface. The shapes of the pimples can be round, elliptical or diamond. The effect is both to soften definition and to induce light scatter to lower contrast. To my mind these are the most satisfactory soft focus attachments, as the better glass types – like the superb Hasselblad Softars – can be used stopped down to small apertures without losing much effect. The optical clarity allows for an image quality approaching that of a true soft focus prime lens, although of a necessarily different nature.

The last category of commercially available diffusing attachments is the differential soft focus type. These consist of a close-up lens with a centre area ground flat, or sometimes cut out. The effect of this is to induce a soft image with very out of focus edges to the negative or transparency. They are very sensitive to lens aperture, and if stopped down more than a couple of stops will start to produce an odd double image. This can be used creatively but is no longer soft focus in the accepted

The degree of soft focus used obviously affects the mood of a picture considerably. It can vary from an almost imperceptible softening to a dreamy, hazy feeling as shown on the **facing page, lower pictures.** Soft focus is something we happily accept when it is used to portray girls, or couples, in a romantic and rural-looking setting but it works much less happily in a bustling town or city environment. Weddings, however, whether in town or country, usually make ideal subjects for soft focus treatment. Backlighting adds to the effect, enhancing the spread of light. Soft focus can, of course, be combined with other effects filters to, for instance, accentuate pastel colours. Except with such subjects as romantic couples, never use soft focus in shots of men, particularly portraits; it looks quite out of keeping with the subject and is invariably unacceptable to him. This applies equally to older men, whereas older women will usually find the effect flattering and pleasing.

SOFT FOCUS ATTACHMENTS

sense. Where these devices are most useful is when attempting a portrait against a confusing background. The effect here can be to render this as very out of focus and thereby more acceptable. The result is not dissimilar to focusing a wide aperture lens on a SLR, but with a degree of soft focus added. In bright light it will probably be necessary to add a neutral density filter in order to retain a sufficiently wide lens aperture.

Do-it-yourself soft focus has been around for a very long time. Prewar articles in the photographic press would describe how crumpled cellophane from a cigarette packet was taped over a lenshood, and then, in order to retain some definition, a lighted cigarette was used to burn a small hole through the centre of the cellophane. This technique is still used in studios today, particularly since the size and shape of the centre hole can be varied so easily. A smoker always has a soft focus facility available.

Of more recent type is the lady's stocking over the lenshood, again with the cigarette burn centre aperture. Unlike crumpled cellophane, the denier and colour of stockings will effect the degree of soft focus and can induce colour cast. Warm tone nylons can give the effect of an 81 series filter in combination with soft focus! I know of several professionals who have gone to the expense of having their favourite nylon 'combination filter' cemented between glass and put into a filter mount. This is one attachment that nobody has yet marketed.

Vaseline smeared over an old UV, or skylight, filter became a vogue in the sixties which still continues today, even to the extent that coloured Vaseline is now sold in photographic shops.

The use of Vaseline as a diffusing medium gives an effect quite unlike anything else. As a starting point, leave a quarter of an inch clear aperture in the centre of an old filter and apply the Vaseline in a circular pattern. Radial smears will add to the effect.

An alternative is to apply greasy finger prints in regular or irregular pattern but again leave a clear centre aperture – unless you are after drastic effect. Do not use Vaseline on any filter glass which you intend to use again in its normal role, as its mount will have to be dismantled for thorough cleaning. Regular exponents of this messy technique invariably have an attachment made up which will hold a 2¼ x 2¼ or 3¼ x 3¼ inch lantern slide cover glass in front of the camera's lens. Vaseline can be removed with lighter fuel, followed by washing-up liquid and warm water.

Another D.I.Y. technique is to use clear nail varnish for spots, circles, radial lines or in combination. I would recommend experimentation on cover glasses before attacking even an old UV filter, as nail varnish dries fast and requires a lot of acetone to remove it completely.

Sellotape over a large lenshood was immediately popularised when Lord Lichfield appeared in a T.V. programme. He used an old photoflood reflector, painted matt black inside, and with two inch clear Sellotape criss-crossed over its front. Again a central aperture should be allowed, in this case of a square or diamond shape. There is nothing to stop you using thinner Sellotape over a standard lenshood, though the results will be different. A wider lens aperture and a longer than standard focal length lens must be used with a large hood, otherwise there is a very real danger of the Sellotape being rendered sharp.

It would be hard to imagine better ingredients for a romantic subject than those in the picture facing page. A woodland setting, a stream, flowers and a beautiful girl have been given just the right degree of soft focus to enhance the mood. We associate doves with peace, hence this is another subject left that works well when softened, as do children – particularly when engaged in relatively peaceful pastimes!

LENSHOODS

It was not long after the birth of photography – well, about forty years to be precise – that photographers discovered the advantages of using lenshoods. Admittedly, most lenses in the earliest days only consisted of between one and four elements, and since coating was still a hundred years or so away, perhaps they should be forgiven for their ignorance.

In spite of deeply recessed lens mounts on some of the cheapest cameras around, camera manufacturers no longer follow the dictum of their forbears: 'Keep the sun behind you', but instead offer automatic focus/exposure/flash, or build in a motor wind as a means of taking better pictures. Expensive and in many ways less effective!

I am always amazed that tourists toting expensive gear – often with several extra lenses in a case – have still to discover the use of a lenshood. Whether one should blame manufacturer or dealer, or both, is a matter for conjecture, yet surely the cost of a collapsible rubber lenshood is now so low as to be almost ludicrous. That this simple item could be omitted from any purchase is beyond my comprehension, but then perhaps I am preaching to the converted. Even in the earliest photographic literature the photographer was exhorted to keep the sun behind the camera, or alternatively, to use his hat to cast a shadow over the lens. Easy enough when most cameras were mounted on a tripod, otherwise there was the need for an assistant, preferably one who wore a hat – and understood about keeping out of shot.

The coming of the 35mm miniature camera with its flare-prone, wide-aperture lenses, brought about a greater awareness generally for the necessity of a lenshood. Accessory hoods of the push-on/clip-on/knock-off type were produced in profusion for the amateur market. Professionals, after the first flush of enthusiasm, went back to not bothering. The aggravation of losing so many knock-off hoods was simply not worth the effort.

Built-in lenshoods have been a feature of larger focal length lenses for some time, and are now appearing on standard lenses. These are the ultimate in terms of convenience, yet because of the design parameters imposed by the dimensions of the lens mount, are often not as efficient as a previous accessory lenshood fitted to the same focal length lens. A further disadvantage is that when a filter, or close-up lens, is fitted, the built-in lenshood becomes proportionately shorter and consequently less efficient. Reversible lenshoods are yet another Leitz innovation from the early 1930s. A hood of this type is invariably deep, wide and, in consequence, very effective.

In ultimate terms of efficiency, a lenshood should be the same shape as the camera format. It is, of course, easier to produce a circular lenshood shape which is why we are stuck with them. There have been compromises between shape and format in the past. The earliest Leitz lenshood, from the nineteen twenties, was a circular shape with a rectangular cut-out in front. This was ultra efficient but meant that the hood had to be a) removed to adjust the iris diaphragm setting, and b) aligned when replaced.

Flare, caused by a light source – often the sun – being in, or just out of frame, spoils many photographs. Even if flare patterns are not evident facing page, image quality invariably suffers. Sometimes we may deliberately wish to include such flare but, if not, a good lens hood of the correct length for the lens in use, is essential.

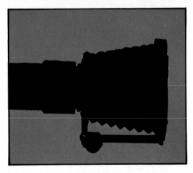

Lens hoods come in a variety of sizes and types. A wide angle lens requires a short, wide hood top to avoid vignetting, and there are extending models available above. The best, albeit most expensive lens hood is probably the bellows hood left which is adjustable for practically all lenses.

It was superseded by a conventional round hood. Some years later Leitz produced larger, round lenshoods with a cut-out back. This reduced the amount of cut-off in the rangefinder/viewfinder windows. Similar hoods have been made by Zeiss, Nikon, Canon and Hoya. Although designed for lenses of up to 100mm focal length, all these hoods were so shallow that they were more appropriate to wide angle lenses. This still applies to the current hoods of this type.

Square and oblong hoods are rather rarer, and usually only available for medium format rollfilm cameras. Invariably with a bayonet mount to avoid skew problems, this type can be compact and efficient – providing that filters etc. are not used on the inner bayonet. The most unusual of these hoods which I have encountered, was an oblong hood with a rotating mount, designed for the 6 x 6cm Praktisix SLR camera. The logic defeats me but it worked well in practice!

Wide angle lenshoods are often neglected by photographers, and certainly when you look at their skimpy dimensions, and sometimes price, this is understandable. Yet the manufacturers do not make these for fun. Under certain circumstances every little helps. Retrofocus wide angle lenses having large areas of glass in front and lots of elements behind, are prone to flare. Even a necessarily shallow lenshood can

prevent a side or top light source from getting into the lens elements. There is also the consideration of affording physical protection to the somewhat vulnerable glass surface. An oversized, and therefore deeper lenshood, can often be fitted to a wide angle lens by means of a step-ring. This may not be as convenient to carry but will be more efficient.

Telephoto and long focus lenses, particularly those with a built-in hood, are the biggest offenders when it comes to inefficiency. As an example: A current proprietary 300mm lens that I own has a lenshood of 30mm length – or 10% of its focal length. A 1950s 312mm telephoto lens was fitted with a 100mm long lenshood as standard, this being over 30% of the focal length. What is more, it needs it! Test pictures taken with the late multi-coated lens, showed a marked increase in contrast when it was fitted with the 100mm hood of the earlier lens.

The first reference I can find to an extendable bellows lenshood is in the James A. Sinclair catalogue of 1910. (It was still available thirty three years later!) Movie cameramen started using this type of hood very early on and still do, but then, look at even a sub-standard format ciné lens, and note the depth of the lenshood. This concern with avoiding lens flare spread into professional photography during the nineteen fifties. Larger format camera makers like Sinar, Arca and Hasselblad began to produce the square compendium, or professional lens shade, as an optional accessory. In recent years this trend has even spread into the 35mm market, through the aegis – literally, of Ambico, who, as far as I know, were the first to produce an oblong bellows hood for still photography. Most hoods of this type have filter provision, either for cemented in glass, gelatins in holders, or nowadays, various plastic devices. Invariably there is also provision for a front mask, à la Leitz, for the longer focal lengths or for specialised cut-out shapes. In practice, a bellows lenshood can be adjusted for maximum efficiency, with any focal length between super wide and ultra long, and at any camera/subject distance between infinity and macro.

A depth of field preview control on the camera is essential to avoid cut-off at smaller lens apertures. Large format hoods are also adjustable in line with camera movements. If the bellows lenshood has any disadvantage it is simply one of bulk, though some units are now made which can be folded for greater portability. All controls are lockable.

The last type of lenshood is basically a filter holder with a (usually) optional lenshood. This is the basis of Cokin, Chromatek, Hoyarex and other filter systems. Filter holders of this type date back a long way, though to the ingenious Jean Coquin must go the credit for their current popularity. Nikon, Hama and Hoya all produce high precision gelatin filter holders with the option of add-on circular lenshoods. These can be suitable for super wide to telephoto lenses. Gelatin filters of 75 x 75mm or 100 x 100mm can be used depending upon the maker. Even Kodak, with its ultimate gelatin filter range, have produced the crude Portré filter holder/lenshood device for many years.

One last word pertinent to lenshoods, and this concerns the blackness of the interior. At one time the better lenshoods were lined with black felt, which, although this could pick up fluff, when kept clean was very black indeed. Modern hoods, with machined interiors sprayed matt black, are not as efficient. They can, however, be lined with black felt. Bellows hoods, though again not as black as felt, by their shape alone will absorb any unwanted light.

COPYING AND DUPING

Just because the sun goes in or it's a lousy day, is no reason to hang up the camera or your filter collection.

All of us have seen what can be done with transparency duping, where there is always a chance that the shot which didn't quite come off could be saved or at least changed into something more acceptable. With the advent of cheap transparency copiers, some of which use the camera's standard lens, there is now no real excuse for the photographer not to try his hand at this technique. In the last resort, there is always the possibility of changing a colour image into black and white – or even vice versa, with the aid of a bit of darkroom magic!

Some of the simpler slide copiers can only use filters behind

the transparency to be copied. This is fine for colour correction and other filters, 'grads', vignettes, centre and colour spots, and any other attachment which is larger overall than the transparency. Because copiers of this type have a translucent diffuser behind the transparency, the effect of a centre spot or shaped mask will not be as marked as in a camera original.

Alternatively, filters and attachments can sometimes be used between the camera's prime lens and an add-on slide duplicator. This invariably affects the focus setting and it may be that the combination will now only focus closer than 1:1. There is also a possibility of vignetting. Gelatin filters can be cut to fit inside the adaptor if required, in which case there will be no focus shift.

Professional slide duplicators like the Illumitran, Elinchrom and Repronar are as versatile as their hefty price tag suggests. The fact that a filter or attachment can be placed between the lens and the subject transparency is a bonus also shared by a conventional bellows unit. In consequence, soft focus, fog, centre and colour spots, varipol and half colour filters may now be used as in a normal picture taking role.

With any of the simpler transparency duplicating devices, the choice of light source is left to the photographer. Whilst daylight or artificial light are the naturals – since a TTL metering system can be used – there is a lot to be said for a constant source, i.e. a small electronic flash unit at a fixed distance from the transparency to be copied. Although this means a certain amount of experimentation with a 'standard' transparency, in the long term it is a better method.

Professional transparency duplicators often use the substitution system. Exposure measurement of the subject

transparency is made with a tungsten lamp, the reading from which is then 'translated' into the correct exposure for the electronic flash used in the final exposure. There is nothing to stop the ingenious from adopting the same method, once the exposure parameters have been ascertained.

Whichever type of slide duplicator is used, there are certain filters and attachments which simply cannot work. These include normal polarisers, infrared and ultraviolet filters, whilst diffraction gratings and crosstars can only be employed by double exposing a separate light source into a dupe or black and white negative. Multiple image prisms and some centre focus attachments will invariably record areas outside of the subject

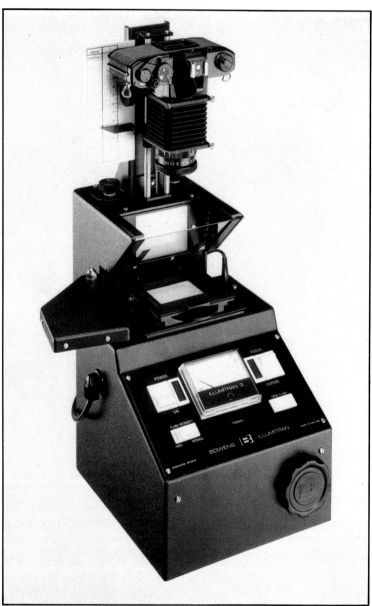

Above left is an Ohnar *transparency copying device that may be fitted with adaptors and thus to the camera body. This particular example contains its own lens system and has zoom facility to allow for enlargement of portions of a transparency. The Bowens Illumitran **above** is a much more sophisticated and costly version of a similar item which includes its own electronic light source plus focusing lamp. With the simpler unit a light source for exposure must be provided, usually a small electronic flash.*

Transparencies can be copied in several ways. There is the sophisticated copier, and the simpler version, featured on the previous page and, of course, copies can be made by making a negative and producing positives from this. It is also possible to copy a projected image. This requires that the camera and lens be set up as close to the optical axis of the projector as possible. With any of the direct copying methods a colour filter, mask or another slide can be combined with the first to create one single transparency in which both images are combined. Many photographers who are interested in duping take photographs specially to use later in combination with another shot. A sheet of kitchen foil, shot through various coloured filters, or with a zoom lens, may not make an exciting subject alone but, in combination with an existing, or yet to be taken, transparency it can provide a very different result. Experimentation is the only way to gain experience.

transparency, as do fisheye and superwide attachments.

The most useful items from the camera bag are Wratten CC colour correction filters, which can be used to alter a colour cast. Light balancing filters such as the 80 or 85 series will only act as a colour filter. A transparency exposed by a totally wrong light source cannot be corrected to normal. This is simply a matter of not being able to put back what is not already there! The same is true for an over-exposed transparency but not for one which is under-exposed. In this case a one, to one-and-a-half, stop error in exposure can often be corrected to a surprisingly high degree. There may be a need to use a colour correction filter if the degree of under-exposure has produced a colour shift in the subject rendering.

The lighter 81 'warming' filters may be used just as in their normal camera role, whilst the blue 82 filters are also useful for the apposite function.

Unfortunately, with any copying process there is an inevitable increase in contrast, which may or may not be acceptable. Several manufacturers make special transparency duplicating films of lower than average contrast. These are only available in bulk lengths, which means loading your own cassettes! A compromise is to use either Kodachrome 25 or, conversely, Ektachrome 160 or 200, these being of slightly lower contrast than other films in the range. All E6 films can be cut in processing by a half stop (maximum), which also reduces contrast. There will be a colour shift towards blue (about CC 10 blue), which must be allowed for.

Provided that your camera has double exposure facility, there is another contrast lowering duping technique which avoids special film or processing. This is known as flashing. The method is to make one exposure of the copier light source with a very heavy neutral density filter, followed by the correct exposure for the transparency to be copied. I must emphasise that this

COPYING AND DUPING

*Facing page is **an example of a** transparency duped together with a texture screen. These screens are available in a wide variety of patterns to suit all types of subject. A quick glance at the pictures on **this page** suggests that they show a city skyline. This, of course, is what they are intended to suggest. They are, in fact, electrical components mounted on a circuit board, combined with transparencies of special effects filters and **left,** also with an outdoor shot which was also filtered! The possibilities presented by a duping set-up, of whatever type or simplicity, are almost endless. As the owner of one of these pieces of equipment, you will find yourself looking at all kinds of subjects with a view to duping. You may even build up a library of such shots, to while away the long, dark evenings, but not, hopefully, at the expense of your photography!*

combination does require a certain amount of experimentation, as the ND filter density directly relates to the ASA speed of the copy film. As a guide, start with 64 ASA film, a Wratten ND 3.0 filter (1000 x factor) and make the flashing exposure at one stop less than for the second exposure. As with any duping technique, it pays to keep copious notes for future reference.

When copying colour transparencies on to black and white film, the same techniques may be used. Once more, high speed film is of lower contrast than slower film. Exposure and development may be altered for contrast reduction: the usual method is to over-expose by one stop and reduce development by 20%.

When copying a colour transparency on to colour negative film for the eventual production of prints, it is better to use internegative film (only available in bulk rolls), if colour fidelity is important. Flashing again gives a slight improvement but alterations in exposure and development will cause colour shifts which often cannot be corrected. Now that a soft grade of colour paper is available, home printers have fewer problems with excess contrast than in days gone by.

There are ways of using filters to change a black and white image into colour. Excluding the specialised techniques of tone separation, most photographers are happy enough to use the methods used by audio-visual producers and colour supplement art directors. This entails monochromatising a black and white image so that it blends tonally with a colour presentation or picture spread. It is as simple as copying a black and white print on to colour film, using a single filter to add colour. It can be as easy as using an 85B to produce sepia tones, or a Wratten 30 for magenta, or an 80B to give blue, and so on, according to the effect required, or to taste, or sometimes lack of it! Strongly coloured and pop filters also tend to obliterate tone and sometimes apparent definition.

Many camera filters can be used on the enlarger, whether to modify an enlarged 'duplicate' transparency, Cibachrome, Ektaflex or other colour, or black amd white print. In each case the nature of the process must be taken into account. For instance, a graduated orange filter will work on the enlarger for an enlarged transparency, Cibachrome or Ektaflex (positive) print, but will induce a lighter complementary coloured area in pos/neg colour print, and in black and white will have the effect of totally holding back the added graduated area.

Monochromatic colour effects can be produced with camera filters on the enlarger, particularly when colour heads simply do not have this range or depth of hue, to say nothing of the 'mixes' available elsewhere.

Spot and fog filters, soft focus devices, vignettes and masks can also be used. The latter is better placed over the subject negative or transparency when mechanisms allow. Even anamorphic and superwide attachments may be used over the enlarger lens (with a suitable mounting ring) to induce distortion in the image. Such are the joys of projection images.

Photography, without any tricks, is capable of producing evocative images. Combination duping right, in which one subject is superimposed on another, can reinforce the idea. The best of these pictures leave something for us to think about. Is the old man remembering the child he was? Or a child he once knew? Or does the picture tell us what the child will become? What has the sea to do with it? Is the memory pleasant or tragic? Solarisation and posterisation are other avenues open to the darkroom worker. There are many different methods of achieving these results, all of which can then be duped, singly or in combination.

ACKNOWLEDGEMENTS

The publishers would like to express their
grateful thanks for technical information
and for the loan of equipment to:

Eumig (UK) Ltd

Introphoto Ltd

Kodak Ltd

Leeds Camera Centre Ltd

Photax (London) Ltd

Polysales Photographic Ltd

Russell's Cameras, Wimbledon

Our special thanks to ▼ Mayfair Photographic
Suppliers (London) Ltd for technical information and
the loan of the **cokin** filter system.